MYTH AND SCIENCE
IN THE TWELFTH CENTURY

A Study of Bernard Silvester

MYTH AND SCIENCE IN THE TWELFTH CENTURY

A Study of Bernard Silvester

BRIAN STOCK

Princeton University Press

Princeton, New Jersey

1972

Copyright © 1972 by Princeton University Press

ALL RIGHTS RESERVED

LCC 72-38385

ISBN 0-691-05201-8

Publication of this book has been aided by a grant from
the Humanities Research Council of Canada,
using funds provided by the Canada Council.

This book has been composed in Linotype Caslon Old Face.
Printed in the United States of America

for
Béatrice

Contents

Illustrations

ix

of the zodiac with their influences towards motion or rest (*mobile / quietum*).

PLATE VI. *Homo microcosmus.* Lucca, Biblioteca Statale, MS 1942, f. 9r. An illustration from the *Liber Divinorum Operum* of Hildegard of Bingen, it presents all the general features of the idea of man as a microcosm which became so popular after 1100. The notion occurs most forcefully in the writings of Bernard Silvester, William of Conches, Hildegard, and Alan of Lille; see the discussion in the Conclusion to Chapter V.

Preface

HISTORIANS of literature and of science have in recent decades shown an increasing appreciation of the fascinating borderland that lies between their two disciplines. Renaissance scholars have done much to illustrate the interdependence of science and other rational and irrational activities, while philosophers of science as widely separated in time and method as Duhem and Thomas Kuhn have emphasized, at a more abstract level, that scientific change and the perception of it are complex processes involving other aspects of culture.

The present book is an attempt to extend this type of approach into the twelfth century, a period in which an impressive revival of literature and science took place. The center of focus is the *Cosmographia* of Bernardus Silvestris of Tours, which was written in the 1140s. This work is analyzed from the twin perspectives of philosophic naturalism and the role of innovation upon traditional modes of thought. As early as 1927 Haskins called for a study of this kind when he wrote: "We still lack a detailed study of the range and depth of Platonic influence in [the early twelfth century]; nor do we know . . . what reactions the new knowledge produced on the older habits of thought." Chapters II, III, and IV of the book treat this problem with reference to Bernard alone, while Chapters I and V assess his relation to other students of natural philosophy in the period, including Thierry of Chartres, William of Conches, and Daniel of Morley.

A critical text of the *Cosmographia*, Bernard's chief work, has been completed for some time but is not yet in print. It was prepared by André Vernet and announced in the *Ecole Nationale des Chartes, Positions des thèses . . . de 1937*, pp. 167-74. This edition, which completely supersedes the redaction of Barach and Wrobel in 1876, is used throughout. I should like to thank M. Vernet for allowing me to make especially large quotations from his text, which he graciously placed at my disposal over a long period of time.

Vernet's text, on the whole, follows the chapter divisions of Barach-Wrobel; where it does not, I have given both references. In addition, owing to the difficulty of Bernard's Latin, I have undertaken the dangerous activity of translating all my quotations. The translations are intended as guides only. My aim has been to place in the hands of students of philosophy, science, or the vernacular literatures a minimal set of tools, both textual and interpretative, for understanding an author whose place in medieval and renaissance thought is clearly seminal.

In addition to the *Cosmographia*, Bernard was the author of a number of other literary works. Unfortunately the final word on his bibliography has not yet been pronounced. In general I have followed Vernet except where more recent evidence has appeared. It is not widely known that his *remaniement* classifies the commentary on *Aeneid* i-vi (published by W. Riedel, Greifswald, 1924) as an "oeuvre d'authenticité possible" but not certain. A critical edition, now in preparation, may dispel the doubt. Until it appears, however, doubtful must remain not only the Virgil commentary but also the interesting commentary on book one of Martianus Capella, which was recently discovered and published in excerpt by Abbé Jeauneau in *Studi medievali*, 1964. It is tempting to think that Bernard, who was one of the most successful didactic poets of the Middle Ages, was also one of the chief literary theorists. Yet, for the moment, the thought must be resisted; too much work remains to be done on twelfth-century commentaries on classical authors. Another work associated with Bernard is a short treatise on composition in MS Wien, Nationalbibliothek lat. 246, published by M. Brini Savorelli in *Rivista critica della storia della filosofia*, 1965. For lack of evidence this must be regarded as an anonymous. As presently established, the proven bibliography of Bernard Silvester consists of some minor poems not mentioned in this study, the *Mathematicus*, the *Cosmographia* (also known as *De Mundi Universitate*), and, very possibly, the *Experimentarius*. Vernet argues that the distribution of manuscripts of the last work is unusual for a French author, but Brini Savorelli makes a strong case for Bernard's hand in at least the meters and the introduction in her edition in *Rivista critica della storia della filosofia*, 1959. If Bernard lived, as Vernet suggests, roughly between 1085 and 1178, his three major works may be viewed in the light which the new astronomy shed on the Platonic cosmology of the early twelfth century.

I should like to thank André Vernet, who kindly read the study, as well as a number of other colleagues who have rendered invaluable assistance. Peter Dronke read Chapters III and IV in an inferior state and made more than a few suggestions for improvement. Over the years I have also derived immeasurable benefit from our stimulating conversations. In addition to having written excellent guides to the School of Chartres, Tullio Gregory and Edouard Jeauneau have provided me with encouragement from time to time. It is difficult to find adequate words to acknowledge the debt I owe to the late C. S. Lewis, under whose supervision I began my research. Perhaps a study, however unworthy, devoted to one of his favorite authors, is the most appropriate gesture. I should also like to express my gratitude to George Rigg for the meticulous care with which he has read my translations, and to my colleagues in the Institute of Mediaeval Studies, J. Sheridan, E. A. Synan, L. E. Boyle and J. R. O'Donnell, for their generous co-operation. Finally, I should like to thank the Very Rev. L. K. Shook for providing an excellent atmosphere for serious research in the Institute and Princeton University Press for the care they have taken in the production of the volume.

The Master and Fellows of Trinity College, Cambridge, and the Canada Council supported the research which made the volume possible. The Institut de Recherche et d'Histoire des Textes, Paris, saved me much time and labor.

B.S.

Toronto
January 1972

Note: Square brackets in the English translations denote material not found in the Latin originals. Within the Latin texts, the normal conventions for square and pointed brackets are observed.

ABBREVIATIONS

AHDLMA

Apuleius, *De Mundo*
   De Deo Socratis
   De Platone

Asc.

Beiträge

Cos.

Chalcidius, *Comm.*

Chenu

CSEL

Gregory

Archives d'histoire doctrinale et littéraire du moyen âge. Paris, 1926–; cited in the year of actual publication.

Apulei Opera quae Supersunt, ed. R. Helm and P. Thomas, vol. III, *Apulei Platonici Madaurensis de Philosophia Libri.* Leipzig, 1921.

Asclepius, in *Corpus Hermeticum,* vol. 2, ed. A. D. Nock and A.-J. Festugière. Paris, 1960.

Beiträge zur Geschichte der Philosophie und Theologie des Mittelalters. Münster, 1891–.

Bernardus Silvestris, *Cosmographia:*
(1) *Bernardi Silvestris De Mundi Universitate libri duo sive Megacosmus et Microcosmus,* ed. C. S. Barach and J. Wrobel. Innsbruck, 1876.
(2) André Vernet, "Bernardus Silvestris. Recherches sur l'auteur suivies d'une édition critique de la *Cosmographia.*" Dissertation, Paris, Ecole Nationale des Chartes, 1938.

Chalcidius, *Commentary* on the *Timaeus,* in *Plato Latinus,* ed. P. J. Jensen and J. H. Waszink, vol. 4, pp. 53-346. London/Leiden, 1962.

M.-D. Chenu, *La théologie au douzième siècle.* Etudes de philosophie médiévale, XLV. Paris, 1957.

Corpus Scriptorum Ecclesiasticorum Latinorum. Wien, 1866–.

Tullio Gregory, *Anima mundi. La filosofia di Guglielmo di Conches e la scuola di Chartres.* Pubblicazioni dell'Istituto di Filosofia dell'Università di Roma, III. Firenze [1955].

Haskins	C. H. Haskins, *Studies in the History of Mediaeval Science*. 2nd edition. Cambridge, Mass., 1927.
Macrobius, *Comm.*	*Ambrosii Theodosii Macrobii Commentarii in Somnium Scipionis,* ed. J. H. Willis. Leipzig, 1963.
MGH	*Monumenta Germaniae Historica.* Berlin and Hannover, 1826–.
MS	*Mediaeval Studies.* Toronto, 1939–.
PL	*Patrologia Latina,* ed. J. P. Migne. 221 vols. Paris, 1844–.
SB	*Sitzungsberichte*
SMed	*Studi medievali.* Torino, 1904/05–; Spoleto, 1960–.
Tim.	Plato, *Timaeus,* in *Plato Latinus,* ed. P. J. Jensen and J. H. Waszink, vol. 4, pp. 5-52. London/Leiden, 1962.
TLL	*Thesaurus Linguae Latinae*

MYTH AND SCIENCE
IN THE TWELFTH CENTURY

A Study of Bernard Silvester

Poesis uero est scientia claudens in metro orationem. . . .

MSS Cambridge, Trinity College B.14.33, f. 10r,
and University Library Mm.I.18, f. 5va

Introduction

THROUGHOUT the greater part of the Middle Ages, *scientia* referred neither to exact science nor to empirically verifiable fact but to all things knowable. Scientific thought and the language of science were inseparable from mythical modes of explaining how the universe arose and functioned. Scientific ideas frequently underwent evolution within the framework of myth and appeared less often as total revolutions in world-view than as internal, structural changes within the myths themselves. In this sense, the *Cosmographia* of Bernard Silvester was the introduction of a relatively new myth of the creation of the world and of man into European philosophical literature.

During the early twelfth century when it was written, certain intellectual developments took place which, by general historical agreement, facilitated the emergence of a scientific sensibility. Owing to the translation of hitherto unavailable doctrines like the Aristotelian physics and Ptolemaic astronomy, a new emphasis was placed on the *quadrivium*, while, within the European intellectual tradition itself, interest in logical rationalism and in mathematics helped to lay the groundwork for a scientific methodology. At the same time a number of important technological innovations were made, particularly in agriculture and in warfare. These served to increase man's control over the natural environment and, as a result, to alter his perception of his place in the natural order. More generally, there was a growth within medieval culture as a whole of a certain existential naturalism, a this-worldliness which balanced the tendency towards mysticism in the Augustinian tradition. This sensibility makes its appearance in literature, in cathedral sculpture, and indirectly in intel-

3

lectual debates. Peter Abelard, for instance, generally recognized to have been the most gifted logician of his generation, argued seriously that universals were not merely
abstractions but were interrelated with physical reality.

These developments should properly be viewed as parts
of a whole. They were made possible, even necessary, by
equally deep changes in the institutional fabric of twelfth-
century society. In France, where many of the outstanding
intellectual and artistic changes originated, the transformation was quite dramatic. During the reign of Louis the Fat,
peace and stability returned to the countryside after more
than a century of continuous invasion. Despite minor set-
backs, the central control of the Capetian monarchy was
strengthened throughout the period and a relatively stable
atmosphere provided for the expansion of cathedral schools
and, later, of universities. The great international political
events of the day, the crusades, brought France, as all
northern Europe, into renewed contact with the Arab
world, whose cultural achievements were in some ways
superior to her own. In these conditions it is not surprising
that a profound religious and social reorientation took place.
Under Bernard of Clairvaux the Cistercians completed the
reforms begun by Gregory VII and the Cluniacs in the
eleventh century, while at St. Denis and Chartres a new
humanism began to take shape. In society at large the
hitherto monolithic feudal system began to be broken
down into a more diversified social structure. The intense
growth in population and the ensuing division of labor
helped to provide France with her first urban centers of
note since the Roman Empire, while the rise of merchant
trading, republican institutions, and a free labor market
altered the bonds between men. For the first time in centuries, town and country became the chief axes of class
conflict. Lastly, with the birth of the towns a different type

of intellecual and style of educational institution made
their appearance.

As economic, social, and institutional factors underwent a
metamorphosis, so did *mentalité*. This aspect of change in
the period, first treated in depth by Marc Bloch, has been
characterized as follows by Fr. Chenu:

> The twelfth century was a turning point in medieval
> civilization; so marked was the transformation that
> took place in the material conditions of life that it has
> been possible to speak of a "technological revolution."
> Encouraged by the breakup of the feudal monopoly
> of the soil, by the economic and political emancipation
> of urban artisans organized into guilds, and by the
> active mobility of men and goods in a market economy,
> the use and spread of new techniques of production
> and commerce profoundly altered not only the ma-
> terial side of life but also the modes of perception,
> sensibility, and representation that pertain to the life
> of the spirit. Did not Aristotle base his analysis of
> change and becoming upon the analogy of the artisan
> and his work?[1]

Few better examples could be found in the twelfth century
of this phenomenon than the interdependence of literature
and science. In both areas the image which man began to
draw of himself restored the balance between the active
and the contemplative life. Man's physical makeup became,
as it had been for Posidonius, an integral part of his divinity. Man's relation to nature, God, and the world was
fundamentally altered.

[1] M.-D. Chenu, *Nature, Man and Society in the Twelfth Century*, ed. and trans. J. Taylor and L. K. Little (Chicago, 1968),
39 (= Chenu, 45; page references in this book are to the French
edition: see List of Abbeviations).

One perspective through which these intellectual changes may profitably be viewed is that of tradition and innovation, of classical form adapting to the new naturalism. On the one hand, there was a purely classical revival, affecting not only literature but law, theology, and the various sciences. On the other hand, the interest in the visible, empirically definable world insured that naturalism interpenetrated the classical revival in numerous ways. One finds the new relation to antiquity expressed in commentaries on the Bible and classical authors; in encyclopedias designed to embrace the accumulated knowledge of centuries but now including a higher degree of information about the real world; in monumental sculpture, in which the saints and the heroes of antiquity are not eternal archetypes, models of wisdom and of action, but begin to resemble the citizens of medieval towns. In a famous metaphor, Bernard of Chartres is reported to have visualized his contemporaries as "dwarfs, standing on the shoulders of the giants."[2] By this he meant that his generation was able to see farther than the ancients, not because they possessed better vision, but because the accumulation of knowledge in their time allowed them a novel perspective on tradition. His own age was a continuation of the classical world in faithfully reproducing its concepts, styles, and cultural ideals. But Bernard was prepared to grant that in other respects it had perhaps surpassed even the ancients.

Within the suggested framework of Bernard's metaphor —and not that of a radical break with tradition as in the Renaissance—the classical debate on myth and science, which had really begun with Aristotle's critique of Plato's

[2] John of Salisbury, *Metalogicon* iii.4; ed. Webb, p. 136, 23-27. On the history of the metaphor, see R. Klibansky, *Isis* 26 (1936), 147-49, and E. Jeauneau, *Vivarium* 5 (1967), 77-99. [See the Selected Bibliography for complete bibliographical data on works cited in the notes.]

Timaeus, was reopened in a new context. The question, first of all, was whether the intellectual forms inherited in tradition could any longer serve as a useful foundation for a scientific understanding of the universe. The responses varied greatly. The tendency towards conservatism in literary format insured that most authors expressed their new ideas in discourses which possessed recognizable links with antiquity. A great many literary forms from the classical and, in particular, the late Latin world were revived for the purpose: the dialogue, the *satura* (or *prosimetrum*), the encyclopedia, the commentary, and, more rarely, the epic and the myth itself. The forms were utilized in ways that often emphasized their distance from antiquity and their relation to literary fashions in their own day. The innovators are frequently called the *moderni,* and the medieval *codices* of such works often contain both the ancient and the modern product. The *Questiones Naturales* of Adelard of Bath are often bound with Seneca's work of the same name,[3] and the *Imago Mundi* of Honorius of Autun and the *Philosophia Mundi* of William of Conches are found with the encyclopedias of Isidore or Bede.[4] Even an apparently uncreative format like the interlinear or marginal gloss could serve as a springboard for original discussion. An example is the commentary of Peter Helias on the grammarian Priscian.

Yet beneath the use of such classical formats for uniting traditional and original ideas lay a deeper problem: whether science, or the individual sciences, would not have to evolve languages which suited their own internal requirements. In particular, as rational modes of thought

---

[3] See Haskins, 41 n. 103.

[4] E.g., MS Paris, Bibl. Nat., lat. 11,130, containing the *Imago Mundi* i-ii (ff. 1-28v), an illustrated *Philosophia Mundi* (ff. 28v-69r), and Bede's *De Rerum Natura* (ff. 69r-78v). For MSS of the *Philosophia Mundi,* see A. Vernet, *Scriptorium* 1 (1947), 243-59.

became more familiar, and as the natural-philosophic corpus, swelled by translations, increased in size, new approaches began to be made to the chief problem between myth and science: the creation of the world and of man. In general there were two approaches, the historical and the structural. In the historical, the natural order was subordinated to historical genesis; in the structural, history was subordinated to a rational order. According to the historical interpretation, the world had a beginning and, presumably, an end; in the structural, the world underwent transformations, but was in essence eternal. Historical genesis emphasized the role of an omnipotent creator in whose beneficent image both the world and man were created; structural genesis, while not denying the existence of the creator, emphasized the creational modalities of the existing world, its laws and principles of procreation. These two approaches of course developed from positions well known in the ancient world (and not without parallels in modern astronomy). Within the context of the limited source materials available in the period, however, each was indebted to a different classical exemplar. For the historical theory, it was the book of Genesis; for the structural, the *Timaeus* in a variety of interpretations. It is common, moreover, to find both approaches brought together in a single work. A good example is Thierry of Chartres' *Commentary* on the opening chapters of the Bible *secundum litteram et secundum physicam*.

As early as the 1130s, many scientific minds were overtly or covertly advocating a structural approach to creation. The problem was not so much the rejection of Genesis as myth, for the whole period, until about 1150, was dominated by Platonic mythologizing. It was the replacement of one myth by another, which, to their minds, possessed inherently better possibilities for scientific development. After 1150, the issues were somewhat different. "The reception of the Ptolemaic astronomy and the Aristotelian physics, as transmitted by the Arabs"[5] combined with a new emphasis on the *quadrivium* rather than the *trivium* to reformulate the whole question of cosmology. The changes also favored larger university centers like Paris over the more intimate cathedral schools like Chartres. Up to the 1140s, however, a certain balance was achieved between myth and science. While not entirely abandoning the framework of mythical cosmogony, authors like Thierry, William of Conches, and Gilbert Porreta began to introduce scientific elements as they understood them. These did not consist of the verification of facts through experiments, although this is suggested from time to time between the lines. It consisted rather in applying strict, logical rationalism to the problem of natural causality. *Ratio* was not only identified with *kosmos*, the Platonic ordering of the elements into a model of the divine, but with the *ordo naturalis*. The essential components of the renovated Platonic cosmology were mathematical and musical harmony, naturalism, and logical consistency within the cosmic system.

Bernard Silvester stands very near the center of this development. As a Platonist he attempted to achieve a goal inherently more audacious than that of the commentators: to rewrite the myth of the creation of the world and of man. A keen student of contemporary natural philosophy, he tried at the same time to introduce into his myth a number of unique features. The result is not only a reworking of a traditional cosmogony, a primitive myth of creation brought up to date. It also mirrors in many subtle ways the deeper intellectual ferment of the period, its inner preoccupations and moods. To carry out this difficult task of synthesis, Bernard adopted the plastic medium of allegory. Using neoplatonic models as his guides, he created a *mythologische Gesellschaft* to enact the drama of creation. Parts of the *Cosmographia*, to be sure, are not free from needless obscurity. Yet it exemplifies perhaps better than many other literary works of the early twelfth century the blend of tradition and innovation implied in Bernard of Chartres' famous metaphor. It was a simple matter for early historians to confuse the author of the *Cosmographia* with Chartres' most renowned humanist.

The method employed throughout the book is the investigation of Bernard's sources, frequently accompanied by direct or indirect manuscript evidence. Yet *Quellenforschung* has not been made an end in itself. Too often medieval authors have suffered unjustly from having their original works reduced to the mentalities of an earlier age or projected into those of a later one. An appreciation of any work of literature implies an acceptance of the period of history in which it was written: its criteria of art, its perspectives on the past, its use of traditional materials in new ways. Until recently, historians have not entirely succeeded in freeing works of the literary imagination in the twelfth century from the Draconian embraces of "the classical tradition" and "scholastic philosophy." The *Cosmographia* is primarily a work of literature, and what is more, the product of a highly individualistic artist. In recognition of this fact, considerable space in what follows is devoted to form as well as to content. The ultimate aim of the study is to use the sources as a key for unlocking the structure of Bernard's myth. For if he was not entirely original as a scientific theorist, his capacity for myth-making was unsurpassed in his time.

CHAPTER I

Narratio Fabulosa

1. Myth, Model, and Science

BERNARDUS SILVESTRIS of Tours very probably wrote his *Cosmographia* sometime between 1143 and 1148.[1] Some seven centuries later an edition based upon only

---

[1] Manitius-Lehmann, *Geschichte der lat. Literatur des Mittelalters* 3 (München, 1931), suggests, 1145-53, the pontificate of Eugene III, who is mentioned at *Cos.* i.3.55-56. Yet the work was probably in progress from an earlier date. John of Spain, whose abbreviated translation of Abu Ma'shar Bernard may have known, was finished by 1133; Steinschneider, *Die europäischen Übersetzungen aus dem Arabischen*, *SB Wien*, vol. 149 (1904), 47. Hermann of Carinthia, possibly Bernard's associate, completed his *De Essentiis* and his translation of Ptolemy's *Planisphere* by 1143; Haskins, 47-48. By this time as well his translation of the longer version of Abu Ma'shar was well advanced; Haskins, 45, and in greater detail, R. Lemay, *Abu Ma'shar and Latin Aristotelianism in the Twelfth Century* (Beirut, 1962), 9-19. The *terminus a quo* for the *Cosmographia* may therefore be as early as the 1130s. The *terminus ad quem* is possibly the winter of 1147-48. R. L. Poole, *Eng. Hist. Rev.* 35 (1920), 328, cites the following gloss for *Cos.* i.3.55 from Bodleian MS Laud. Misc. 515, f. 188v: "*Eugenius*. Iste Eugenius fuit papa in cujus presencia liber iste fuit recitatus in Gallia et captat ejus benivolenciam." But is this gloss to be trusted? There are at least two reasons to doubt that it should. First, the MS was written after 1250, a somewhat late witness for the event. We must assume that it was taken from an earlier copy, now lost. Moreover, if one reads the whole gloss instead of isolating this statement, it emerges as a highly unintelligent commentary on the *Cosmographia*, showing no very great understanding of the book's sources or meaning. Why then should it be trusted without question on the problem of dating? Lastly, is the *Cosmographia* not somewhat lengthy to be *recitatus*, and would the faithful who attended the Council of Reims in 1148 not have been offended by its astrology?

two unreliable manuscripts[2] was put into print by C. S. Barach and J. Wrobel. Both immediately after its appearance in the Middle Ages and after its publication in 1876, the encyclopedic myth made a considerable impact on the learned literary scene. The editor of the critical text, André Vernet, has counted dozens of manuscripts, and historians have been able to trace Bernard's influence on a wide variety of medieval and renaissance authors, including Hildegard of Bingen, Vincent of Beauvais, Dante, Chaucer, Nicolas of Cusa, and Boccaccio—whose annotated copy of the work we possess[3] [Plate I]. Yet critics have been unable to agree on an interpretation. Abbé Clerval, one of the earliest to study the myth, described it as "un des poèmes philosophiques les plus curieux du XIIe siècle,"[4] while more recently Fr. Chenu has referred on more than one occasion to its "ambiguity."[5] Perhaps more than any other work of the period, the *Cosmographia* has been capable of inspiring partisan interpretations.[6] At the same time, all

[2] Wien, Nationalbibl., lat. 526 and München, Bayer. Staatsbibl., Clm. 23,434. The *Cosmographia* was, in fact, partially published in three earlier editions: V. Cousin, *Ouvrages inédits d'Abélard pour servir à l'histoire de la philosophie scholastique en France* (Paris, 1836), 627-36; B. Hauréau, *Histoire de la philosophie scholastique* I (Paris, 1872), 407-17; W. Stubbs, *Radulfi de Diceto decani Lundoniensis opera historica* II (London, 1876), lxxviii-ix. In the introduction to his edition (p. 141) Vernet notes wryly that while Cousin's readings were inexact, "la ponctuation est en général excellente et C. S. Barach aurait été bien inspiré de la suivre," a sentiment that has doubtless been shared by many a modern reader of Bernard.

[3] Firenze, Bibl. Med. Laur., MS plut. xxxiii,31, f. 59va. Cf. F. Munari, *Philologus* 104 (1960), 279, n. 3.

[4] *Les écoles de Chartres au moyen âge du Ve au XVIe siècle* (Chartres, 1895), 171.

[5] *AHDLMA* 22 (1956), 76; Chenu, 114-15.

[6] These are summarized by T. Silverstein, *Modern Philology* 46 (1948-49), 92-116, esp. 92-93, and more briefly by M. McCrimmon, "The Classical Philosophical Sources of the *De Mundi Uni-*

who have studied it agree that it is an important book: under the veil of allegory it presents a synthesis of central doctrines in the medieval and renaissance philosophy of nature, man, and the world.

Although we know little of Bernard's life, contemporary and later witnesses record his success as a teacher of the humanities [Plate II]. Typical of them is Matthew of Vendôme, who recalls learning to compose Latin verse under Bernard's supervision at Tours, presumably between 1130 and 1140.[7] Bernard refers to the region of Tours twice in the *Cosmographia*.[8] He is therefore assumed to have taught there for a period of his life. His only other literary associations are with Chartres. Most medieval copies of the *Cosmographia* contain a letter of dedication to Thierry, who became Chancellor of Chartres in 1141. Yet, as Poole points out in his summary of the evidence, "there is nothing to suggest that he was ever connected with Chartres"[9] as a student or teacher. Bernard's dedicatory epistle merely asks Thierry for his approval of the *Cosmographia* before he publishes it under his own name. Hermann of Carinthia, with whom Bernard may have collaborated in the *Experimentarius*, also sent to Thierry his translation of Ptolemy's *Planisphere*.[10] Bernard's letter is really only evidence that he attempted to win the favor of a powerful yet liberal figure, widely known for his in-

---

versitate of Bernard Silvestris" (diss., Yale Univ., 1952), and P. Dronke, *SMed* 6 (1965), 415-16.

[7] Me docuit dictare decus Turonense magistri
     Silvestris, studii gemma, scholaris honor.

Ed. Wattenbach, *SB München, philos.-philolog. und hist. Kl.*, 2 (1872), 581, lines 69-70; cited and discussed by E. Faral, *SMed* 9 (1936), 70.

[8] *Cos.* i.3.261-62 (= Vernet, 264-65); i.3.351-52.

[9] *Eng. Hist. Rev.* 35 (1920), 331.

[10] Haskins, 47.

terest in science and for his occasional defense of unpopular theses. Whether Bernard is connected directly to Chartres or not, however, historians have been essentially correct in interpreting his humanism within its cultural ideals.[11] Bernard belonged very much to the generation of Thierry, William of Conches, Gilbert Porreta, and John of Salisbury. In his mind, as in theirs, an interest in new ideas went hand in hand with a rediscovery and fresh reading of the classics.

The *Cosmographia* is possibly the most complex literary product of the early twelfth century. As it is clearly a composite form, it may be useful at the outset to isolate the individual elements in it and to discuss them separately. These may then be reunited and the work better appreciated as a whole. In general, two distinct structures are at work. There is both a dramatic *myth*, enacted by a group of allegorical personifications, and a resulting *model* of universal order, relating the macro- to the microcosm. In other words, there is both a story of the creation of the world and of man and a resulting design whose parts are analyzed in relation to each other. While it is not always possible or desirable to separate these elements—Noys, for instance, is both an actress in the drama and a principle in the model —a rough division between them allows one to perceive the interplay between form and content and to better comprehend Bernard's dexterity of composition.

First, then, the myth. Bernard prefaced the *Cosmographia* with an *argumentum*, but it must be followed with caution.[12] It tells us that "in the first book, called *Megacosmus*, Natura complains in tears to Noys, God's providence,

[11] See in particular Gregory, 175-278; Chenu, 19-51, 108-41.

[12] Bernard's preface is inaccurately called the *breviarium* by Barach and Wrobel. Unfortunately, it has also been accepted by historians as an accurate guide to the work. In point of fact, the brief summary omits for the most part *Cos.* i.4, ii.5-9, and ii.12-14.

about the confusion of *hyle* or prime matter and implores that the worldly order be brought to a more attractive conclusion."[13] The remainder of i.1, written in hexameters (an unusual verse form for Bernard), consists of Nature's complaint: it describes in vivid detail the turmoil of chaos before the harmonious stability of the four elements is established. In i.2, in prose, Noys continues the dialogue with Natura. She agrees in principle to fulfill the request, theorizes about her relation to God, then turns to the practical business of creation, separating the four elements and moulding them into a stable structure for the world's body. After a digression in which Noys, never modest, discourses on her own powers, the world-soul, *endelichia*, descends in emanation from the heavens. The union of body and soul takes place under Noys's guidance, completing i.2.

Once the body and soul of the universe are "married," its contents unfold before the reader in i.3 in elegiacs. Noys, who is presumably presiding over this event as well, is nonetheless mentioned in the catalogue of all things in the world. The reader is thus given the impression—maintained throughout the *Cosmographia*—of astrological determinism operating in co-existence with a certain amount of free will. Bernard sets forth the nine orders of angels, the zodiac, the divisions of the earth, and its contents, including mountains, rivers, trees, fruit, spices, paradises, domestic vegetables, flowers, fish, and birds. When this little encyclopedia is finished, he presents, in i.4, an explanation of how the universe runs. The cosmic globe possesses an eternal source of life-giving power which flows down from the heavens in the form of heat and light. The cosmos itself is eternal, a notion which he defends by uniting, not altogether successfully, material from a number of different sources. In the hierarchy of *genii* or *numina* that transmit ideas,

---

[13] Ed. Barach-Wrobel, p. 5, lines 16-20.

principles, and life-forces from above, primacy of place is given to Noys. Then follow *mundus*, the living creature of the world itself, *endelichia*, the world-soul, Natura, and *imarmene*, fate. These are all interrelated in a syncretistic fashion.

Book one may thus be divided into three sections: i.1 and i.2, on creation itself; i.3, on the contents of the universe; and i.4, on the quasi-scientific processes by which the cosmos functions.

In *Microcosmus*, book two, Noys promises to create man as the summation of her work. In ii.3, she first bids Natura seek out two other goddesses whose help will be indispensable: Urania and Physis. Natura searches for Urania in the heavens and finds her, not too surprisingly, indulging in astrology. Urania agrees to co-operate and explains to Natura some of the difficulties which the individual soul will encounter, as well as the diverse properties it will acquire, in descending to inhabit temporarily the human frame. In ii.5-9, Urania leads Natura on a long journey through the stars. After visiting a mysterious, neoplatonic palace called Tugaton, they descend to earth through the planetary spheres. At ii.9, just below the lunar sphere, they pause at a place called Granusion, where they encounter Physis with her two daughters, Theory and Practice. While Physis conducts what appear to be experiments into the natures and causes of phenomena, Noys arrives on the scene. After delivering an oration on the dignity of man (ii.10), she proceeds to supervise the work of the other three goddesses in creating man as a microcosm (ii.11-12). Physis, now raised to an important role in the drama, first complains about the inherent difficulty of making man from the left-over elements; then, aided by Urania and Natura, she puts man together rather like a mechanical fabrication. In ii.13-14, man, the *fabrica Nature primipotentis*, is described in detail, thus providing a literary balance to the poetic un-folding of the *megacosmus* in i.3.

In general, then, book two may be divided into two major acts, dealing respectively with the astral journey and the creation of man. It is also possible to divide the last act into two scenes, one treating man's actual formation from the elements, the other the manner in which he functions.

This, in brief, is Bernard's myth. Clearly, within it, a model of the universe and of man is envisaged, but, as suggested above, this model is inseparable from the manner in which it is presented. Moreover, within the myth two different types of source material may be distinguished, each contributing in a different way to the ultimate result. The first is the story of creation itself. For this Bernard's chief source was Plato's *Timaeus*. The second is the philosophical and scientific information that fills out the skeletal model of the *Timaeus*. For this Bernard turned to a wide group of classical and contemporary authors.

To deal first with Plato: Bernard drew from the *Timaeus*, which he read in the late third-century translation of Chalcidius, not only many essential ideas, but, more importantly, the conception of myth imbedded in the dialogue. Bernard did not entirely assume, as did Plato, that "the world is only a likeness of the real," but he did clearly support the view that "any account of it can be no more than a 'likely' story."[14] To put the matter slightly differently, there are in the *Cosmographia*, as in the *Timaeus*, two senses of myth. In the first, just mentioned, it is assumed that

no account of the material world can ever amount to an exact and self-consistent statement of unchangeable truth. In the second place, the cosmology is cast in the

[14] F. M. Cornford, *Plato's Cosmology* (London, 1937), 28.

17

form of a cosmogony, a 'story' of events spread out in time. Plato chooses to describe the universe, not by taking it to pieces in an analysis, but by constructing it and making it grow under our eyes. . . . Some have regarded the mythical character of the dialogue as a 'veil of allegory' which can be 'stripped off,' and have imagined that they could state in literal terms the meaning which Plato has chosen to disguise. . . . [Yet] there remains an irreducible element of poetry, which refuses to be translated into the language of scientific prose.[15]

Like Plato, Lucretius, and, most appropriately, Manilius, Bernard Silvester is a cosmic poet. The *Cosmographia* cannot be reduced to a mere summary of the doctrines it contains if its artistic structure is to be left intact. Like the *Timaeus*, it must be considered an attempt to build a cosmic order before the reader's eyes.

The attitude towards myth in Bernard and his contemporaries will be discussed at greater length in the second part of this chapter. With regard to the model of universal order presented in the *Cosmographia*, it may be useful at the outset to point out certain broad similarities. Like Plato, Bernard conceived the ordering of the world to be based on the action of a beneficent creator and his vicegerents who were also gods. He saw genesis essentially as a problem of Intelligence (Noys) and Necessity (Natura, Urania, Physis, etc.). Within this framework, he developed some of Plato's favorite themes: the idea of man as a microcosm of the universe, the union of the world-soul and the earth, the interrelation of motion, time, and eternity, the notion that the soul undergoes a type of education before it enters the body, and, based upon the above, a group of parallels between man's configuration and the

---

[15] *Ibid.* 31-32.

world's. Yet, in spite of these obvious points of comparison, the *Cosmographia* is in some fundamental ways unlike the *Timaeus*. One reason is that it is based on a translation which breaks off abruptly at 53B, near the beginning of Plato's second account of creation "from a different point of view." Another, more important reason is that Bernard often intermingles Plato's views with those of his interpreters. The latter often reflect attitudes and opinions quite different from Plato himself.

If there is a single characteristic which unites Bernard's other sources besides Plato, it is that they are all encyclopedic. Moreover, they may be thought to represent a stage of cosmological thought which, coming after the mythical cosmogony, attempts to explain in scientific terms what it means. In this sense, their works may be called *structural encyclopedias*, since the structure of the cosmogony—proceeding from fundamentals like matter and form to the immense diversity of the universe—often lurks just beneath the surface. Chalcidius' *Commentary* on the *Timaeus*, perhaps Bernard's major single source, is a good example. The work is an encyclopedic treatise based upon the original and, like it, divided into two major topics, Intelligence (chapters 8-267) and Necessity (268-355). Under these headings however Chalcidius does not construct the universe before the reader's eyes. Rather he takes it apart. His commentary is a comprehensive exposition of the *Timaeus*, taking each separate theme in the myth as a topic for synthesizing the thought of a number of ancient schools. The reader is thus presented with an entirely different literary form from the original. While based upon the idea of myth, the commentary turns the notion around and presents instead a demythologization. Throughout the Middle Ages, moreover, Chalcidius' commentary was thought to be an indispensable tool for understanding Plato. The two structures, the myth and the demythologization, were accepted as interdependent, resonating parts of a whole. With respect to the *Cosmographia*, the important point is that Bernard incorporated both the idea of a mythical cosmogony and that of a commentary on it. In the course of telling the story of creation, he explains what creation is all about. At times, in fact, Bernard may be guilty of allowing *mythos* to be submerged in *encyclopedica*.

Thus, in addition to drawing on the idea of mythogenesis as in Hesiod, Genesis, Plato, or Ovid, Bernard should be viewed as a structural encyclopedist. There are numerous models on which he may have drawn: Pliny's *Natural History* ii, the *De Mundo* of Apuleius, and the *De Rerum Natura* of Isidore or of Bede; commentaries like that of Macrobius on Cicero or Martianus Capella on the seven liberal arts (in which the encyclopedia is presented in allegory as in the *Cosmographia*); and, perhaps as well, works like the *Premnon Physicon* of Nemesius of Emesia, in the eleventh-century translation of Alphanus of Salerno, and even the *Periphyseon* of John Scottus Eriugena. In its general pattern, however, the *Cosmographia* resembles most closely the structural encyclopedias written in the twelfth century: the anonymous *De Constitutione Mundi*, the *Imago Mundi* of Honorius of Autun, the *Questiones Naturales* of Adelard of Bath, and the *Philosophia Mundi* and *Dragmaticon* of William of Conches. In all these works, as in the *Cosmographia*, certain assumptions are made about the division of the sciences or the theory of knowledge. The real world is seen to possess a rational design, the result of cosmogony, which the encyclopedia imitates through the ordering of its facts. The world is not primarily apprehended in its naturalistic diversity—although this is often a strong, balancing undercurrent—but as a logical pattern, a harmonious arrangement of discrete elements. Even in the illustrations which accompany these works, this relationship is maintained.[16] They do not present the world as it really is, but in a schema relating the elements, the humors, the seasons, and man. They are, like the encyclopedias, "symbolic cosmologies" [Plate III A, B, and C].

Bernard's association with the encyclopedists is clear from the term *cosmographia*, employed as a title in many manuscripts. The term's original meaning was "geography" or "cartography."[17] Isidore of Seville applied it to the five books of Moses,[18] and, in the twelfth century, the usage hovers between that of a mythical cosmogony and a spiritual geography.[19] The relationship may also be demonstrated by comparison with other twelfth-century encyclopedias. In particular, the encyclopedic aspects of the *Cosmographia* bear a strong resemblance to the *Philosophia Mundi* of William of Conches, written between 1135 and

[16] See M.-T. d'Alverny, *AHDLMA* 20 (1953), 31-81; H. Bober, *Journal of the Walters Art Gallery* 19-20 (1956-57), 65-97.

[17] E.g., Cassiodorus, *De Institutione Divinarum Litterarum*, cap. 25; *PL* 70, 1139C-D; *Ravennatis Anonymi Cosmographia . . .*, ed. M. Pinder and G. Parthey (Berlin, 1860).

[18] *Etymologiae* vi.2.1; *PL* 82, 230B.

[19] J. K. Wright, *The Geographical Lore of the Time of the Crusades* (New York, 1925), 127. Two renaissance cosmographies with medieval roots are Peter Apian's *Cosmographicus Liber* (1524) and Sebastian Münster's *Cosmographica* (1544). When Christopher Columbus sailed for America, he took with him a slightly expanded version of a twelfth-century cosmography written by Pierre d'Ailly (1350-1420) and entitled the *Ymago Mundi*; see the edition of E. Buron (Paris, 1930). The medieval tradition is aptly summarized in the beautiful *Liber Cosmographie* of John de Foxton in MS Trinity College, Cambridge, R.15.21, dated 1408. In the prologue, f. 1ra, John, who calls himself "Capellanus," states: "Qui nomen immerito *Cosmographia* nominatur et dicitur a cosmus quod est mundus et graphia quod est descriptio, unde cosmographia, id est mundi descriptio."

1145.[20] Both works begin with fundamentals, William with the Trinity and the four causes of creation (i.1-14), Bernard with a portrait of the original longing of matter for form (i.1-2). The rest of book one of the *Philosophia* is virtually analogous to most of *Megacosmus* and the last half of *Microcosmus* (ii.9-14). William describes the *anima mundi*, the demons and angels, the elements, and the creation of living things (i.15-23), which correspond roughly to *Cosmographia* i.2-3 with a premonition of ii.9. *Philosophia* ii.1-16, an outline of the upper atmosphere, the stars, the galaxies, and other astronomical topics, is paralled by *Cosmographia* i.3 and ii.5-8. William's fascinating discussion of planetary motion, the seasons, and the eclipses in the same book seems to have been divided between *Cosmographia* i.4 and ii.6-8, although here, admittedly, the parallel is much less precise. *Philosophia* iii, however, is directly analogous to *Cosmographia* i.3-4: both treat air, the five zones, and the problem of heat, light, and the sun, to which Bernard gives a more astrological interpretation at ii.6. Finally, *Philosophia* iv.8-41, treating sex, birth, infancy, man's physical makeup, and the history of the world are paralleled roughly by *Cosmographia* i.3 and ii.9-14. The only part of Bernard's work that finds no echo in William's is the astral journey of Natura and Urania.

The *Cosmographia*, then, may be viewed as a composite literary form. First, it is a *myth* written in alternating verse and prose sections; as such it is similar to the cosmogonies of classical poetry, the *Timaeus*, and, in their mythical sense, the opening chapters of Genesis. Secondly, it is a *model* of universal order, an encyclopedia that presents the results of the creation story. As such it gathers into its com-

---

[20] A. Vernet, *Scriptorium* 1 (1947), 244. Cf. P. Dronke, *Anuario de estudios medievales* 6 (1971), 129-30, who suggests a date before 1130.

plex fabric information from a wide variety of classical and contemporary authorities. In addition to these two elements, the myth and the model, there is a third. For the sake of simplicity it may be called the scientific. Bernard was not himself a major scientific theorist, nor, with the possible exception of the *Experimentarius*, did he engage directly in the activity of translating. Yet the *Cosmographia* reflects the growing natural-philosophic interests of the period in many ways. First of all, Bernard's allegorical figures nearly all represent physical forces. Physis and Urania represent the disciplines associated with their names in Bernard's time, and the *sensilis mundus* is peopled with a whole host of deities who also play a part in the physical schema. Secondly, Natura, in addition to symbolizing the natural forces that guide fatalistic causality, clearly represents *ratio scientiam quaerens*, reason seeking out knowledge. She is, so to speak, the *ratio* of Manilius, readapted to the twelfth-century scene. Thirdly, Bernard helped to revive the classical idea of physical as opposed to moral allegory. In the *Cosmographia* the sun, the moon, and the stars are divine. Astrological deities guide the universe, and their motions, with their resultant physical forces, constitute natural laws. Thus the abstractions at the center of the work are not moral but philosophical truths. Fourthly, Bernard is interested in the real, empirically definable world for its own sake. One finds in the *Cosmographia* the same balance between an ideal order and a sensuous experience of the world that one finds so vividly expressed in Romanesque and Gothic sculpture.[21] Lastly, the structuring of the myth, its reworking of traditional materials, held certain important implications for natural philosophy. For Bernard, the intellectual advances of his own day were a source of great

[21] See Lynn White Jr., *Amer. Hist. Rev.* 52 (1947), 421-35.

optimism. In his mind the dusk of the late antique gods signified the rise of rational science.

Bernard's optimism resulted in part from the excitement generated by the recovery of many works of Greek learning through both Greek and Arabic channels in the second quarter of the century.[22] Awakened to the possibility of rediscovering ancient learning, northern Europeans began to travel to various points of contact with the Greek and Arabic world: to northern Italy, to the kingdom of Sicily, to Constantinople, and to Syria. In Bernard's time the most important centers of translation were in Spain. In the liberal atmosphere that followed the recapture of Toledo in 1085 the collaboration of Christian, Muslim, and Jew bore rich rewards. Raymond, bishop from 1125 to 1151, patronized the reintroduction into Latin of numerous philosophical works, while Dominicus Gondisalvi, archdeacon of Segovia, participated in the translation of Avicenna, ibn Gabirol, Alfarabi, and Algazel. John of Seville gave the Latin West its first versions of Ptolemy's *Centiloquium*, as well as the astrological treatises of Abu Ma'shar, Omar, Thebit, and Messahala. Plato of Tivoli translated the astronomy of Albattani and Ptolemy's *Quadripartitum* by 1138, and his *Liber Embadorum*, finished by

[22] I make no attempt to summarize the now vast literature on this question, except to point out that Haskins, from whom, chiefly, my summary is derived, did not sufficiently emphasize the part played by twelfth-century naturalists in introducing Aristotelian and Ptolemaic conceptions through indirect channels; on this question, see the excellent but neglected address of A. Birkenmajer at the VIe Congrès International des Sciences Historiques in Oslo, 1928, entitled, *Le rôle joué par les médicins et les naturalistes dans la réception d'Aristote au XIIe et XIIIe siècles* (Warszawa, 1930). A more recent summary is provided by Lemay, *Abu Ma'shar*, ix-xl. These works emphasize Arabic channels; on the transmission of Aristotle directly from the Greek see, in particular, L. Minio-Paluello, *Traditio* 8 (1952), 265-304.

1145, helped to introduce Arabic trigonometry into the north. Hermann of Carinthia and Robert of Chester appear to have worked together to latinize the *Koran* for Peter the Venerable. Hermann's text of Ptolemy's *Planisphere* is the only version of that work to have survived. Robert's astronomical tables, his version of Morienus' *De Compositione Alchemie* and his rendering of Alkhwarizmi's *Algebra* were completed by 1145. Spain, of course, was not the only center: from the eleventh century, Salerno, Antioch, and Sicily had been active. Nor is much known in detail about the translators, men like Iacobus Veneticus Grecus, Raymond of Marseilles, and Moses of Bergamo. Yet more than any other single factor, the translations were responsible for "the renaissance of the twelfth century."

One of the topics to be discussed below is Bernard's relation to this movement. The problem is complicated by the fact that the translation of a given work did not insure that it passed immediately into the school curriculum. A good example is furnished by the *Libri Naturales* of Aristotle. Available, in theory, from about 1150, they were not incorporated fully until nearly a half-century later.[23] A distinction must therefore be made between the enthusiasm the new science generated among the Latins and the actual influence it exercised in their works. The one must not be mistaken for the other. Like Adelard of Bath, the first Englishman of the century to take an interest in natural science, Bernard often reflects the intellectual developments of his time without giving evidence that he participated fully in them. Although Adelard is the more scientifically oriented of the two, their lives show certain similarities. For instance, the *Cosmographia*, like Adelard's *De Eodem et Diverso* and *Questiones Naturales*, brings

[23] D. A. Callus, *Proceedings of the British Academy* 29 (1943), 279.

25

the new learning into relation with the old, and unites both in an essentially classical format. The tension in *De Eodem* between Philocosmia, who loves this world, and Philosophia, who loves the ideal world, is matched by Bernard's simultaneous involvement in the real world and his detachment from it. While both authors are keenly interested in the new astronomy, which they know at first hand, neither betrays a genuine acquaintance with Aristotle. Their Aristotelianism is derived chiefly from the traditional *phisici* and *medici*. Along with Thierry of Chartres, William of Conches, and Daniel of Morley, however, they comprise a separate and highly original tradition of twelfth-century naturalism. Commenting on Adelard's failure to reflect in his writings the Arabic works in which he professed so keen an interest, Haskins concluded that he had derived "not so much facts or theories as a rationalistic habit of mind and a secular philosophy."[24] Haskins did not consider another possibility, namely that Chartres might have influenced Toledo. Yet this perspective would account more satisfactorily than the assumption of unidirectional influence for the continual attempts of many authors to unite the Latin and Arab positions into a universal cosmology.

This, in a word, was Bernard's aim. In order to accomplish it, he tried to bring together what he considered the two major sciences of his time, medicine and astronomy. His chief source for medical theory, it is assumed, was Constantinus Africanus, the eleventh-century translator of Hippocrates and Galen.[25] In Constantinus's abridgement of Ali ibn Abbas, medical theory was presented, as in Galen, as a development of general physical doctrines interrelating the universe and man, and it was in this form that Bernard

---

[24] Haskins, 39.
[25] On Constantinus's reception in the West, see H. Schipperges, *Sudhoffs Archiv für Geschichte der Medizin* 39 (1955), 62-67.

assimilated them into the *Cosmographia*. The chief sources for astronomy among the Latins were Chalcidius, Macrobius, and book eight of Martianus Capella's *De Nuptiis*; among the Arabs, Abu Ma'shar (ca. A.D. 786-866), whose *Maius Introductorium in Astronomiam* was made available in excerpt by John of Seville in 1133 and *in toto* by Hermann of Carinthia by 1141.[26] In Bernard's mind moreover medicine and astronomy were parts of a universal science, whose systematic features are discernible throughout the *Cosmographia*. The division of the work into two parts, treating the celestial or elemental (macrocosmic) and the sublunary (microcosmic) worlds was an acknowledgement of this principle—which Daniel of Morley, writing somewhat later, summarized aptly in stating

> qui igitur astronomiam dampnat, phisicam necessario destruit.[27]
> (he who thus condemns astrology, by necessity destroys physics.)

Medico-astronomical theory was also the framework within which Bernard, faithfully following Galen, revived the late classical idea of the natural order as a mediating element between God and the world.

Of the two sciences, Bernard considers astrology, that is, applied astronomy, the more important. In his mind it is an all-embracing theory of heavenly motion and by its laws the lower world is governed. Bernard had already displayed this interest in his *Mathematicus* (i.e. *The Astrologer*); he was to give it another direction in the *Ex-*

[26] On Abu Ma'shar's introduction in the twelfth century, see Lemay, *Abu Ma'shar*, 3-132. Lemay perhaps overstresses the degree to which Abu Ma'shar actually influenced the Chartres group; but see below, Ch. V.

[27] *Liber de Naturis Inferiorum et Superiorum*, ed. K. Sudhoff, *Archiv für die Geschichte der Naturwissenschaften*, 8 (1918), 32.

perimentarius, a treatise on divination through geomancy.[28] In the *Cosmographia* astrology is the queen of the predictive sciences. Its relation to medicine is summarized briefly by Abu Ma'shar himself in the *Introductorium*, i.1. Presenting astrology as the loftier discipline, as does Bernard, he nonetheless takes pains to point out its interdependence with medical theory:

> The object of medicine is as follows: first, to make a close investigation of the materials of bodies according to the natures of the elements; then, to mix [them] in the bodies, carefully observing their proportions; and lastly, to explain motions on the basis of the natural necessity of the mixtures through the intensification and diminution of their accidents. The object of astrology . . . is [first] to measure the motions of the elements from the motions of the stars and the changes of time; then to measure the motions of the cosmos itself; then, of its parts, [and to do all these] both generally and specifically. Just as the physician is first instructed by the sensations of his experience, then turns to the natural properties of the species . . . , so the astrologer turns from a certain sensible instruction of experience to the natural [relations] of heavenly bodies. . . . And thus he possesses the definite power and natural force of the stars and planets by reason of their effects.
>
> Medicine and astrology then seem to be rather universal [in their application]. . . . Medicine, starting from their composition, status, and accidents, deals with the nature of the elements and the changes of bodies; but astrology, as a whole, reaches its consummation in the motion and natures of celestial bodies

---

[28] On Bernard's geomancy, see L. Thorndike, *A History of Magic and Experimental Science*, vol. 2 (New York, 1929), 110-15.

and their effects throughout the lower world. The physician pays attention to changes in the elements; the astrologer follows the motions of the stars in order to understand the causes of fundamental change.[29]

In view of the general level of interest in astronomy in the period, this sort of statement could be expected to have a profound effect on a temperament like Bernard's. The enthusiasm which it may have generated is reflected in the letter which his friend, Hermann of Carinthia, sent to Thierry with his translation of Ptolemy's *Planisphere* in 1143. Reviewing the birth of astronomy, Hermann states that exact knowledge arose from the empirical measurement of the motions of celestial bodies.[30] By studying the

[29] *Introductorium in astronomiam Albumasaris abalchi octo continens libros partiales* [Venezia, 1506], f. a.4 recto: "Est autem medicine . . . officium. Primo corporum materias elementorum secundum naturas subtiliter perspicere, deinde in corporibus seruata proportionabilitate commiscere, commixtionum demum ex naturali necessitatis accessu at recessu accidentium motus tractare. Officium autem astrologie . . . ex motu stellarum elementorum motus temporumque alterationes atque tum mundi ipsius tum partium eius: hic generaliter, hic specialiter metiri accidentium motus. Ut igitur medicus sensilibus primum experimentis instructus, deinde ad nature proprietates prouectus specierum . . . sic astrologus ex sensibili quadam experimentorum institutione ad naturales celestium corporum prouectus . . . sicque stellarum et siderum cuiusque vim et naturam effectuum ratione certam habet. . . . Medicina vero et astrologia magis vniversalis videretur. . . . Medicina siquidem in elementorum naturis et in alterationibus corporumque ex eius compositione, statu, et accidentibus exercitatur; astrologia vero in celestium corporum motu et naturis atque per mundum inferiorum effectibus tota consumitur. Medicus quidem elementorum alterationibus operam dat. Astrologus stellarum motus sequitur elementarie ad alterationis causas." This text, which will be cited throughout, is John of Seville's version. Minor corrections have been made silently.

[30] *Claudii Ptolemaei opera*, ed. J. L. Heiberg (Leipzig, 1907), vol. 2, pp. clxxxiii-iv.

heavens, man was gradually able to understand nature and free himself, in part, from complete subjection to natural catastrophes. In addition, through science, Ptolemy solved a problem of great philosophical importance: identity and difference.[31] In Hermann's letter there is thus a meeting of the problems of Platonic cosmology and Ptolemaic astronomy: the latter is seen to be the complement of the former. Although influenced by Hermann, Bernard saw these relationships slightly differently. He agreed that Platonic cosmology was completed by astrology, but, unlike Hermann, he made man's senses and the physical sciences the bases for philosophical knowledge. His own original interpretation of the medical theories of Constantinus Africanus, with their sensorial bias, played a large role in his mind.

The *Cosmographia* is therefore a new cosmogony primarily in the sense of being a radical reworking of traditional material to suit the needs of a new horizon. In incorporating a certain amount of rationalism into the work, however, and in intermingling it with the natural lore which he drew from a variety of encyclopedias, Bernard never lost sight of the fact that he was writing a work of literature. It is his deliberately literary goals that separate him ultimately from the more overtly scientific writers of the period, even though on many occasions his doctrines differ little from theirs. This is another way of stating that in the *Cosmographia* the mythical predominates over the scientific. The philosophic abstractions, the *dramatis personae*, enact the creation of the world and of man as a cosmic epic. Von Bezold described Bernard's *Mathematicus*, a presumably earlier work, as a mixture of dialogue, drama, and epic.[32] While the *Cosmographia* is more

---

[31] *Ibid.* clxxxv.

[32] *Das Fortleben der antiken Götter im mittelalterlichen Humanismus* (Bonn/Leipzig, 1922), 84, 86.

complex, the same elements are at work. They give it its literary as opposed to rational flavor. But the subordination of the scientific to the humanistic is not simply the result of a loose union of the *quadrivium* and the *trivium*. It reveals an attitude towards myth which, as noted above, is a rejuvenated classical idea. Bernard clearly believed that myths like the *Timaeus* and Martianus' *De Nuptiis* concealed beneath their surface abstract truths. The *Cosmographia* is an attempt to construct a similar literary edifice. To understand this intention fully, therefore, some attention must be paid to the more general attitudes towards myth in the earlier twelfth century.

2. Twelfth-Century Approaches to Myth

If the ancient and late classical worlds, like the modern, were rather evenly divided on whether myths, allegories, or fables might conceal beneath their surface secret moral or philosophical information, the Middle Ages, until the 1140s, had no doubt whatsoever. The tendency towards allegory already highly developed in neoplatonism was extended between the ninth and the twelfth centuries until it emerged as a general method for dealing with all types of texts.[33] In the early twelfth century, individual disciplines

[33] There is no comprehensive account of literary theory in the twelfth century. In general, for the earlier period, see H. Wolfson, *The Philosophy of the Church Fathers*, vol. 1 (Cambridge, Mass., 1956) and J. Pépin, *Mythe et allégorie* (Paris, 1958); between the ninth and twelfth centuries, see M. Grabmann, *Die Geschichte der scholastischen Methode* (Freiburg i. B., 1910-12), C. Spicq, *Esquisse d'une histoire de l'exégèse latine au moyen âge* (Paris, 1944), and B. Smalley, *The Study of the Bible in the Middle Ages* (Oxford, 1952). The essay by H. de Lubac, *Recherches de science religieuse* 34 (1947), 180-226 is valuable, but his later study, *Exégèse médiévale*, 4 vols. (Paris, 1959-64) should be used with caution. Figural typology in literature was the subject of several studies by E. Auer-

like law, theology, and, to a lesser degree, literature, began to take on the characteristics of separate subjects in the school curriculum, but they had not developed methods of classifying and analysing facts which corresponded to their own exigencies. Out of the *trivium* developed a common approach to different sorts of literary documents, and out of the *quadrivium*, a common fund of knowledge with which to carry out interpretation. In particular, scholars commenting on classical texts during the intellectual revival of the early twelfth century introduced their theories of the hidden meanings of myths from a framework for exegesis most highly refined by theologians. The methods being developed for the sacred texts became, with slight modifications, those employed for secular texts.

In commenting on secular literary or natural-philosophic texts, the threefold or fourfold system of exegesis was generally simplified. One normally finds only two senses clearly distinguished: the literal and the allegorical.[34] The literal corresponded to the grammatical sense. It dealt with the meanings of difficult words or phrases, etymologies, and historical facts. The allegorical sense, as in theology, varied greatly. Its chief concern lay with the moral-philo-

---

bach; see in particular *Scenes from the Drama of European Literature, Six Essays* (New York, 1959), 11-76, and *Typologische Motive in der mittelalterlichen Literatur* (Krefeld, 1953). On this subject see D. W. Robertson, Jr., *A Preface to Chaucer* (Princeton, 1963), 286-364, and the general article of Uda Ebel in H. R. Jauss and E. Köhler, eds., *Grundriss der romanischen Literaturen des Mittelalters*, vol. 6, tome 1 (Heidelberg, 1968), 181-215. On Bernard Silvester himself, see J. R. O'Donnell, *MS* 24 (1962), 233-49.

[34] An exception is Alan of Lille, *Anticlaudianus*, prologue, ed. Bossuat (Paris, 1955), p. 56, lines 7-10: "In hoc enim opere litteralis sensus suauitas puerilem demulcebit auditum, moralis instructio perficientem imbuet sensum, acutior allegorie subtilitas proficientem acuet intellectum." But can one really separate the "moral" and the "allegorical" senses in the *Anticlaudianus*?

sophical meaning of the text but it was not limited to that. In particular, as interest in science grew and new, hitherto unknown texts began to appear, it gradually developed as well into the secret rational or naturalistic meaning of the text. An active school of naturalistic exegesis developed at Chartres under Bernard, Thierry, Gilbert Porreta, and William of Conches, and the number of extant commentaries of this type in classical texts all over Europe (many awaiting their editors) testifies to a very widespread phenomenon. They indicate that, in general, the revival of legal, classical, and Biblical studies went hand in hand with an interest in natural philosophy; that through the application of logic and the discovery of new facts, myths began to be demythologized and the value of myth itself to be reassessed.

A document recently discovered by Abbé Jeauneau admirably illustrates all of these tendencies.[35] It consists of a literary and philosophical commentary on a part of the first book of Martianus Capella's early fifth-century *Nuptials of Philology and Mercury*. The commentary is found in a unique manuscript, Cambridge University Library Mm. I.18, ff. 1-28r, and it breaks off abruptly at *De Nuptiis* i.37. The distribution of the commentary is also uneven. It does not deal with the whole of the story of even *De Nuptiis* i, which concerns Mercury's search for a bride and his eventual choice of Philology on the advice of Virtue and Apollo. Folios 1-6ra of the commentary are devoted exclusively to Martianus i meter 1 (*Tu quem psallentem* . . .), which obviously appeared in the eyes of the commentator to comprise a synthesis of Platonic philosophy similar to that presented in rather more numerous exegeses of Boethius, *Consolatio Philosophiae* iii, meter 9.[36] From folio 6 to 17rb the commentary deals again with a

---

[35] *SMed* 5 (1964), 844-49, 855-64.
[36] See P. Courcelle, *AHDLMA* 12 (1939), 5-140; H. Silvestre,

relatively small portion of the text, i.2-8, in which Martianus, the narrator, explains to his nephew the sort of tale he is going to tell and the search for a bride for Mercury actually begins. From this point the commentary is slightly less concentrated, passing line by line through each succeeding section of book one.

The complexity of the commentary has led Jeauneau to remark that it is one of the most important expositions of Martianus in the Middle Ages.[37] Its interest for this study is that it brings under one cover Platonic cosmology, a theory of myth, and *encyclopedica*—the very elements out of which the *Cosmographia* is built. As the work is not easily consultable, its contents may be summarized briefly. It begins with a discussion of the musical harmony of nature and man (ff. 1va-2ra), including an exposition of the *integumentum* of Bacchus and Apollo (ff. 2rb-2va). Then it turns to the concord of the four elements and their analogies in man (ff. 2va-3vb),[38] using as illustrations, in part, the fables of Tiresias and Pollux and Castor (ff. 3vb-4ra). A lengthy treatise on the division of the sciences (ff. 5ra-5vb) and the cardinal virtues (6ra) follows. Then, returning to his initial preoccupations, the author treats the union of Jove and Juno in Martianus allegorically as the harmonious interplay of the four elements and the natural cycle of life (ff. 7ra-8ra). Afterwards, fate and God's omnipotence are discussed, and there is a section devoted to the good and to faith, finishing with an explication of the

---

Revue d'histoire ecclésiastique 47 (1952), 44-122; R.C.B. Huygens, *Sacris Erudiri* 6 (1954), 373-427; E. Jeauneau, *Rivista critica della storia della filosofia* 14 (1959), 60-80. The best brief article is still that of J. Handschin, *Zeitschrift für Musikwissenschaft* 9 (1927), 193-208.

[37] *SMed* 5 (1964), 844.

[38] Published in part (f. 3ra) by Jeauneau, *ibid.* 857-58.

myth of Nereus (ff. 8ra-10ra). This in turn is followed by a commentary on Chalcidius' views on *hyle, silva,* and other cosmological issues, and includes a fascinating discussion of the way in which the *archetypus mundi* is revealed *sub integumento* in the fable of Argus (ff. 10rb-vb). Following this, there is a long explanation of various notions employed by Martianus: *fama* (10vb-11ra), youth (11rb-11va), the liberal arts (11va-12rb), divination (12rb-13ra), *entelechia* (13ra-13va), *psyche* (13va and at numerous later stages), the origin of the soul (13vb),[39] eternity (14ra), *ratio* (14ra-rb), Tritonia, Delius, Urania, *divina pagina*, Vulcan, the five senses, and *memoria* in quick succession (ff. 14ra-16va), *virtus* (16vb-17vb), the classical oration and its parts (17vb), *fortuna* (18va), and musical terminology (18vb).

The commentary turns at this point to astronomy and astrology, dealing successively with the problem of the waters above the firmament (ff. 19rb-va),[40] the makeup of the heavens, the spheres, and the four elements (19vb-20vb), *fortuna* again, in the context of astrological determinism (21ra-b), the zodiac (21va), the four seasons (21vb), and the *anima mundi* (22ra). What may be described as the last section of the commentary consists of an exposition of *De Nuptiis,* book i, meter 2.21-22. It includes a discussion of music (ff. 22rb-23ra) and philology (23rb), and also treats prefiguration in the Bible (24ra), Apollo and his mythographical associations (24rb), the Muses (25ra-b), and the voyage to demand Jove's approval, not without parallels with the vision of Rachel (25va-b).[41] The opinions in the commentary, while covering many subjects, are not often striking in originality. The classical authorities consist of Plato, Chalcidius, Macrobius, and the

[39] *Ibid.* 859-60. [40] *Ibid.* 860-62.
[41] *Ibid.* 862-64.

encyclopedists, while echoes of William of Conches are prominent among the *moderni.* Jeauneau thinks that the commentary was written by Bernard Silvester.[42] Even if it is not, it illustrates a view

[42] In the article cited, 845-50, Jeauneau argues for Bernard's authorship. The evidence is as follows: (1) the author of Mm.I.18 refers to a commentary on Virgil, and passages of the Martianus commentary resemble those in the *Aeneid* commentary, assigned by some to Bernard; (2) the author of Mm.I.18 refers to Orléans as a familiar place; and (3) both the text of Mm.I.18 and Bernard Silvester are associated with Chartres. The author of the Martianus commentary even refers to the controversy on whether there are waters above the firmament (Genesis i.6-7), arguing against the refutation of this idea in William of Conches' *Philosophia Mundi.*

The evidence, however, makes better sense if turned around. First of all, Bernard's authorship of the Virgil commentary is uncertain. It is mentioned in a fifteenth-century library catalogue (see P. Lehmann, *Mittellateinische Bibliothekskataloge,* vol. 2, p. 15, line 35), and the MS on which Riedel based his edition is a single fifteenth-century copy, Paris, Bibl. Nat., lat. 16,246, ff. 44r-68r. While further research has revealed other copies (see G. Padoan, *Italia medioevale e humanistica* 3 (1960), 227-40), it has not greatly strengthened the case for Bernard's authorship. The other known copy, MS Crakow, Bibl. Jagell., 1198.DD.12, is also late, and to complicate the matter further, the Paris MS also contains the *Poetria* of Alberic of London, supposed by some to be the author of the *Third Vatican Mythograph,* a work which the author of Mm.I.18 appears at times to be citing; see notes 85 and 86 of this chapter. Furthermore, later references to the commentary do not strongly associate it with Bernard. In his edition of Coluccio Salutati's *De Laboribus Herculis* (Zurich, 1951), B. L. Ullman provides an index to alleged citations of the commentary. But Salutati, who cites most of his other authorities by name, nowhere mentions Bernard, and Ullman's *fontes* do not provide convincing rapports.

There are also some independent reasons against attributing Mm.I.18 to Bernard. (1) He never taught at Orléans and is only connected to Chartres, which the author of Mm.I.18 may know, by the thinnest of evidence. (2) So far as is known, he wrote no commentary on Plato, and the author of Mm.I.18 makes repeated references to one; see Jeauneau, *art. cit.,* 846. (MS Trinity Colof literature and philosophy currently in fashion at both Chartres and Tours. The most elaborate discussion of literary typology in the treatise occurs in the *accessus*. After listing the contents, the author presents a series of definitions of types of allegory, including some loose notes on the uses of myth. While not in any sense a comprehensive, philosophical document, this passage is one of the fullest contemporary statements extant of allegorical theory. The text is as follows:[43]

---

lege, Cambridge, O.7.7 contains a twelfth-century copy of the *Cosmographia* to which is appended, in the same hand, a short commentary on Plato using its images, ff. 26r-27v, but this can hardly be construed as a full exposition of the *Timaeus*; see Stock, *MS* 34 (1972), 152-73.) Therefore, if the author of the Virgil commentary also wrote the Martianus commentary, he was probably not Bernard. (3) There are important doctrinal differences between the *Cosmographia* and Mm.I.18. For instance, Bernard did not defend the ridiculous thesis that waters exist above the firmament; his conception of the *aplanos* is discussed in Ch. IV. (4) Except for its orthodoxy on this last point, the Martianus commentary might well be associated with the school of William of Conches; on William's unlocated lectures on *De Nuptiis*, see M. Grabmann, *SB München, philos.-hist. Abt.* 10 (1935), 25-26. (5) The *Ysagoge in Theologiam* in MS Trinity College, Cambridge B.14.33, ff. 3r-111v, written in an English hand of the early twelfth century, contains word for word with its diagram at ff. 9r-10v the division of the sciences of Mm.I.18, ff. 5ra-b. This remarkable document, which antedates all known copies of the commentaries attributed to Bernard, contains a complete theology based upon a glossing of the Hebrew text of the Bible, which it cites. It was published by Landgraf, *Spicilegium Sacrum Lovaniense* 14 (Louvain, 1934). On the authorship, see D. E. Luscombe, *AHDLMA* 43 (1969), 7-16.

[43] f. 1rb; ed. Jeauneau, *art. cit.*, 856-57. I have relied, on the whole, on Jeauneau's transcription and repeated his notes. Minor changes include repunctuation, retention of the original orthography and, in the first line of the cited passage, the preference for the actual MS reading in favor of Jeauneau's "Genus doctrine figura est."

Genus figura doctrine est. Figura, autem, est oratio quam inuolucrum dicere solent. Hec autem bipertita est: partimur namque eam in allegoriam et integumentum. Est autem allegoria oratio sub historica narratione uerum et ab exteriori diuersum inuoluens intellectum, ut de lucta Iacob. Integumentum uero est oratio sub fabulosa narratione uerum claudens intellectum, ut de Orpheo. Nam et ibi historia et hic fabula misterium habent occultum, quod alias discutiendum erit. Allegoria quidem diuine pagine, integumentum uero philosophice competit.

Non tamen ubique, teste Macrobio, inuolucrum tractatus admittit philosophicus. Cum enim ad summum, inquit, deum stilus se audet attollere, nefas est fabulosa, uel licita, admittere. Ceterum cum de anima uel de ethereis aeriisue potestatibus agitur, locum habent integumenta. Unde Virgilius humani spiritus temporalem cum corpore uitam describens integumentis usus est. Qui idem introducens sibillam de deis agentem inquid: "obscuris uera inuoluens,"[44] id est, diuina integumentis claudens. Plato quoque de mundano corpore aperte locutus, cum ad animam uentum est, dicit figuraliter eius materiam numerum esse.[45] De stellis quoque euidenter pronuntians, mistice de spiritibus dicturus ad inuolucrum se conuertit, dicens quia celi et terre filii sunt Oceanus et Thetis.[46] Ergo et iste (= Martianus) humane nature deificationem pandens nihil absque misterio efferens ut prudens theologus fatur.

A [literary] figure is a kind of instruction. More-

---

[44] *Aeneid* vi.100. On medieval interpretations of this text, see P. Courcelle, *Fondation Hardt . . . Entretiens* III (1955), 95-136.
[45] *Tim.* 35A-36D; pp. 27-28.
[46] *Tim.* 40E-41A; p. 35, 1-6.

over, a figure is a literary discourse which is normally called a mythical covering. It is subdivided into two types, *allegoria* (theological allegory) and *integumentum* (philosophical myth). Now an allegory in this sense is a literary work in the form of an historical narrative, enveloping an understanding true and different from external appearance, like the struggle of Jacob. But a philosophical myth is a literary work which encloses its true significance in the form of a fictitious narrative, as in Orpheus. Both the historical and the fictional modes contain a secret mystery which will be discussed elsewhere. In sum, allegory is suitable for Holy Scripture while myth is suitable for philosophical writing.

As Macrobius bears witness, a philosophical treatise in itself does not permit the use of myth everywhere. For he states that when the style dares to approach the highest divinity, it is wrong to use even a permitted [type of] fiction.[47] On the other hand, when treating the soul, the heavens, or the celestial forces, myths have their place. Virgil, describing the temporal existence of the human spirit with the body, uses mythical coverings in this way. The same authority, introducing a prophetess treating of the gods, speaks, "enveloping the truth in obscurities," that is, enwrapping divine matters in a covering. Plato, as well, after speaking openly about the human body, when it comes to a question of the soul, says figuratively that its material is number. Also, speaking clearly of the stars when he was about to speak mystically of spirits, he has recourse to myth, stating that Oceanus and Thetis are the sons of heaven and earth. Thus as well, Martia-

---

[47] Literally, "the permission or the use of the fabulous is forbidden," garbling Macrobius, *Comm.* i.2.13-14 (cited in n. 60 of this chapter).

nus, an experienced commentator, unveiling the apotheosis of human nature, presents nothing without an inner meaning.

This is an uncomplicated analysis of the types and uses of allegory, intended for the classroom and based upon a late classical exemplar: the famous discussion of the kinds of fabulous narratives in Macrobius, *Commentary on the Dream of Scipio*, i.2.6-16. That the author should employ Macrobius in the *accessus* to a commentary on his near contemporary, Martianus Capella, is characteristic of expositions of classical texts in the period. In addition to being linked in the twelfth-century imagination as theoreticians of myths and dreams, whose revelations of mystery were in some ways similar, they comprised the two chief sources for doctrines on astronomy before translations like those of Hermann of Carinthia and John of Spain made available more exact Arab sources.[48] What the above passage says about allegory is neither very original nor difficult to follow, but it employs a number of technical terms of exegesis which require explanation and render a simple translation inadequate.

Before discussing them, some attention should be paid to the idea of poetry conceived as a general imaginative experience in the commentary. Poetry is here defined by analogy with theology: just as God, as poet-creator, makes both order and harmony in the universe and invests religious writings with secret mysteries, so the myth-maker invents a literary allegory beneath whose exterior moral or natural truths are concealed. Just as Scriptural truths pass from their eternal creator to the temporal earth through the medium of the Word, so poetry presents moral or physical doctrines in a manner pleasing and un-

[48] C. Leonardi, *I codici de Marziano Capella* (Milano, 1959-60), 476 (= *Aevum* 33 [1959], 476).

derstandable to the reader. The poet is not so much the creator as the medium and arranger of the literary work: the *artifex*. This conception of the poetic experience, an adaptation of Plato's notion of literature's essential falsehood to Aristotle's justification of its utility, was passed on to the Middle Ages by the neoplatonists. In poetic practice its essential features are found in Lucretius, Manilius, and in the Christian-Latin poets of the fourth and fifth centuries who versified the cosmogony of Genesis. Its theory is concisely summarized in a single statement in the ninth century by John Scottus Eriugena:

> Just as poetic art, through untrue stories and allegorical representation, constructs its moral and physical doctrine towards the arousing of the human spirit— for this is proper for heroic poets, who praise the deeds and habits [of men] figuratively—so theology, as if by a certain poetry, shapes Holy Scripture by fictions of the imagination towards the counsel of the soul.[49]

Eriugena has reversed the comparison, but has included all the essential elements: the notion of poetry both as figure and as instruction; the analogy from theology—in this case from poetry to theology as, somewhat later, in William of Conches—in which both experiences share a common theory of myth; and, what becomes of central interest in the twelfth century, the idea that not only moral but also physical doctrines may be concealed by allegory.

The conception of the poet as philosopher, prophet, and

---

[49] *Expos. J. Scot. super Ierarchias S. Dionysii*, cap. 2.1; *PL* 122, 146B-C: "Quemadmodum ars poetica per fictas fabulas allegoricasque similitudines moralem doctrinam seu physicam componit ad humanorum animorum exercitationem—hoc enim est proprium heroicorum poetarum, qui virorum fortium facta et mores figurate laudant—ita theologica veluti quaedam poetria sanctam Scripturam fictis imaginationibus ad consultum nostri animi . . . conformat."

viaticum to occult knowledge became fully developed in the revival of Platonism in the first half of the twelfth century.[50] A classic description of the poet's role occurs in the *accessus* to the commentary attributed to Bernard Silvester on the first six books of the *Aeneid*. Here, Virgil is both *poeta et philosophus*:

> Insofar as he is a philosopher, he writes concerning the nature of human life, and this is his method of proceeding: under the cover of allegory he describes what the human spirit, placed for a time in the human body, undertakes or undergoes. In writing this work he . . . respects two arrangements in the narrative: as a poet, the artificial, as a philosopher, the natural. For *integumentum* is a type of demonstration which beclouds the understanding of the truth under a fictitious narrative. For this reason it is also called *involucrum*. And a person takes from such a work what is useful according to his own capacity [to interpret it].[51]

[50] Cf. Camb. Univ. Lib., MS Mm.I.18, f. 10ra. Amid a comparison of the fable of Nereus to the Bible, the commentator states: "Nouit namque omnia uates que sunt, que fuerant, que mox uentura trahantur. Nam ingenium habet mensuram ad capienda quedam futura et rationem ad presentia et memoriam ad transacta tenenda." The idea is put another way at f. 8vb: "Quod uero in mundo scribitur diuinitas sic accipe: mundus hic sensilis liber quidam est, habens in se diuinitatem, in se scriptura." Cf. the discussion of *divina pagina*, f. 15ra. Bernard does not actually refer to the poet as prophet in the *Cosmographia*. Alan of Lille, however, summarizes the notion of the poet as a medium in the *Anticlaudianus*, v. 273; ed. Bossuat, p. 131: "Carminis huius ero calamus, non scriba uel actor. . . ." Alan may be the earliest poet of modern Europe to assume this role. It is traditionally assigned to Dante; see the excellent study of B. Nardi, *Dante e la cultura medievale* (Bari, 1942), 258-334, and more generally E. R. Curtius, *Europäische Literatur und lateinisches Mittelalter* (Berne, 1954), Excursus xxi.

[51] *Comm. Bern. Silvestris sup. sex libros Eneidos Virgilii*, ed. G. Riedel (Greifswald, 1924), 3: "Scribit enim in quantum est phi-

This statement, like the *accessus* to the Martianus commentary cited above, is an attempt to integrate the creation of a literary work into the realm of experience by employing moral and physical allegory. The myth is considered in two ways: as a simple narrative and as a structure of ideas whose meaning is to be sought in relation to life itself. The myth not only instructs and delights, but provides a means whereby, in a moral and physical sense, man may come to know himself better. Moreover, it should be stressed that the poet, as *philosophus*, has the same access to hidden physical doctrines as the natural philosopher. In his *Liber de Naturis*, Daniel of Morley refers to Hesiod as *naturalis scientie professor*.

These relationships may be better appreciated by returning to the Martianus commentary and discussing the issues it raises, its sources, and the two chief exegetical terms, *involucrum* and *integumentum*, which it shares with the Virgil commentary.

In using the term *figura*, first of all, to characterize allegorical discourse, the author introduces a definition which recalls the Roman grammarians. Quintilian, who summarizes their theories, states that a figure of thought or of speech is "a rational change in meaning or in language from the ordinary and simple form."[52] Late Latin gram-

---

losophus humanae vitae naturam. Modus vero agendi talis est: sub integumento describit quid agat vel quid patiatur humanus spiritus in humano corpore temporaliter positus. Atque in hoc scribendo . . . utrumque narrationis ordinem observat, artificialem poeta, naturalem philosophus. Integumentum vero est genus demonstrationis sub fabulosa narratione veritatis involvens intellectum, unde et involucrum dicitur. Utilitatem vero capit homo ex hoc opere secundum sui agnitionem. . . ." Cf. R. McKeon, *Modern Philology* 43 (1945-46), 222-23, who neglects, in my opinion, the force of naturalistic as opposed to moral allegory.

[52] *Institutio Oratoria* ix.1.4; ed. L. Radermacher (Leipzig, 1925), vol. ii, p. 133: " 'figura' . . . ⟨est⟩ conformatio quaedam orationis

marians agree with him that *allegoria*, in the literal sense, is a figure of speech through which the original is willfully distorted, using "wit, sarcasm, contradiction and proverb."[53] The twelfth-century commentator, proceeding from grammar to rhetoric and dialectic, first integrates his sense of allegory with classical linguistic theory, then turns to the moral or philosophical sense of allegory which is his real interest. His discussion from this point is inseparable from its chief source, Macrobius' *Commentary on the Dream of Scipio.*

In the section of the *Commentary* which forms the basis for this discussion (i.2.6-16), Macrobius is actually developing, somewhat inaccurately, a schema of Plotinus against the Epicureans, who wished to exclude all imaginary events from serious discourse.[54] In his hasty division of fables, allegories, and myths, Macrobius employs the term *fabula* in a new sense, that of myth. Chalcidius had used the term to translate *mythos*, but primarily in the sense of story or fable.[55] Parallels for Macrobius' usage may be found in Firmicus Maternus and in Martianus Capella.[56] Latin, possessing no special term for myth, gradually pressed into service *fabula* (or *fabella*) and its adjective *fabulosus*. In philosophical theology, Macrobius states, *fabulae* are divided broadly into two groups, depending on whether their function is to give pleasure or instruction.[57] In some of these

---

remota a communi et primum se offerente ratione"; trans. Butler (Loeb).

[53] *Ibid.* viii.6.57, citing the translation of Butler, vol. 3, p. 333 f.

[54] *Comm.* i.2.3; p. 4: "Epicureorum tota factio aequo semper errore a vero devia et illa aestimans ridenda quae nesciat. . . ."

[55] See Waszink, index, p. 368, s.v. μῦθος.

[56] See *Iulii Firmicii Materni Matheseos libri VIII*, ed. W. Kroll and F. Skutsch (Leipzig, 1913), index, s.v., and *De Nuptiis*, ed. Dick-Préaux, index, s.v., and of course Cicero, *passim*.

[57] *Comm.* i.2.7; p. 5.

fictions, like those of Aesop, the matter is wholly false, while "the argument in others, by contrast, is built upon a foundation of truth. However, this very truth is represented by a certain fictitious arrangement and this type, to be precise, is called *narratio fabulosa*."[58] Not satisfied with these distinctions, Macrobius again divides fabulous narratives into two types: in the first, the plot involves material unfit for philosophers and disrespectful to the gods; in the second, "a notion of sacred mysteries, covered with respectable ideas and dressed up with appellatives, is disclosed under the pious veil of allegory."[59] These are the types of myths suitable for serious philosophical commentary.

Macrobius then turns to the sort of material which allegorical myths should treat; on this point the anonymous twelfth-century commentator paid close attention. Macrobius says that "commentaries do not admit the fabulous, even of the approved kind, in every discourse, but are accustomed to employ them whenever they speak of the soul, aereal or ethereal powers, or the other [planetary or stellar] divinities."[60] The allegorical myth, however, is not employed in treating "the highest and most important of all divinities, who among the Greeks is called either the Good or the first cause or Mind—containing the original parts of the universe, called ideas, originating and coming

[58] *Ibid.* i.2.9; p. 5: ". . . at in aliis argumentum quidem fundatur veri soliditate sed haec ipsa veritas per quaedam composita et ficta profertur, et hoc iam vocatur narratio fabulosa. . . ."

[59] *Ibid.* i.2.11; p. 6: ". . . sacrarum rerum notio sub pio figmentorum velamine honestis et tecta rebus et vestita nominibus enuntiatur."

[60] *Ibid.* i.2.13; p. 6: "Sciendum est tamen non in omnem disputationem philosophos admittere fabulosa vel licita, sed his uti solent cum vel de anima vel de aeriis aetheriisve potestatibus vel de ceteris dis loquuntur."

from the supreme God."[61] Macrobius concludes this section with a statement whose "special language" of mystery and religion must have held a wide appeal for a group of writers, like those at Chartres, who were experiencing, not only a revival of the structural study of myth, but also of Hermeticism:[62]

de dis autem, ut dixi, ceteris et de anima non frustra se nec ut oblectent ad fabulosa convertunt, sed quia sciunt inimicam esse Naturae apertam[63] nudamque expositionem sui, quae sicut vulgaribus hominum sensibus intellectum sui vario rerum tegmine operimentoque subtraxit, ita a prudentibus arcana sua voluit per fabulosa tractari. Sic ipsa mysteria figurarum cuniculis operiuntur ne vel haec adeptis nudam rerum talium Natura se praebeat, . . .

But concerning the rest of the gods, as I said, and the soul, philosophers turn to the mythical, not without

[61] *Ibid.* i.2.14; p. 6: ". . . ad summum et principem omnium deum, qui apud Graecos τἀγαθὸν, qui πρῶτον αἴτιον nuncupatur . . . vel ad mentem, quem Graeci νοῦν appellant, originales rerum species, quae ἰδέαι dictae sunt, continentem, ex summo natam et profectam deo."

[62] *Ibid.* i.2.17-18; p. 7.

[63] Is Macrobius echoing the more brilliant statement of the same idea by Seneca, *Naturales Questiones* vii.30.6; ed. F. Haase (Leipzig, 1893), ii, 316-17?: "⟨sic⟩ rerum natura sacra sua non semel tradit. initiatos nos credimus: in vestibulo eius haeremus. illa arcana non promiscue nec omnibus patent: reducta et interiore sacrario clausa sunt. ex quibus aliud haec aetas, aliud quae post nos subibit, dispiciet." A late twelfth-century poem on the same theme is edited and somewhat misinterpreted by F.J.E. Raby, *Speculum* 43 (1968), 72-77. The lines of Bernard Silvester cited on p. 72 are not indebted to Macrobius but to Abu Ma'shar; Macrobius does not state (pp. 74-75) that serious fables may not delight and instruct at once.

purpose or to divert themselves, but because they know that a free, unclothed display of herself is unacceptable to Nature. For, just as she has withdrawn her meaning from the understanding of common men through the varied covering and concealment of her essential qualities, so she has decided that her secrets are to be discussed by experienced men through myth. These very mysteries are hidden by the devices of allegory, in order that she, being Nature, may not display herself nude even to the adepts of such rites.

To an educated, bicultural reader of the fifth century, Macrobius would seem to have united in this section of his commentary a number of different threads of Hellenistic thought. But to a twelfth-century Platonist, lacking the complex originals out of which Macrobius' loose fabric was woven, the discussion of allegory appeared to be, not only a totality in itself, but a starting point for further theory and discussion. Macrobius' central points recur frequently in twelfth-century commentaries: the idea of the poet as prophet, leading the reader to deeper knowledge of the text or of himself by means of allegory; the myth itself, the structure that results from his creative activities, as opposed to a strictly logical discourse; the personification of Nature, a Hermetic goddess who reveals her secrets through the medium of the poet, the high-priest of creation as a divine work of art; and the technical terms, only metaphors in Macrobius—like *tegmine operimentoque*—which become, in the twelfth century, points of definition and reference. Most importantly, through neoplatonism two different sorts of activity become legitimized: first, the demythologization of ancient fables and myths to elicit their hidden meanings; secondly, the making of new myths, the actual creation of structures that seek to symbolize the true nature of reality. In the resonance between these two interdependent, yet not interchangeable, literary forms, the commentators provide a language for understanding the new and original literary myth of the *Cosmographia*.

There are some fundamental similarities and one striking difference between Macrobius' original and the twelfth-century commentary on it. Like Macrobius, the later commentator presents a demythologization which is much more overtly scientific in its interests than the text it exposes. Neither Cicero's *Dream of Scipio*, from the *Republic*, nor Martianus' *De Nuptiis*, book one, are, in the ordinary sense, scientific documents. Yet both commentaries are eclectic encyclopedias of natural philosophy. Macrobius is one of the classic repositories of Greek learning in the Middle Ages. The Martianus commentary is a representative collection of scientific doctrines from the earlier twelfth century. In many respects their views on individual issues are variants of a similar position. Yet there is a basic difference between the two. The Martianus commentary does not make a division between frivolous and serious allegory but between religious and secular. It reserves *allegoria*, a term inadequately rendered by its English or Romance language cognates, for the Bible. To describe secular myths it employs *integumentum* and *involucrum*. (*Involucrum*, it should be noted, appears to refer to all myths, but the distinction between religious and secular is developed in what follows.) While a certain analogy of methods is implied, the author is careful not to confuse the two kinds of allegory. In his mind they refer to two fundamentally different kinds of narrative, *historia* and *fabula*, factual and fictitious. The commentator does not see the logical impossibility of proposing a structural methodology for handling all types of myth while asserting that one group has an especially intimate affinity with truth. Other commentators, like William of Conches, approached this question in a freer spirit. The important point however is the analogy: through the *trivium*, the "science des *verba*" and the *quadrivium*, the "science des *res*,"[64] the enigmas of myths yield to the hard cold facts. The twelfth-century approach to myth, presented here in general outline only, thus possesses all the features of a consistent, systematic literary theory. Twelfth-century documents which actually treat these problems are relatively rare. There is however another way of attacking the whole question: by tracing through the earlier periods the progressive expansion of sense of the two central terms, *involucrum* and *integumentum*.[65]

The Latin meaning of *integumentum*, a physical covering of some kind, survives in the little used English word "integument," but, like *involucrum*, for which it is virtually a synonym in the twelfth century, its technical significance in the medieval critical vocabulary has been lost. In classical Latin, neither term appears to have been used often, and both possessed an unphilosophical primary sense. Cicero however employs them both as figures of speech in a manner which precisely foreshadows their later development. In *De Oratore*, Cotta praises Crassus (and thus Cicero himself) for having the good sense to suggest that a moderate amount of rhetoric enhances any good speech, saying

[64] Chenu, 48.

[65] The material from printed sources in the following account is from the *TLL*: for *integumentum*, vol. vii,1, fasc. xiv (Leipzig, 1963), pp. 2088-89; for *involucrum*, vol. vii,2, fasc. ii (1959), pp. 260-61. A useful article on *involucrum* is M.-D. Chenu, *AHDLMA* 22 (1956), 75-79. On *integumentum*, especially in William of Conches, see E. Jeauneau, *AHDLMA* 24 (1958), 35-100. On both terms see as well H. de Lubac, *Exégèse médiévale*, vol. ii.2 (1964), 182-208, and H. Brinkmann in A. Zimmermann, ed., *Miscellanea Mediaevalia* 8 (Berlin/New York, 1971), 314-39.

modo in oratione Crassi divitias atque ornamenta eius ingenii per quaedam involucra et integumenta perspexi.[66]

I sensed just now during Crassus' speech the riches and embellishments of his inventive power as through some wrappings and coverings.

While both terms retain the physical meaning as "covering," there is also suggested a Platonic metaphor, as if Crassus, by wrapping his meaning in such delicate, rhetorical veils, has paralleled the concealment of formal reality from the senses of man by the phenomenal appearance of things.

In the late Latin or patristic period, *integumentum* is a rare word which spawns a number of related terms, all bearing a physical meaning.[67] *Involucrum*, by contrast, soon enters the vocabulary of Christian Latin and its physical sense is subordinated to, or combined with, new abstract connotations. In place of a physical covering it comes to represent a type of covering beneath which thought is deliberately concealed, as a parallel to the covering of the soul provided by the body. As a cover of this kind, *involucrum* is both *allegoria* in the limited, grammatical sense and in the wider moral sense. The evolution of this meaning, moreover, is not difficult to trace, since it is a tributary to a mainstream of Christian metaphor. Paul, for instance, states that at the end of time, "this perishable being must be clothed with the imperishable and what is mortal must be clothed with immortality."[68] The Vulgate translates Paul's term "to clothe" by *induere*, which is

---

[66] *De Oratore* i.35.161; cf. Jeauneau, *AHDLMA* 24 (1958), 38 n. 3.

[67] E.g., *integulatus*, "covered with tiles"; A. Souter, *A Glossary of Later Latin to 600 A.D.* (Oxford, 1949), 233.

[68] I Cor. 15:53, trans. *New English Bible*.

close to Macrobius' Platonic metaphors *vestire* and *tegere* as well as to the nominal forms *velamentum, tegmen,* and *operimentum.* Christian patristic use of the metaphor, moreover, also parallels Macrobius' usage. Ambrose, for example, states that "mens hominis . . . quasi involucro quodam corporis tegitur"[69] (the soul of man . . . as if by a certain wrapping of the body, is concealed); and adds, paraphrasing Paul, that immortality will intervene at the end of time "cum huius corporis anima deposuerit involucrum. . . ."[70] (when the soul has put aside the covering of the body). Augustine is capable of using the word with both a physical and an abstract sense. Discussing the degradations of the flesh, he states that "sapiens . . . ab omnibus involucris corporis mentem, quantum potest, evoluit"[71] (the wise man . . . turns his mind away from all the superficialities of the body as much as he can). But he can also extend the enigmatic sense of the term beyond that of Ambrose: "cum involucrum . . . similitudinis quaerentibus discipulis explicaret, non ait 'ager est Africa,' sed ait, 'ager est mundus' "[72] (when he explained the hidden meaning of the simile to those disciples who were posing questions, he did not say, "the place is Africa," but said, "the place is the world"). And again: "ubique Christus aliquo involucro sacramenti praedictus est a prophetis, Ecclesia aperte,"[73]

---

[69] *Inst. Virg.* iii.18; cited in *TLL*, vol. vii,2, fasc. ii, p. 260, s.v. "*involucrum*," section 1,b.

[70] *Cain et Abel* ii.9.36 (*TLL*).

[71] *Contra Acadic.* i.18.23 (*TLL*).

[72] *C. ep. Parmeniani* i.14.21 (*TLL*).

[73] *De Beata Vita* i.4 (*TLL*); not to forget the beautiful use of the metaphor by Prudentius, *Cathemerinon* v.33-36; ed. M. P. Cunningham (Turnhout, 1966), p. 24:

> Felix qui meruit sentibus in sacris
> caelestis solii uisere principem,
> iussus nexa pedum uincula soluere
> ne sanctum inuolucris poluerat locum.

(Everywhere Christ is foretold by the prophets by some sacramental metaphor, the Church, openly).

Only in the twelfth century does *integumentum* come to be used with the same plasticity as *involucrum*. In general, it signifies the "allegorical covering" of a secular fable or myth. There are however few if any general rules in its application. Jeauneau observes that "the interpretation of an *integumentum* is not brought about through the concrete application of certain universally valid formulae. The sense which is suitable to attribute to a myth depends on the context in which it is found and also, in a good part, on the imagination of the master who is commenting."[74] This concept of variable exegesis is born out by a wide variety of texts. A simple-minded commentator in the late twelfth-century likened *integumentum* to the hard, outer covering of a nut which had to be broken open before the fruit could be savoured.[75] Another commentator, more orthodox, explored the pejorative possibilities. Assuming that dangerous thoughts on the education of women could be gleaned from the *Timaeus*, he suggested that "distortions" might appear, *sub integumento*, in a too liberal reader.[76] In general, however, *integumentum* recreated the

[74] *AHDLMA* 24 (1958), 43 (my trans.).

[75] *S. Fulgentii Episcopi super Thebaiden*, ed. Helm, *Fulgentii . . . Opera* (Leipzig, 1898), 180: "Quam ob rem, 'si parua licet componere magnis,' non incommune carmina poetarum nuci comparabilia uidentur. In nuce enim duo sunt, testa et nucleus, sic in carminibus poeticis duo, sensus litteralis et misticus. Latet nucleus sub testa; latet sub sensu litterali mistica intelligentia." This short commentary, found in MS Paris, Bibl. Nat., lat. 3012, ff. 60v-64r, may now perhaps be dated in the twelfth century; see Stock, *Traditio* 27 (1971), 468-71.

[76] MS Paris, Bibl. Nat., lat. 16,579, f. 4v. The term, however, does not normally have a pejorative connotation. Cf. Camb. Univ. Lib., MS Mm.I.18, f. 5va: ". . . poesis dat eis exteriorem integumentorum narrationem." Cf. f. 14vb: "Duo autem aminicula solet

spirit, if not the letter, of Macrobius' statement. Myths, poems, dreams,[77] and other literary works could contain moral or scientific senses to be unlocked by exegesis. Peter Abelard provides an eloquent example. He employs both terms, *involucrum* and *integumentum*, throughout the *Introduction to Theology*, stating categorically that neither the opinions of Plato nor the Platonists are acceptable unless attributed to the holy spirit through the very attractive covering of myth.[78] For both philosophers and prophets are traditionally accustomed to present their doctrines somewhat indirectly. Statements which seem on the surface to be lacking in sense may on closer inspection be found to be "full of great mysteries."[79] "Macrobius, the

habere animam: teguntur enim uitia et bonum." Cf. f. 21rb: ". . . extra involutionem integumenti . . ." There are numerous other examples.

[77] A good example of Platonist dream-theory is provided by the *Liber Thesauri Occulti* of Paschalis Romanus, ca. 1163. It begins by describing dreams as integuments which reveal the future, then goes on to state, i.2; ed. S. Collin-Roset, *AHDLMA* 30 (1964), 147: "Nam in sompniis vita et mors, paupertas et divitie, infirmitas et sanitas, tristicia et gaudium, fuga et victoria levius quam in astronomia cognoscuntur, quia perceptio astronomia multiplicior est ac difficulior." Cf. i.14; p. 160: "Est itaque fantasia tanquam fabula, . . . in tegumentis et obscuritate involuta." Similar views are stated in an anonymous commentary on Macrobius written in the twelfth century; Paris, Bibl. Nat., lat. 18,421, f. 10v, and in the commentary on Macrobius by William of Conches.

[78] *Introductio* . . . , cap. 19; *PL*, 178, 1021C: "His ex Platone breviter collectis, atque ad nostrae fidei testimonium satis, ut arbitror, diligenter expositis, consequens, existimo, ad sequaces ejus commeare, ut ea quae ab ipsis quoque de anima mundi sunt dicta, nulla ratione convenienter accipi posse monstremus, nisi Spiritu sancto per pulcherrimam involucri figuram assignentur." A comparison between Abelard's *Introductio* and William's commentaries on classical authors would possibly be very instructive, as their approaches to many problems connected with myth appear to be similar.

[79] *Ibid.* 1021C.

commentator on Cicero and no mean philosopher himself, illustrates, in fact, how much philosophy always disdained to make public its secrets in naked words—especially when discussing the soul or the gods—but had the habit of speaking through certain mythical wrappings."[80]

But is the moral or philosophical the only context in which *integumentum* is used? William of Conches seems to reveal another. If one accepts the distinction between religious and secular allegory made in the Martianus commentary as a twelfth-century norm, then the introduction of new, often rival notions in physical theory or cosmology was not apt to be greeted without controversy. William provides one example of intellectual retreat in the face of criticism in the revision of his *Philosophia Mundi* into the more orthodox *Dragmaticon*. But was not a more subtle outlet for the growing scientific energies of the period furnished by allegory? At a time when science was virtually identical with *ratio*, one possible direction for rational activities lay in the structural study of myth. The fact that the growth in interest in science occurred during a vogue of Platonism meant that allegory could in part express alienation.[81] William reveals this tendency better in his commentaries on classical authors than in his encyclopedic dialogues, where the confrontation with authority is often direct. In his commentary on Macrobius, for instance, he attempts to restore the original meaning of the text which

[80] *Ibid.* 1022B-C: "Quantum etiam semper philosophia arcana sua nudis publicare verbis dedignata sit, et maxime de anima, de diis, per fabulosa quaedam involucra loqui consueverat, ille non mediocris philosophus, et magni Ciceronis expositor, Macrobius, diligentissime docet."

[81] Cf. Jeauneau, *AHDLMA* 24 (1958), 55, my trans.: "In the thought of the twelfth-century masters, *integumentum* is not only a learned diversion, a witticism. It is a precious tool, thanks to which one may eliminate from Plato, from Boethius, or any other authority, the suspicion of heresy."

the author of the Martianus commentary, aware of doctrinal problems, tries to distort. Macrobius, he states, was really aiming at a comprehensive theory of myth. The important distinction is not between religious and secular but between frivolous and serious myths. All serious myths possess "an argument," "a plan which examines something."[82] This *ratio*, alike for Christians and pagans, is revealed *sub integumento*. All myths may thus be reduced to a few fundamental structures and a similar principle of exegesis may be employed. William does not exclude natural-philosophic documents from this typology. As a parallel to Biblical and literary criticism, he proposes on more than one occasion that cosmological writers discourse either *fabulose, astrologice,* or *astronomice.*[83] Thus, through his commentaries on Plato, Boethius, Macrobius, and Priscian, he tries to compare disparate mythical structures using reason as his guide in much the same way as Abelard attempted to compare differing theological positions.

[82] [*Glosae super Macrobium*], Berne, Bibl. Mun., MS 266, ff. 2ra *et seq.* The text is here cited from the Berne MS only; for a description of the other MSS, though not of successive versions, see E. Jeauneau, *AHDLMA* 27 (1961), 17-28; on the meaning of the commentary, *idem* in R. R. Bolgar, ed., *Classical Influences on European Culture A.D. 500-1500* (Cambridge, 1971), 95-102. "Per illam fabulam. (= per illam demum fabulam, Macrob., *Comm.* i.1.3.7) . . . fabula enim est quicquid non est ita. (f. 2vb) Nec omnibus fabulis. (= nec omnibus fabulis philosophia repugnunt, *Comm.* i.1.2.6) Posuerat argumentum Colotis contra Platonem tale scilicet quod non oportet fabulam confingi a philosopho. Hac ratione Macrobius resistens tali argumento probat aliquando genus figmenta convenire philosophis. . . . Dicitur enim argumentum ratio que probatur aliquid. Argumentum etiam dicitur quod libet fictum verisimile. . . . Dicitur etiam argumentum aliquid aliud intellectum" (f. 3va). A somewhat different version of this material is presented in Vatican, Pal. lat. 953, f. 82ra-b.

[83] *Phil. Mundi* ii.5; *PL*, 172, 59A-B; *Glosae super Plat.*, cap. 66; ed. Jeauneau, p. 138. For further references, see Jeauneau, *Glosae*, p. 138, n. a.

In addition to presenting a comparative theory of myths, William attempts to invest classical, mythical stories with physical meanings. In this development however he is not alone. The idea of physical allegory, related to the growth of astrology in the Alexandrian period, gradually infiltrated twelfth-century Platonism from different directions. One route was provided by late antique astrological writers like Firmicus Maternus; another by *Hermetica* and the growing corpus of Arab astrological works. One finds a considerable amount of physical allegory in the *Third Vatican Mythograph*, where it sits somewhat uneasily beside the moral and philosophical views. An equally good example however is provided by the Martianus commentary in Cambridge. Here, as in William, the relation between scientific, literary, and Biblical texts is established through Platonism and the analogy of methods it implies:

> In *Libris* enim *Naturalibus* sciens, intueris naturas animalium . . . , sic et in diuina pagina intueris, in quantum fas est, eterna bona.[84]

> For, learning from the *Libri Naturales* [of Aristotle] you will discover the natures of living things . . . , just as, in Holy Scripture, you will discover, insofar as is allowed, the eternal moral goods.

The physical interpretation of classical myths provides an excellent example of the way in which a traditional form could be used to accommodate contemporary, scientific interests. Both William in the Macrobius commentary and the author of the Martianus commentary, for example, present a naturalistic explanation of the genealogy of the gods. In the Cambridge version, there are four different allegorizations of the birth of Bacchus. In the first, Jove's copulation with Semele is seen to be the union of *ignis superior*

[84] Camb. Univ. Lib., Mm.I.18, f. 15ra.

56

with the earth, resulting in the natural fertility of the vine. Jove came to earth *sub humana forma*, just as fire, defined as his nature directed towards lower things, acts upon the earth. This was Jove's *humana natura* (human because *humana* is, in the mind of the commentator, grammatically related to *humor*, liquid, and the legend relates that Jove revealed himself in a thunder storm). After the union, Semele was pregnant with Bacchus just as the earth each year is made fertile and produces wine—and so the allegory continues, each new episode having a physical significance.[85] An equally charming example is furnished by the *fabula de Tiresia*, through which the changes of the seasons are explained. According to legend, Tiresias was blinded by the gods when he was seven years old for revealing to men secrets which they ought not to have known. In the commentary, Tiresias is bisexual. In winter he is male and hence unproductive; in the spring, female. The seven years of his blindness symbolize the seven unfertile months which separate autumn from spring.[86]

[85] *Ibid.* f. 2rb: "Iupiter sit hoc loco ignis superior, quasi iuris pater quia omnia cohibet. Terra autem dicitur Semele, quasi sine melo. Cum enim alie spere ex motu reddant sonum, ipsa motum non habet atque ideo nec sonum. In Semele ergo agit Iupiter sub humana forma quando in terram agit ignis, inferiorum natura. Humana enim forma est pluuia, uix pruina grando. Forma quidem dicitur et humor et quelibet natura quia discernitur res per suam naturam. Humanus autem dicitur humor quasi humi, id est, inferiorum elementorum natura. Ignis quidem est inferiorem humorem et attrahere et remittere. Tunc Bacco Semele repletitur, quasi naturali producendi uinum potentia terra fecundatur." A similar, though somewhat less complex allegory is related by William of Conches, *Glosae super Macrobium*, MS Berne 266, f. 3ra, corresponding to the last of the four allegories in the Martianus commentary. Cf. *Mythographus Vaticanus tertius*, cap. 12-13; ed. Bode (Cellis, 1834), 243-47.

[86] The relationship to the *Third Vatican Mythograph* is in this case quite close. The following may be compared:

These two examples could easily be multiplied. Their importance for this study is not so much in their own right, but what they reveal about the interpenetration of classical and scientific motifs. Through them, it becomes clear that the conception *involucrum/integumentum* is not only a Platonic metaphor revived and transformed but the key to a problem known in the ancient world and reintroduced in the twelfth century: the type of discourse suitable for representing moral and natural-philosophic truths. In Ber-

---

MS Mm.I.18, f. 3va-b:

Tu concordias ligas . . . elementa vicibus [*De Nuptiis*, i.1] : id est alternis temporibus. . . . Vicibus: aliis duobus alternis temporibus scilicet uere et autumpno. His enim animalia coeunt; que aperte illa exprimit de Tiresia fabula. Tiresias namque mundana perhennitas interpretatur, quod quidem tempus est coequeuum mundo. Tiresias masculus existit: dum tempus hiemali frigore clausa terra, nil parit. Duos serpentes coeuntes uirga percutit, dum uno tempore alia bina et bina se conmiscentia feruore tangit. In mulierem de uiro mutatur, dum in uere fecundit de sterili hieme conuertitur. Sexus enim mulieris uer gerit, quia et in eo terra parturit et animalium sexus uterque coit. Septimo anno in terra serpentes permiscentur, dum mense vii animalia iterum in coitu iunguntur. A martio namque uerno mensis septimus est autumpnalis septembris, unde autem septem nomen habet.

Myth. tert. 4.8; ed. Bode, 169:

Habet enim fabula, Tiresiam serpentes duos coeuntes vidisse. Quos quum virga percussisset, in feminam mutatus est. Tum vero post temporis seriem, septimo videlicet anno, eosdem vidit concumbentes, similiterque iis percussis, in formam pristinam est restitutus. Ob hoc quum de amoris qualitate Juno et Jupiter certamen habuissent, eum judicem elegerunt. Ille virum tres unicas amoris habere, novem vero feminam dixit. . . . Tiresias itaque *aestiva perennitas* interpretatur; unde et in figura temporis ponitur. Tempus igitur mensibus hiemalibus dum, terris frigore constrictis, germina nulla producit, masculam quodammodo obtinet formam. Vere autem ingresso, animalia jam lascivam exercentia et coeuntia videns, percutit ea virga, id est fervoris aestu; tuncque in sexum femininum, id est, in aestivam transit fecunditatem.

58

nard's *Cosmographia*, Platonism may be seen at different levels. It is discernible, first of all, in the idea of including the allegorical configurations of physical forces in a Platonic myth. At another level, however, it may also be observed in the physical conceptions themselves, for Bernard consistently presents ultimate realities like matter as allegorical mysteries. But the problem of myth and science also has larger implications. Viewed through its perspective, much of the early twelfth-century debate on *ratio* or *auctoritas* may perhaps be seen in a new light. For, while conservative ecclesiastics may have opposed science for its own sake, more adventurous (and no less Christian) thinkers had to look beyond this limited framework to the question of the language of science as it was handed down in medieval tradition.

The 1130s and 1140s appear to have been a crucial period for this controversy. With the growth of rationalism, the appearance of new texts, and the disengagement of science as a discipline from its moral and theological background, Platonism could not help but come under attack. The structural analysis of myth by Abelard, William of Conches, and their contemporaries was an attempt to solve the problem, but in their time no single solution dominated the field. There were rather two tendencies, sometimes discernible within the work of a single author. One approach took myths seriously and attempted to work within their framework for discourse. That is another way of saying that they placed the *trivium* above the *quadrivium*. This group includes most of the authors mentioned above, who attempted, like William, to demythologize the ancients, or, like Bernard, to write *narratio fabulosa*. A generation later, their theory was concisely summarized by Moses Maimonides.[87] The other approach consisted of an extensive reaction

[87] *Rabi Mossei Aegyptii Dux seu Director dubitantium aut perplexorum* ... [Paris, 1520], f. 3: "Scias etiam quod naturalia simili-

against myth. While less well documented, its essential features may be discerned well before 1150. A good example is provided by a manuscript at Cambrai.[88] A work of the first half-century, it consists of a *Tractatus de Astronomia* divided into four books. In addition to propounding advanced views on the subject, it contains a vicious criticism

---

ter non possunt exponi ab homine expositione perfecta, nec potest homo facere, vt sciatur pars principiorum suorum sicut sunt. Et tu scis quod dixerunt sapientes, et nomen in opere de Beresith (= scientia naturalis, f. 3) in duobus. Et si poneret homo omnes illas rationes, esset expositor et ideo fuerunt dictae illae rationes in libris prophetiae in parabolis. Et loquuti sunt in eis sapientes in parabolis et similitudinibus, vt ambulent in eis per viam librorum sanctitatis."

[88] Cambrai 930, *inc: Incipit liber Maimonis in astronomia a Stephano philosopho translatus*. The four books are respectively ff. 2-15r, 15r-26v, 26v-38r, 38r-49v. Although the MS breaks off before the end of book iv, the author seems to be near the end of his discussion. Geometrically correct illustrations in red are found at ff. 4v, 20r, 26v, 27v, 30v, 31v, 32r, 35r, 36r, 38v, 43v (two ill.), 45v, 47v, 48r. Another MS, particularly interesting for the milieu of Tours and Chartres, is found in Paris, Bibl. Mazarine, 3642 Rés. Haskins, who studied it in detail, noted its connection with Hermann of Carinthia and possibly Tours, p. 52: "If we read in the preface 'Turonum' with one MS (Mazarine 3642, f. 55) [of Hermann's treatise *On the Astrolabe*], . . . the B. or Ber. of the dedication becomes Bernard of Tours. . . ." Haskins apparently did not notice an independent treatise on cosmology in the same MS, ff. 69va-80va. The work, described by Molinier (*Catalogue . . . de la bibliothèque Mazarine*, vol. 3, Paris, 1890, 151-52) as *De philosophia Tulli* should perhaps be entitled *Liber de Philosophia et Astronomia*, even though it is clearly inspired by Macrobius. Written in a thirteenth-century hand, and bearing the marks of imprecision and haste, it is divided into three books (ff. 69va-73ra, 73ra-78vb, 79ra-80va), and treats, among other things, a typical list of mid-twelfth-century themes: the creation of the world (69rb-70rb), the *anima mundi* (70rb-va), the *demones* (70va-vb) the elements (70vb-71ra-b) and astronomical subjects. The MS is clearly a later copy, of which ff. 95-121 may be the original.

of Macrobius. An example from among Bernard Silvester's sources may be taken from Hermann's translation of Abu Ma'shar. In the second book of the *Introductorium*, the author refers to the "Arabes vero nihil in fabulas sperantes"[89] (Arab [thinkers] who place no confidence at all in myths). Later in the treatise, he refers to those who follow *involucrum atque error*.[90] Hermann could translate these texts without fear of contradiction. He well knew that Ptolemy was the most radical and authoritative of those who attacked the mythical cosmogonies of the ancient world.

Perhaps the most perfect example of the crisis of sensibility provoked by the differing attitudes toward myth is furnished by the *Liber de Naturis Inferiorum et Superiorum* of Daniel of Morley, written around 1175. Daniel explains that he fled the stultifying atmosphere of Paris, with its emphasis on law and theology, for Toledo, so that he might study the *quadrivium* under the *sapientiores mundi philosophos*. He then accuses the Latins of wilful obscurity in scientific matters:

Therefore it is to be entreated and exhorted many times that, as nothing obscure is contained here [in the *Liber de Naturis*], one ought not to hurry to condemn the simple and lucid statements of the Arabs, but to pay attention, since the Latin philosophers, laboring unfruitfully over such matters, have, through ignorance, put forth obscure figures, enwrapped in their own circumlocutions, with the result that the uncertainty of error is concealed beneath the shadow of ambiguity.[91]

[89] *Introductorium* ii.1; f. b.3 recto.
[90] *Ibid.* viii.1; f. [g.7] verso. The Venice edition has *in volucrum* for *involucrum*.
[91] Ed. Sudhoff, *op. cit.*, 6-7: "Exorandus igitur atque multipliciter

If only one could take Daniel at his word, but one cannot! As this passage admirably illustrates, the *Liber de Naturis* is written in anything but a clear style. It is as rhetorical as the *Cosmographia*. Throughout, Daniel employs time and time again the very methods he says he rejects. He numbers poets among the presocratics as founders of physical theory[92] and utilizes the *fabulosa astronomia* of William of Conches.[93] The best example of his indecisiveness occurs near the beginning of book two. Reconciling the Biblical account of sublunary creation with natural philosophy, he takes as his point of departure Psalm 45:2: "Lingua mea calamus scribe"[94] (Write, my tongue, like a pen). Yet this very text was cited by a poet who held no reservations about neoplatonism, Alan of Lille, at the climax of his major literary myth, the *Anticlaudianus*.[95]

Needless to say, the debate on myth and science was not settled in the twelfth century. It continued up to the seventeenth, receiving a definitive critique in Francis Bacon.[96] While rejecting, for good reasons, medieval methods of textual criticism, many renaissance humanists, like Boccaccio and Salutati, displayed a keen interest in literary allegory. From their works it is a short step to Vico's attempt to discover the hidden meanings of primitive myths and, in a broader perspective, to the attempts of modern structural anthropologists.

---

exhortandus est, ut quamuis hic nihil contineatur obscurum, non iccirco planas atque dilucidas Arabum sententias contempnere festinet, sed attendat, quod Latini philosophi, circa talia inutiliter laborantes, obscura per ignorantiam figmenta quibusdam ambagibus obuoluta protulerunt, ut ita sub umbra ambiguitatis error incertus tegeretur."

[92] *Ibid.* 12-13. [93] *Ibid.* 18.

[94] *Ibid.* 23. [95] Cited above, n. 50.

[96] On this subject, see the excellent study of P. Rossi, *Francis Bacon, from Magic to Science* (London, 1968), 36-134.

CHAPTER II

Nature's Complaint

*Pays singulier, supérieur aux autres, comme l'art
l'est à la Nature, où celle-ci est réformée par
le rêve, où elle est corrigée, embellie, refondue.*

—Baudelaire, *L'invitation au voyage*

1. *Natura*: Initiator of Cosmic Reform

To TURN from the twelfth-century theory of myth to Bernard Silvester himself, the dramatic action of the *Cosmographia* begins with Nature's complaint and consists of a dialogue between her and Noys up to book i.2.47, at which point the task of subduing the unruly elements is undertaken. In the initial scene, Natura complains to Noys about the unpleasant state of chaos in the world and Noys, rebuking her gently, promises to do what she can to make the universe a more harmonious order. Although an educated, twelfth-century reader would have had little trouble in perceiving that Noys (= νοῦς) was derived in some way from the *mens divina* of late classical thought, he might not have been able to discern from Bernard's opening lines alone the full meaning of Natura. One reason for this is that Bernard's introduction of Natura into medieval Latin literature as an allegorical goddess presiding over the creation of the world and of man was something of an innovation.[1] Natura had been mentioned—allegorized and unallegorized—in previous medieval poetry of course, but she had never taken the major role in an epic. A more im-

---

[1] Cf. E. R. Curtius, *Zeitschrift für rom. Philologie* 58 (1938), 180-97, whose views are oversimplified.

portant reason arises from the fact that Natura in the *Cosmographia* is not only a revived classical idea; she personifies notions and even sentiments current in the twelfth century. During this period there was an astonishing growth in discussions of nature from different points of view—grammatical, legal, theological, and scientific.[2] It is possible to regard this movement as a purely intellectual phenomenon, divorced from the society in which it took place. Yet this view overlooks one of the most distinctive features of the twelfth-century approach to the problem of nature: the ways in which pre-existing theory is evidently being modified to suit existing practice. The development of law, political theory, and natural philosophy in northern Europe at the same time as the reintroduction of classics like Justinian, Aristotle, and Ptolemaic astronomy ensured that a complex interplay of ideas took place. The appearance of a goddess Natura in a cosmological epic is therefore not an accident. Speaking of the whole movement, Tullio Gregory remarks: "The value which the contemplation of the physical world came to assume, the new sensitivity of poets and philosophers towards nature, studied and versified as the principle of universal order, autonomous within the context of its own creative being, gave an incontestably special quality to the whole culture of the twelfth century, a quality, moreover, which is rather difficult to reduce—as indeed some have tried—to a simple literary fact."[3] In a different vein,

---

[2] On *natura* in antiquity see A. Pellicer, *Natura* (Paris, 1966), and, for the Middle Ages, the same author's article in the *Novum Glossarium Mediae Latinitatis* (*Mox-Nazara*) (Copenhagen, 1965), cols. 1090-98. A philological-philosophical analysis of *natura* to the middle of the twelfth century is undertaken by T. Gregory in *La filosofia della natura nel medioevo* (Milano, 1966), 27-65.

[3] Gregory, 215 (my trans.).

Fr. Chenu has spoken of the new sensibility towards nature "bloqué par les conformismes littéraires et culturels."[4] Similar views have been advanced on the legal and political side.[5] A multidisciplinary approach, somewhat overdue,[6] is clearly needed [Plate IV].

Bernard's goddess Natura is therefore first to be considered in the broadest context as the personification of a group of interrelated concepts in the earlier twelfth century. Later in the *Cosmographia* Bernard summarizes these attributes aptly in a single phrase—*Natura, mater generationis*—which he took from Abu Ma'shar.[7] Natura's ab-

---

[4] Chenu, 27.

[5] E.g., B. Tierney, *Journal of the History of Ideas* 24 (1963), 307-22; G. Post, *Studies in Medieval Legal Thought* (Princeton, 1964), 494-561.

[6] Lynn White Jr., *Amer. Hist. Rev.* 52 (1947), 435 states: "Modern science, similarly, as it first appeared in the later Middle Ages, was more than the product of a technological impulse: it was the result of a deep-seated mutation in the general attitude towards nature, of the change from a symbolic-subjective to a naturalistic-objective view of the physical environment." For an attempt at the social construction of this phenomenon, see the same article, n. 35. Important from a theoretical point of view from among these early approaches is the neglected study of F. Borkenau, *Der Übergang vom feudalen zum bürgerlichen Weltbild* (Paris, 1934), in which the problem of the social reconstruction of *der Begriff des Naturgesetzes* is treated on pp. 15-96. Borkenau's sources unfortunately do not go back further than the thirteenth century.

[7] *Introductorium in Astronomiam*, i.2, f. a.5, recto: "natura . . . mater generationis." Abu Ma'shar's conception, however, is rather more Aristotelian than Bernard's. In this chapter he discusses *generatio* and *corruptio*, presenting an Aristotelian background for his astrological views. He defines *natura* as one of three kinds of fundamental forces causing motion, summarizing her innate properties as follows: "Quoniam et illius nature nec huiusmodi virtus inest et huius natura eiusmodi virtutis receptiva ex quo actu et passione mundi

stract meaning in the *Cosmographia* is however her minor function. She is much more important as a dramatic character. Here, her part is more subtle and difficult to define. First, she transforms in a dramatic context the Hermetic/ Macrobian notion of Nature as a mysterious goddess who disdains to reveal her secrets openly but clothes them in allegory. Neither Bernard's secrets nor his reasons for adopting allegory are the same as his authorities', but Natura, as a dramatic character, reveals them gradually as the *Cosmographia* proceeds to its climax. Secondly, the reader follows Natura's point of view throughout the work. He becomes acquainted with the secrets of heaven and earth as Natura does. Thus the reader, so to speak, is educated at the same time as Natura, who represents dramatically the spirit of progressive enlightenment which accompanies increasing knowledge of and control over the natural environment. Natura does not really become the "nature" which stabilizes the universe until the universe itself is ordered and she fully understands how it works according to the latest theories. When the *Cosmographia* begins, Natura is presumably in a state of relative ignorance.

What is the purpose of Natura's complaint? It is twofold: first, that the world, which is in a state of chaos, should be ordered into a more harmonious whole; secondly, that the new order should be a moral improvement on the old.

In the quickly flashing, even confusing images in which Natura presents her description of primordial chaos in i.1, it is not easy to keep these requests apart, but in view of the moral allegory which is incorporated into the *Cosmo-*

---

natura permixtio sit generationum eiusdem mater" (f. a.5, verso). In *Cos.* ii.9, Bernard combines this idea with a fertility metaphor derived from Chalcidius and Martianus; see Ch. IV, n. 107.

graphia it is necessary to do so. First, setting the scene, Bernard states that Silva, the mother-figure of material things, is holding the *confusa primordia rerum*, the primal elements of the universe in chaos, within the confines of the old sphere.[8] Then Natura asks Noys whether she has not

> mollius excudi silvam, positoque veterno,
> posse superduci melioris imaginem forme. . . .[9]

the capacity to hammer out matter more softly and, when what is old and worn-out is put aside, to draw forth the image of a better form.

In *veterno*, Bernard consciously repeats the idea that the present state of the world is a *vetus globus*. Although he does not tell us at this point whether the world is eternal or not, he implies that it developed cyclically, one stage succeeding to another. The present unruly state of the elements, conscious of its own imperfection, begs, through Natura, to be able to proceed to a new and better form:

> Rursus et ecce cupit res antiquissima nasci,
> ortu silva novo circumscribique figuris![10]

For behold, the most ancient of things desires to be born again; matter desires to be circumscribed with forms from a new beginning!

God, moreover, essentially benign, far from being jealous of creation,

> in melius, quantum patitur substantia rerum,
> cuncta refert. . . .[11]

---

[8] *Cos.* i.1.1-2: "cum Silva teneret/ sub veteri confusa globo primordia rerum. . . ."

[9] *Cos.* i.1.8-9.　　[10] i.1.35-36.　　[11] i.1.13-14.

remakes everything in a better way, as far as the substance of things allows.

Referre suggests that the cosmos is not being made but remade; that is, in addition to the Platonic notion of the creator making the world in the image of a divine model in the beginning, Bernard seems to be suggesting the astrological idea that cosmic reform occurs at a definite time when, according to the positions of the heavenly bodies, the order of the universe dissolves and is remade again from the chaos of the four elements.[12] In short, Natura is pleading with Noys to inaugurate a new stage in the history of the world—a history which is cyclical and progressive—in which the elements of the former age will be used to build the new.

Presiding over chaos, Natura describes matter and the four elements inhering in it. The portrait of primordial chaos virtually comprises the rest of her speech. The description, which is more poetic than philosophic, is best analysed through its images: Natura juxtaposes the Platonic mother-figure, holding the atomistic particles of matter in her lap, with the image of matter in the ordinary, unabstract sense of the term, as stuff which is malleable and can be beaten into a new shape. At the same time, Bernard repeats the terms *cultus, cultius,* suggesting not only that the cosmos desires to be ordered into a more harmonious, proportionate form, to present a better dressed appearance, but to be improved in the sense of cultivation, even civilization. The combination of cosmological and cultural images, and the suggested relationship between

---

[12] The obvious source is Plato, *Tim.* 29E; p. 22: "Optimus erat, ab optimo porro inuidia longe relegata est. Itaque consequenter cuncta sui similia, prout cuiusque natura capax beatitudinis esse poterat, effici uoluit."

them, is unlike any other description of primordial chaos in medieval Latin. Here, in part, is Natura's speech:

Silva rigens, informe chaos, concretio pugnax,
discolor usie vultus, sibi dissona massa!
Turbida temperiem, formam rudis, hispida cultum
optat et a veteri cupiens exire tumultu
artifices numeros et musica vincla requirit. . . .
Quid prodest quod cuncta suo precesserit ortu
Silva parens, si lucis eget, si noctis abundat,
perfecto decisa suo, si denique possit
auctorem terrere suo male condita vultu?
Ante pedes assistit Yle cum prole suorum
invidiam factura tibi quod cana capillos,
informi squalore suum deduxerit evum. . . .
Debetur nonnullus honos et gratia Silve:
que genitiva tenet gremio diffusa capaci.
Has intra veluti cunas infantia mundi
vagit et ad speciem vestiri cultius orat.
Has lacrimas tener orbis habet, nutricis ut ipso
decedat gremio Silvamque relinquat alumnam.
Assistunt elementa tibi poscentia formas,
munus et officium, propriis accommoda causis,
affectantque locos ad quos vel sponte feruntur
consensu deducta suo. . . .[13]

Silva—a stiff, formless chaos, a bellicose compound, the discoloured face of Being, a mass dissonant to itself! Being turbid, she desires tempering, being ugly, beauty, being uncultivated, refinement. Desiring to escape from her ancient tumult, she asks for skilful proportions and the harmonious bonds of music. . . . What profits Silva that she has preceded every-

---

[13] *Cos.* i.1.18-46.

thing in her origin if, as our parent, she needs light and abounds in darkness, if, cut off from her own perfection, she is able, in a word, to terrify her own creator with her ill-founded face? At her feet waits Hyle with her whole train of descendants, in order to arouse envy against you, [Noys], since, white in hair, she [= Hyle] has spent long years in distasteful squalor. . . . Not a little respect and thanks ought to be Silva's, [for] in her capacious lap she holds whatever has been produced and scattered loosely about.

The infant of the cosmos, as from within a cradle, cries out, and begs to be dressed more suitably for display. The tender cosmos sheds these tears so that it may withdraw from the lap [of its wet-nurse], so that it may leave fostering Silva. The elements, accommodated by their own causes, lie in wait for you, asking for the forms, duties and office; or, led down by their own consent, they strive after those places towards which they are naturally borne.

For a reader unaccustomed to the familiar metaphors of twelfth-century Platonism, this poetic description may appear full of obscurity. An understanding cannot be attained without a close look at Bernard's source material. Before turning to it, however, it is worth noting that Natura has made her appearance in the drama in a minor, if well-known, medieval topos: the dialogue-debate between a divinity and an earthly participant. This device, which was in vogue during the late classical period, is employed in two of Bernard's chief models. In the *Consolation of Philosophy*, from which Bernard derives the images of harmony in Natura's speech, the debate takes place between Philosophy and Boethius, who is awaiting execution in his cell. In Martianus' *De Nuptiis*, it comprises one of the elements in the love affair between Mercury and Philology.

Both sources had an equal attraction for Bernard. His Natura, like Boethius, is earth-bound; she represents the curious, inquisitive imagination, anxious to learn the secrets of the universe. Like Philology in the *De Nuptiis*, however, Natura is an abstraction, a personage above the human level but below that of Noys and Urania. She is, in fact, instructed by others throughout the *Cosmographia*. (Mercury and Philology were frequently explained by twelfth-century commentators on Martianus as representing *sermo* and *ratio*.[14] While it is not possible to see an exact parallel, Noys does in fact do most of the instructing while Natura is the initiator of cosmic reform.)

The sources for Bernard's opening verses are difficult to unravel. In general, the language reflects a combination of Platonic and Ovidian elements, united through Boethius. Bernard visualizes chaos somewhat like Ovid in the beginning of the *Metamorphoses*:

> Ante mare et terras et, quod *tegit* omnia, celum
> unus erat toto naturae vultus in orbe,
> quem dixere *chaos*, *rudis* indigestaque *moles*
> nec quicquam nisi *pondus* iners *congestaque* eodem
> non bene iunctarum discordia *semina rerum*.[15]

Before there was any earth or sea, before the canopy of heaven stretched overhead, nature presented the same aspect the world over, that to which men have given the name chaos. This was a shapeless, unco-ordinated mass, nothing but a weight of lifeless matter, whose ill-assorted elements were indiscriminately heaped together into one place.

[14] E.g., Camb. Univ. Lib., MS Mm.I.18, f. 1r-v. On the history of this notion, see G. Nuchelmans, *Latomus* 16 (1957), 84-107.

[15] *Met.* i.5-9; trans. M. Innes (Penguin). Natura, of course, is not allegorized in Ovid.

While the (purposefully) italicized words and phrases are directly echoed by Bernard, it is difficult to state with precision just where his debt to Ovid lies. An argument can be made for his having taken the idea of a hexameter cosmogony from him, but Bernard's hexameters are in fact more like Lucan's.[16] As with Plato and Virgil and, most of all, *Consolatio Philosophiae* iii, meter 9, it is perhaps preferable to speak of "agreement" rather than "debt."[17]

[16] J. E. Sandys, *Hermathena* 12 (1903), 436.

[17] It would be very difficult to pinpoint Bernard's sources for the description of chaos in i.1. For instance, he may well have drawn on patristic summaries of earlier verse cosmogonies. Chalcidius, treating *de genitura mundi, Comm.*, cap. 266 (pp. 280-81), comes close to Bernard's language. An even better example is provided by Lactantius, *Diuinae Institutiones* i.5.8-15. In his refutation of pagan polytheism, Lactantius refers to Hesiod's description of chaos, "quod est rudis inordinataeque materiae confusa congeries," (*CSEL* 19, part 1 [1890], p. 14). Virgil and Ovid, he continues, are closer to monotheism; Ovid, in particular, sees cosmogenesis arising "a deo, quem 'fabricationem mundi,' quem 'rerum opificem' uocat," but adds that this takes place "natura ducente" (*ibid.* 15-16). It is also difficult to know just where Bernard is transforming images from the classical and late Latin poets. For instance, in suggesting that matter, needful of form, should be "carved out," is he not echoing *Aeneid* vi.847-48? :

> excudent alii spirantia mollius aera
> credo equidem, vivos ducent de marmore vultus. . . .

There is also a great temptation to suggest that Bernard knew the opening lines of Manilius' *Astronomica*. Two early MSS of the work are extant: Bruxelles, Bibl. Roy., 10,012-10,013, ff. 1-99v, from the tenth or eleventh century, and 10,615-10,729, ff. 107-22, from the twelfth or thirteenth. In his edition (London, 1903-30), vol. 5, p. viii, Housman also mentions a late MS, Leiden, Bibl. Rijk., Voss. lat. 390, which contains "Manilius and after him 'liber somnium Salomon, seu prognosticorum somnium. oratio de praesentia et utilitate medicinae. centiloquium Ptolemaei.' " This type of *mélange* of Platonic and natural-philosophic works might easily have

A clearer, more self-conscious debt to Claudian may be demonstrated. The borrowing is not from Claudian alone; it is shared with Pliny[18] and certain scattered images in

---

been copied from a lost twelfth-century exemplar. (On the knowledge of Manilius as late as the tenth century, see D. B. Gain, *Latomus* 29 [1970], 128-32.) Moreover, the atmosphere of *Astronomica* i is very like the *Cosmographia*. Natura in Manilius learns the secrets of nature (i.11-15) and the phrase *rerum primordia* occurs in a description of poetry's capacity to reveal the physical and astronomical wonders of the world, i.125. Yet many of these similarities may be accidental and the phrases gleaned from *florilegia*. The topos of the secrets of nature occurs in Seneca (cited above, Ch. I, n. 63), and may be taken as well from Cicero, *De Natura Deorum* ii.61; ed. Mueller (Leipzig, 1898), p. 101: "Quid vero? hominum ratio non in caelum usque penetravit?" It occurs as well in Apuleius, *De Mundo*, [*praefatio*], p. 136, lines 2-15 and in Macrobius (see the above discussion). The type of poetic mixture which could be produced is aptly illustrated in some verses of Walter of Châtillon (?), ed. A. Wilmart, *Revue bénédictine* 49 (1937), 143, from an anonymous collection of twelfth-century poems in Bibl. Charleville MS 190:

> Ab antiqua rerum congerie,
> cum pugnarent rudes materies
> moles fuit huius elegiae
> ordinata.

[18] While adopting, in general, the idea that nature in one of her aspects serves man, Bernard shrinks from identifying her with deity as Pliny does in the *Naturalis Historia* ii.1; ed. C. Mayhoff (Leipzig, 1906), vol. i, p. 128: "Mundum, et hoc quodcumque nomine alio caelum appellare libuit, cuius circumflexu degunt cuncta, numen esse credi par est, aeternum, inmensum, neque genitum neque interiturum umquam . . . idemque rerum naturae opus et rerum ipsa natura." Some have thought that Bernard drew the idea of Natura as craftsman (*Natura artifex*) from Pliny (*Nat. Hist.* ii.66; *ibid.* 190, line 166; *Cos.* i.4.125). While this is possible, it should also be noted that the idea is reasonably widespread in the twelfth century; e.g. William of Conches, [*Glosae super Priscianum*], Bibl. Nat., lat. 15,130, f. 3va: "natura . . . artifex." For a late illustration of Natura as the *artifex* of man, see Plate IV. A rare, twelfth-

Chalcidius.[19] Its context, however, is in Claudian, whose influence on twelfth-century allegorical verse has perhaps not been sufficiently clarified.[20] Although a minor figure in Roman literature, Claudian was at home with two literary forms which subsequently became very popular: the dream vision and the allegory. In Claudian these elements are often merely ornaments, figures in a panegyric. Yet sometimes they are placed in a fascinating philosophical context. Claudian expressed two ideas in poetry which obviously attracted Bernard: a faith in the pagan gods for mitigating the vicissitudes of fortune, and opposition to the Epicurean notion of the arbitrariness of fate. It is possible, though fanciful, to think of Bernard transforming the first idea into the notion that the heavenly divinities, representing physical forces and appearing as stars, control motion in the celestial regions and influence human destiny in a manner which contradicts the machinations of blind Fortune. In her speech, in fact, Natura says that the ordering of matter will counterbalance the disruptive effects of the *ludicra cece machina Fortune*. As with this notion, however, Bernard presented the second in Stoic terms, transmitted in part by Lucan.[21] Throughout the *Cosmographia*,

---

century representation of Natura in relation to grammar is found in Bruxelles, Bibl. Roy., MS 19,116, f. 3r.

[19] See Waszink, index greco-latinus, s.v. *natura*.

[20] Interesting commentaries on Claudian are found in MSS Paris, Bibl. Nat., lat. 8082 and lat. 18,552.

[21] E.g., *De Bello Civili*, i.72-74; ed. C. Hosius (Leipzig, 1905), p. 4:

Sic cum compage soluta
saecula tot mundi suprema coegerit hora,
anticum repetens iterum chaos. . . .

Cf. *De Bello Civ.* ii.1-15, on which an eleventh-century copy of a *glossa ordinaria* in Paris, Bibl. Nat., lat. 9346 suggests a terminology not unlike Bernard's. Lucan's *leges* and *foedera* become the *ordinatio naturae*, his *parens rerum* the *conditor et natura*, and on *sive* the idea of a planned universe is directly related to man's free will.

Claudian speaks of a goddess Natura on many occasions,[22] but a special place must have been reserved in Bernard's mind for her appearance in *The Rape of Proserpine*. Throughout the poem Claudian juxtaposes images of order and disorder; they form the basis from which the rape derives its moral irony. In book one, Proserpine, awaiting the arrival of her mother, Ceres, embroiders the ordered world of nature on a gown.[23] In book two, dressed in it, she approaches the doom which Jove and the Fates have prescribed for her. Her rape by Pluto is thus made to symbolize the ravishing of a naturally pure cosmos by the elements of the underworld, or disorder. More importantly from Bernard's viewpoint, Claudian returns to this theme in book three, where the rape is interpreted by Jove as the loss of the art of agriculture by mankind. In other words, Ceres, in grief over the loss of her daughter, has deserted

---

parens rerum an additional marginal gloss (omitted from I. Endt, *Annotationes super Lucanum*, Leipzig, 1909, p. 40) states: "Questionem proponit poeta utrum secundum Stoicos mundus a deo gubernatur id est regatur an secundum Epicureos fortuna id est casibus agitetur. Sed ipse more poetarum medium se inter illos ponens indiffinitum reliquit." In another gloss in a MS of the twelfth-century, Paris, Bibl. Nat., lat. 10,315, f. 11v, *informia regna* from the same source becomes *chaos* and, what is more surprising, *materiamque* becomes *mundum*.

[22] See E. R. Curtius, *Zeitschrift für rom. Philologie* 58 (1938), 180-97.

[23] i.248-53; ed. Koch (Leipzig, 1893), 269:

> Hic elementorum seriem sedesque paternas
> insignibat acu veterem qua lege tumultum
> discrevit Natura parens et semina iustis
> discessere locis; quidquid leve, fertur in altum;
> in medium graviora cadunt; incanduit aer;
> legit flamma polum; fluxit mare; terra perpendit.

the techniques of man. Within the context of universalizing
the rape, Jove reiterates in the same book a traditional account of how civilization was born in the first place.

In the reign of Saturn, Jove says, men did not have to
work, since the soil was naturally fertile and replenished
itself. While he did not personally begrudge men the good
life, he felt that too much luxury and abundance were
dulling their minds. Therefore,

> provocet ut segnes animos rerumque remotas
> ingeniosa vias paulatim exploret egestas
> utque artes pariat sollertia, nutriat usus.[24]

[he asked necessity, the mother of invention], to pro-
voke their dull spirits and, little by little, to search out
the hidden causes of things, so that inventiveness
might give birth to the arts and techniques and practice nourish them.

Since Ceres, he continues, has now left her responsibilities,
the earth is no longer a fit place to live. Natura now comes
to him *cum magnis . . . querellis*, complaining that she, who
was until recently the *genetrix mortalibus*, has now taken
on the characteristics of an unlovable stepmother. Here,
in her own words, is her complaint:

> Quid mentem traxisse polo, quid profuit altum
> erexisse caput, pecudum si more pererrant
> avia, si frangunt communia pabula glandes?
> haecine vita iuvat silvestribus abdita lustris,
> indiscreta feris?[25]

What advantage is it [to man], even if he derives his
intelligence from the heavens and [alone among the
beasts] holds his head up erect, if he has to wander
like a beast through trackless wastes, if, like them, he

---

[24] iii.30-32; p. 283.   [25] iii.41-45; p. 284.

crushes acorns for food? What joy is such a life, hidden away in woodland marshes, indistinguishable from the beasts?

Jove adds that he heard this complaint so often from Natura that, pitying mankind, he instructed Ceres to wander over land and sea. In the course of her journeys she taught Triptolemus the art of agriculture, from whom it spread to all mankind.

This story is so well known that it is tempting to suggest that there is an undercurrent of it in Natura's complaint. There are however some fundamental differences. First, Bernard's images suggesting the emergence of civilization or agriculture are perhaps closer to that in Virgil, *Georgics*, i.125-59.[26] In particular, Bernard seems to have assimilated and transformed Virgil's notion that Jove intentionally made farming difficult in order to enhance the social value of work. In the *Cosmographia*, the major and minor divinities are almost always engaged in ceaseless activity, and Bernard's conception of the universe and man as self-reproducing mechanisms is directly related to their internal labor. Secondly, although Claudian's Natura is presented in images similar to Bernard's, the images deal mainly with commonplaces like Nature's control over the four elements. In another important respect the two goddesses are quite different. In Claudian, Natura is essentially a passive force, reflecting the will of the gods in spite of its injustice; in Bernard she is an active, inquisitive spirit, towards whose education the elements and the cosmos are ordered.

The images in which Bernard first presents Natura suggest, in fact, that he has drawn on at least two other interpretations of the way in which cultural progress and tech-

---

[26] The clue is *Georgics* i.124: "nec *torpore* passus sua regno *veterno*," and i.152: "aspera silva" (my italics).

nology change the life of man. A clue to his main source is
provided later in the *Cosmographia*. When man has been
fully created as a microcosm, he states:

> cuditur artifici circumspectoque politu,
> fabrica Nature primipotentis, homo.[27]

Man, the contrivance of first-power Nature, is fashioned for his craftsman [= Physis] and for one circumspect to polish.

The clue is *fabrica*, used extensively to describe man as an

---

[27] *Cos.* ii.14.1-2, a difficult couplet. There are two possibilities
for *politu*, a word Bernard appears to have invented: (1) as an ablative, fourth declension noun, whence *artifici circumspectoque* would
be construed as adjectival modifiers; and (2) as an ablative supine,
with *artifici circumspectoque* as dative substantives. The latter has
been chosen because it makes better sense in the context and appears
to follow Bernard's stylistic usage. Although he employs *politu* nowhere else, he uses *artifex*, as a noun and as an adjective, on a number of occasions. Normally it is a noun, and one of his favorite
metaphors is that the world and man are "fashioned" for their
artifex, either God or the individual goddess involved at that point.
Thus, in i.4.125, he speaks of "artifex Natura," but in ii.13.32
[Physis], "artifex" and in ii.13.106-07: "Physis igitur, sollers ut
erat artifex. . . ." With the last instance in mind, it would appear
that Bernard is contrasting the role of Natura, on behalf of whose
complaint man is envisaged, and that of Physis, who, at this point,
is his craftsman. The dative form *artifici* also occurs at ii.1.1, where
a similar contrast is made between the roles of Noys and Natura.
Lastly, in *politu*, is Bernard not very close to *politia*, Cicero's term
for Plato's commonwealth? Such an interpretation would account
for a possibly adversative sense of *-que* and suggest that the *homo* is
not only the *fabrica* of Natura and the handicraft of Physis, but
"what is more," needs further refinement "by someone knowledgeable." It is also worth noting that Cicero parallels part of the expression in *De Natura Deorum* ii.55; ed. Mueller, p. 96, line 30:
[homo], "incredibilis fabrica naturae." On the existence of two
tenth-century MSS of the *De Natura Deorum* in the Tours Library,
see C. H. Beeson, *Classical Philology* 40 (1945), 219-20.

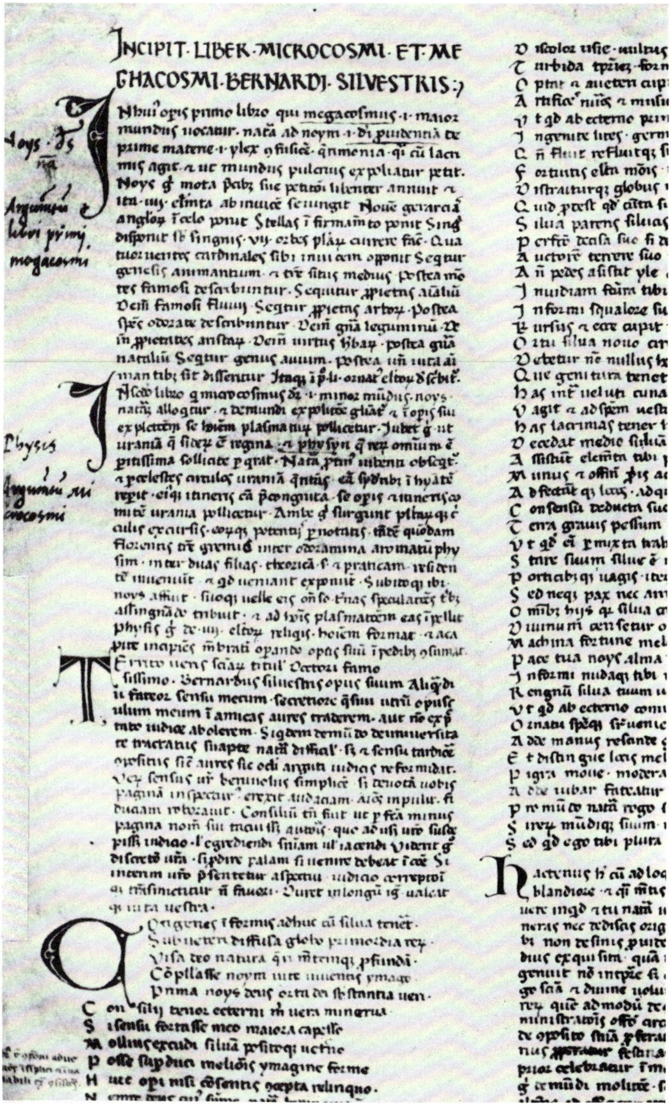

INCIPIT · LIBER · MICROCOSMI · ET · ME
GHACOSMI · BERNARDI · SILVESTRIS ·

[Two columns of medieval Latin text in a heavily abbreviated gothic/caroline hand, with marginal annotations by Boccaccio; the bulk of the manuscript text is not legibly transcribable.]

PLATE I. A copy of the *Cosmographia* annotated by Boccaccio. Firenze, Biblioteca Medicea Laurenziana, MS Plut.
XXXIII, 31, f. 59va.

PLATE II. A fourteenth-century "portrait" of Bernard Silvester. Oxford, Bodleian, MS Digby 46, f. 1v.

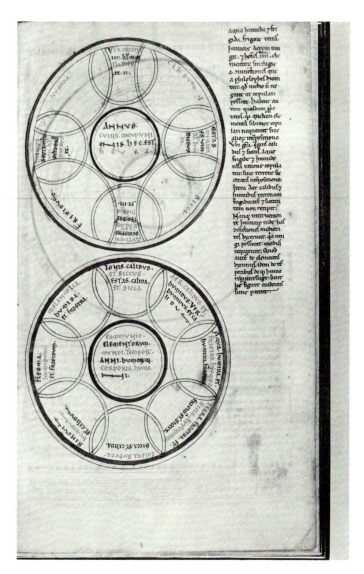

aqua humida 7 fri
gida. frigore uttil.
humore Aerem uni
gr. 7 hoid. in ele
mentoz surzugie
a. uunctione que
a philosophif dram
tur. qd medio si ne
gatur ut copulari
possint. habour au
rem quaidam ppe
utes. qa quedam ele
menta subuuer copu
lari nequeunt sine
alioz unpofitione.
Ubi gria. Ignis cali
dul 7 siccul aque
frigide 7 humide
ulla umone copula
tur. sine terrene sic
cterai unpofitione.
ferm Aer calidus 7
humidul terrenam
frigiditaté 7 siccita
tem non recipit.
Hanaz uttri ueniem
tr humore mde hal
uunctionel medietal
ret durccut. qa um
gi possum. medium
requirunt. Quod
autre de elementil
dpimus. tam de te
ponibul de qz humo
ribz untelligre. Siac
be figure auidemi
sine parem.

PLATE III A. Schematic representations of the four elements, the four humors, and their qualities in the *mundus*
and in *homo*. Baltimore, Walters Art Gallery, MS W.73,
f. 8r.

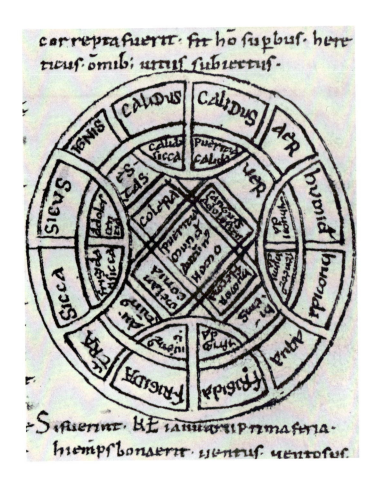

PLATE III B. Another symbolic representation of the elements and the humors. Paris, Bibliothèque Nationale, MS lat. 5247, f. 9rb.

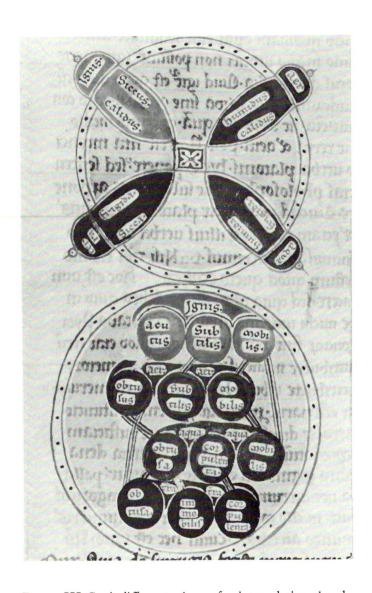

PLATE III C. A different schema for interrelating the elements in the creative process; from a *Dragmaticon* of William of Conches. Paris, Bibliothèque Nationale, MS lat. 6415, f. 6rb.

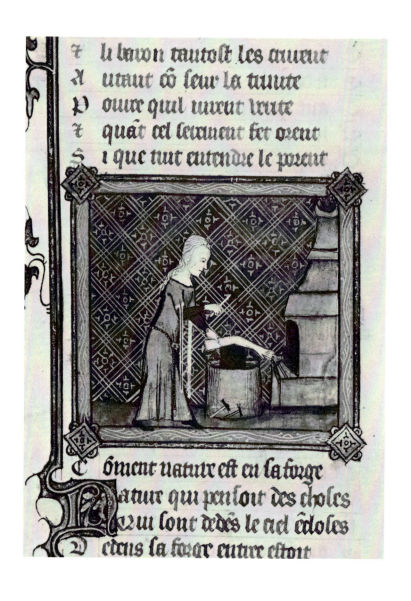

li baion tautoſt les aruent
utaut cō ſeur la tuute
ouue qiul uueut lcute
quaͤt cel ſeruuent ſer oreut
i que tut eutendie le poreut

ōuient uatuie eſt eu ſa forge
atuie qui penſout des choles
uu ſout dedes le ciel ēcloſes
edeus ſa forꝛ euture eſtoit

PLATE IV. *Natura artifex* from a ms of the *Roman de la Rose*. Bruxelles, Bibliothèque Royale, MS 11,187A, f. 98v.

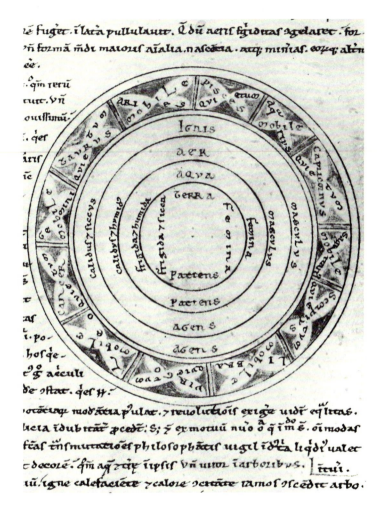

Plate V. A Hermetic schema of creation. Paris, Bibliothèque Nationale, MS lat. 13,951, f. 19v.

PLATE VI. *Homo microcosmus*. Lucca, Biblioteca Statale,
MS 1942, f. 9r.

imitation of the greater world and the finest product of his *fabricator*, God, by the fourth-century astronomical writer, Firmicus Maternus. In the opening chapter of book three of his *Matheseos*, the most comprehensive astronomical-astrological compilation available to medieval authors before the translation of Abu Ma'shar, Firmicus presents the *Thema Mundi*, in which he outlines the stages of world history and their relation to the positions of the stars. Bernard, however, did not only consult Firmicus on the subject. He appears to have read the account of the same problem in Macrobius, *Commentary*, ii.10. Both of these discussions, moreover, seem to be linked in his mind to Plato's "great year," the time at which the stars regain their original positions relative to each other and recommence their ordered movements. Plato does not link the "great year" to cultural progress and history in *Timaeus* 39 D, but Firmicus and Macrobius, steeped in neoplatonic commentary and in astrology, both did. The problem for them was not simply that the stars should regain their positions, but that the whole of the cosmic order should suffer a cataclysm —somewhat like those described by Hesiod and mentioned briefly by Plato in *Laws*, book one—out of which a new stage of history should ultimately be produced. Firmicus and Macrobius had quite different opinions on both the age of the earth and the progress of civilization, and Bernard seems to have drawn images from each without completely committing himself to their arguments. One reason for this was that he had his own highly individualistic idea of how civilization advanced.

Of the two accounts, the smaller debt is to Macrobius, *Commentary*, ii.10. Here, discussing Cicero's casual mention of natural catastrophes which erupt from time to time, Macrobius reflects briefly on an important idea: the age of the earth and its relation to man's technical progress. His argument is as follows. The world could not really be eternal, although there are strong arguments in favor of this view, because civilization, as recorded in history, is of a comparatively recent date. If the world were eternal, why does Greek history go back no further than two thousand years? If so many ages have passed, why were not culture and technical innovation discovered sooner? In other words, while philosophers argue that the world must always have existed, historical evidence suggests a gradual progress from a definite point in time. Nor can a strong argument be drawn from the cyclical nature of history. The rise and fall of civilizations is a wholly natural phenomenon, determined by the alternations of fire and moisture with respect to the stars.

There are numerous reasons why this account might have appealed to Bernard. First, it attempted to reconcile the notion of the world's eternity, which had sustained no little debate in his day, with the idea of creation, as civilization, beginning at a single point in time and gradually progressing. Secondly, it proposed that civilization itself, or rather the rises and falls of various civilizations, were the consequence of natural events. Thirdly, it suggested an optimistic view of human history as a whole. If technical progress was a recent phenomenon, then, by transferring the notion, his own age occupied an important place in history. This idea is similar to Bernard of Chartres' famous metaphor, "standing on the shoulders of the giants," and Silvester seems to be aware of it in his attempt to imitate Macrobius' language in one particular passage of the *Commentary*:

Nam quis facile mundum semper fuisse consentiat, cum et ipsa historiarum fides multarum rerum *cultum* emendationemque vel ipsam inventionem recentem esse fateatur, cumque rudes primum homines et incuria *silvestri* non multum a ferarum *asperitate* dissimiles meminerit vel fabuletur antiquitas. . . .[28]

For who would readily agree that the world has always existed when the testimony of historical accounts implies that the development, improvement, and even invention of many crafts is of recent date, when the ancients recall or relate in legends that, in the beginning, men were uncultivated and, in their rustic crudeness, not unlike wild beasts.

Bernard uses the same language—*cultus, rudis, silvestris,* and *asperitas*—to describe the unrefined state of matter as did Macrobius to portray the uncultivated state of man before the arrival of civilization. Macrobius' notion that the world was created in time, however, is rejected by Bernard. He prefers to think of the cosmos being reconstituted from time to time out of eternally subsisting elements. In this, as well as other aspects of his opening lines, he seems more indebted to Firmicus' *Matheseos,* iii.1.1-19. Firmicus attempts more successfully than Macrobius to integrate astrological prediction into a theory of cosmic reform. He also includes two ideas which Bernard drew upon heavily throughout the *Cosmographia*: one, the relatively large role assigned to Natura in the cosmic process; and two, the view that a science of the heavens is not incompatible with free will. Firmicus also makes a greater effort than Macrobius to treat man as a microcosm in a scientific sense. Thus, while Macrobius, the later source, was better known to Bernard and his contemporaries—dozens of twelfth-century copies of it exist and numerous, unedited commentaries —Bernard seems to have made a conscious choice of Firmieus, an earlier and, strictly speaking, more scientific mind.

[28] ii.10.6; p. 125 (my italics).

What is perhaps the most interesting feature of Firmicus' *Thema Mundi* is the transition he makes from myth
to science. *Matheseos* iii.1 opens with a brief account of
the astronomical theories of Aesculapius and Anubius.
Firmicus immediately informs the reader that these should
not be accepted without verification:

> Sed ne quem hominum fabulosa commenta decipiant
> et qui putet a prudentissimis viris genituram istam sine
> causa esse compositam, omnia a nobis debent specialiter
> explicari, ut secreti istius prudentissima ratio omnibus
> hominibus diligentissimis expositionibus intimetur.[29]

Lest however the fabulous accounts of men should de-
ceive anyone, and one think that the account of the
world's birth was contrived by such perceptive men
without a cause, we must explain everything in detail,
in order that the most carefully worked out plan of
this secret [type of presentation] may be intimated to
all men by a most assiduous exposition.

The point Firmicus is trying to make is that astrology,
as a science of the heavens, verifies statements which would
otherwise have to be accepted as myths. While not rejecting myth as a legitimate mode of conveying facts, he adds
a degree of rationalism. If the cosmos, created by God, is
a beautiful work of art, its order is knowable. While no
meaningful statements may be made about the original
constituents of the myth—in this case the planets and their
influences—the order is susceptible to analysis; it is ex-
plicable and even predictable. Although he may have derived it from other authorities as well, this point of view,
with little change, was adopted by Bernard in the *Cosmographia*.

[29] *Matheseos* iii.1.8; ed. Kroll & Skutsch, vol. i, p. 93.

The cornerstone of Firmicus' incorporation of a rational explanation of the heavens into mythical accounts of their changes is the rejection of the notion that the cosmos was created at a definite point in time:

> There was never a definite origin of the cosmos. Neither did the world's origin take place on a certain day, nor did anyone intervene at a fixed moment when the universe was formed through the plan in the divine mind and its foreseeing laws. Nor indeed has the fragility of human inquiry been able to extend itself so far as to conceive or explain the origin of the world by a simple cause....[30]

Firmicus then presents the theory that the *apocatastasis* or *redintegratio* of the cosmos comes about by fire and flood, the latter following the former. In doing so, he employs a phrase which Bernard placed, almost word for word, in a slightly different context in i.1:

> Nulla enim re ⟨ab⟩ alia exustae res poterant renasci nec ulla re alia ad pristinam faciem formamque revocari, nisi admixtione aquae concretus, pulvis favillarum omnium genitalium seminum collectam conceperit fecunditatem.[31]

> For things which are consumed by fire can in no way be reborn nor in any way be recalled to their pristine appearance and shape unless, coalesced by the admixture of water, the dust of the ashes of all the birth-giving seeds produce a collective fertility.

[30] *Ibid.* iii.1.9; i. 93: "Non fuit ista genitura mundi; nec enim mundus certum diem habuit ortus sui nec aliquis interfuit eo tempore, quo mundus divinae mentis ac providi numinis ratione formatus est, nec eo usque se intentio potuit humanae fragilitatis extendere, ut originem mundi facili possit ratione aut concipere aut explicare...."

[31] *Ibid.* iii.1.9; i, 94.

In i.1, Bernard not only uses the terms *concretio* and *rursus* . . . *nasci*, but refers to the seeds about to produce a new order as the *genetiva*, and transforms *facies* into a brilliant metaphor to describe the face of Silva terrifying her maker.

Firmicus' account of the stages of human cultural history is not reproduced *in toto* in the *Cosmographia*. As with Macrobius, Bernard selects words and phrases and works them into a new pattern, one that is not wholly recognizable until the cosmic drama is done. In Firmicus' description of the world's origin and progress, each planet is responsible for a successive stage of history, onto which it imparts definite characteristics as it holds dominion over the earth in an astrological relationship with the moon. The first planet is Saturn, whose influence is not to be confused with the more famous age of Saturn in Hesiod and Virgil.[32] In the course of presenting Saturn's effects, Firmicus makes use of ideas which Bernard employs in i.1. The moon, he says, caused the first periodic revolution of the cosmos in conjunction with Saturn,

> for since the first origin of the world was uncultivated, repulsive, and savage in its rough habits, and since cultivated human reason [*lit.* the plan or reason of cultivated humanity] had deserted these barbarous men, who had come upon the first signs of light, hitherto unknown to them, [the astrological sages] wished this horrid and uncivilized time to be Saturn's, so that, in

[32] For an outline of Saturn as an astrological figure in medieval literature, see R. Klibansky, E. Panofsky, and F. Saxl, *Saturn and Melancholy* (London, 1964), pp. 127-95. Bernard's account of Saturn in *Cosmographia* ii.5, discussed below, Ch. IV, differs from that of Abu Ma'shar, cited (in English only) in the same volume, pp. 130-31. The authors perhaps refer somewhat too vaguely to Bernard Silvester on pp. 185-86.

imitation of this star, mortality, framed in the beginning stages of life, might endure acquaintance with savagery and the inhuman roughness of wild beasts.[33]

Later, in *Cosmographia* ii.5, Bernard makes reference to the rough ways of Saturn in a possibly contemporary context. In the second stage, Jupiter supersedes Saturn and an appropriate amelioration of the human condition takes place. In a *cultior vita*, man learns manners and loses his savagery. In the third, the moon in conjunction with Mars allows man, who has now entered the right path of life, to conceive all the civilizing adornments of the arts and other skillful constructions (*omnia autem artium et fabricationum ornamenta*).[34] In the fourth, under Venus, man, now governed by providence against the evil inherent in himself, is further improved by the addition of eloquence (*sermo doctus*) and an understanding of nature (*naturalis scientia*).[35] In the last period, under Mercury, mankind's *ingenium* is further increased, but, instead of using his wisdom to benefit the world, the improbity of evil (*malitiae . . . inprobitas*) causes him to invent and hand down many nefarious devices for wrongdoing.[36] Firmicus concludes this summary of the *genitura mundi* by affirming that man's body, being a little cosmos, is also destroyed by fire and flood, and that the whole process of cosmic generation and regeneration is directed by Natura:

[33] *Matheseos* iii.1.11; i, 94: ". . . quia enim prima origo mundi inculta fuit et horrida et agresti conversatione effera, et quia rudes homines prima et incognita sibi vestigia lucis ingressos politae humanitatis ratio deserebat, Saturni hoc agreste et horridum tempus esse voluerunt, ut ad imitationem huius sideris ⟨in⟩ initiis vitae constituta mortalitas agresti se conversatione et inhumana feritatis exasperatione duraret."

[34] *Ibid.* iii.1.12; i, 95.   [35] *Ibid.* iii.1.13; i, 95.

[36] *Ibid.* iii.1.14; i, 95.

Sic omnifariam ad imitationem mundi hominem artifex Natura composuit, ut, quicquid substantiam mundi
aut dissolvit aut format, hoc etiam hominem et forma-
ret et solveret.[37]

Thus Natura, the craftsman, put together man in the
imitation of the world in every way, so that, whatever
either dissolves or forms the substance of the world
might also form and dissolve man.

This idea, somewhat transformed, is clearly in Bernard's
mind throughout i.1.

To summarize, then, Bernard's opening verses present
images which suggest not only that the world is about to
be made in its creator's design, as in Plato, by a group of
his vicegerents, but that, in an ill-defined way, the creation
of the world is also a cosmic reform, predictable from the
stars and the cyclical course of history. The main actors
in this drama are Natura, Noys, and Matter. In classical
poetic descriptions of chaos Bernard found many of the
elements out of which he composed his own picture. Yet
it is more complex than any of his predecessors, utilizing
both Claudian's images of *Natura parens omnium* and
echoing the story of the world's cultural history as presented in Macrobius and Firmicus Maternus. In short,
Bernard suggests that while *mundus* in one of its aspects
is eternal, it has been altered from time to time by cata-
clysms of the elements. In the allegorical drama about
to unfold, a new state of the cosmos and man will reflect a new stage of civilization. If one recalls at this
point that Macrobius mentions that this sort of truth is
often presented by poets *sub poetici nube figmenti*,[38] then
Bernard's juxtaposition of the image of an ancient cosmos
with recent, revolutionary change—a theme to which he

---

[37] *Ibid.* iii.1.16; i, 96.   [38] ii.10.11; p. 126.

returns often—takes on a possibly added meaning. The new *mundus*, waiting like a babe for its clothes, may be interpreted not only as Plato's cosmos in a primitive sense but as the world of the twelfth century. Standing on the shoulders of the previous authorities on the mythical development of civilization, Bernard is perhaps recreating, as an undercurrent to his *Cosmographia*, the spirit of his own times. His allegory of Natura, then, is not only the story of her initiation into the secrets of the universe. It is the myth of how both the world and man emerged from the "primal forest"[39] into a new culture.

2. *Noys*: Messenger and Providence of God

The second personage who makes an appearance in the *Cosmographia* is Noys. Although Natura's role in the drama is a large one, it is overshadowed by hers. Throughout it is Noys who appears at crucial times and provides the *ratio*, the plan of action, by which theory is translated into practice. In i.2, she brings order to the warring elements and unites the body and soul of the world; in ii.9-10, she provides a similar plan for the microcosm, man.

Although her function in the work is thus a central one, historians have been unable to agree on just what it is. Von Bezold, whose interpretation of the *Cosmographia* influenced a whole generation of scholars, wrongly ascribed masculine gender to her,[40] a mistake repeated by Gilson in

[39] A term first employed, rather fancifully, by C. Langlois, *Bibl. de l'Ecole des chartes* 54 (1893), 243, and more recently with exactly Bernard's meaning by P. Dronke, *SMed* 6 (1965), 414.

[40] *Das Fortleben der antiken Götter* . . . , 79: "der Noys." Cf. Adelard of Bath, *De Eodem et Diverso*, ed. H. Willner, *Beiträge* 4.1 (Münster, 1903), 12: "Nam et antequam coniuncta essent, universa quae uides in *ipsa noy* simplicia erant" (my italics). Cf. Daniel of Morley, *Liber de Naturis*, ed. Sudhoff, p. 7: "in Noy id est in mente divina. . . ."

his attempt to vindicate Bernard as a Christian writer.[41]
E. R. Curtius reacted strongly against Gilson's views, but
neglected the philosophic background on which they were
based.[42] T. Silverstein, in an effort of compromise, suggested that Noys was neither *verbum Dei*, as Gilson had
maintained, nor a pagan fertility figure, as Curtius had asserted, but "a separate fabulous construction," based on
two separate traditions, "the female figure of Sapientia in
the Solomonic literature of the Bible, that is, the Book of
Wisdom and related sections of the Ecclesiasticus," and
"the figure of Minerva, from many sources but mainly
from Martianus Capella."[43] Provided that one does not
try to reduce Noys' mythical context to straightforward
propositions, all of these views provide useful clues to her
meaning.

Noys has three major functions. First, she is, as Gilson
suggested somewhat out of context, the providence of God.
This is the title given to her in Bernard's *Argumentum*.
Secondly, she is the messenger of God, and in this function she has a third role, related to Bernard's notion of
astrological prediction. In other words, she is not only the
logos which transmits God's design to the world; she occupies a place in the construction of the world, foretold in
his mind and predictable from the stars. These interrelated
functions moreover must be deduced from a relatively
scanty description of her powers. Bernard only speaks about
Noys twice at length in the *Cosmographia*, both times in
i.2. Of the two accounts, the first is the more informative.

[41] *AHDLMA* 3 (1928), 12.
[42] *Zeitschrift für rom. Philologie* 58 (1938), 188-89. Cf. H.
Liebeschütz, *Vorträge der Bibliothek Warburg 1923-24* (Leipzig /
Berlin, 1926), 133-43.
[43] *Modern Philology* 46 (1948-49), 110. Cf. M.-T. d'Alverny,
Mélanges . . . de Lubac ii (Paris, 1965), 121 n. 39.

It occurs in the dialogue with Natura which opens the drama and comprises Noys' answer to her complaint:[44]

"Vere," inquit, "et tu, Natura, uteri mei beata fecunditas, nec degeneras nec desciscis origine, que, filia Providentie, mundo et rebus non desinis providere. Porro Noys ego, Dei ratio profundius exquisita, quam utique de se alteram se usia prima genuit, non in tempore sed ex eo quo consistit eterno, Noys ego, scientia et divine voluntatis arbitraria ad dispositionem rerum, quemadmodum de consensu ejus accipio, sic mee administrationis officia circumduco. Inconsulto enim Deo priusquam de composito sententia[45] proferatur, rebus ad essentiam frustra maturius festinatur. Sua rerum nativitas divina prior celebratur in mente, secunda est que sequitur actione. Quod igitur de mundi molitione sanctis ac beatis affectibus et consilio conceperas altiore, ad efficentiam non potuit evocari presentem adusque terminum supernis legibus institutum: rigida et inevincibili necessitate nodisque perplexioribus fuerat illigatum, ne quem mundo desideras cultus et facies presentius contigisset. Nunc igitur, quia tempestive moves et promoves causisque ad ordinem concurrentibus, tuis desideriis deservitur."

"You, Natura," I say, "[are] truly the blessed fertility of my womb; you neither degenerate nor deviate from your origin nor, as the daughter of providence, cease to provide for the world and the things in it. But I, Noys, a more carefully worked out design of God, whom primal being undoubtedly produced from itself as its second self, not in time, but out of that by which he exists eternally, I, Noys, the knowledge and

---

[44] *Cos.* i.2.3-23.   [45] *sententiam*, Vernet.

arbitrator of the divine will for the arrangement of the cosmos, carry out the duties of my office as I receive them from his judgment. For, if God is not consulted before a plan is brought forward concerning what is composed, [the result] is hurried, in vain, and brought too quickly into existence for the universe (*rebus*). His divine nativity of the cosmos is first celebrated in his mind before that which follows is brought into existence by his act. Therefore, what you had conceived about the construction of the cosmos through sacred, blessed desires and loftier deliberation could not be carried to its conclusion according to the end set down in laws above. Lest the cultivation and configuration which you desired for the world should have been brought together too soon, [the cosmos] had been [first] bound with complex knots and ineluctable necessity. But now, since you move and advance at the right time according to laws which contribute towards order, He is glorified by your desires."

Two of the central ideas in this speech repeat motifs from Nature's complaint: the longing of matter for form, of disorder for order, and the notion that the world has arrived on the threshold of a new stage of cultural history. The other ideas are presented in complex language that intermingles various currents of Platonic expression in Bernard's time. In order to understand them more fully, they may be prefaced with a simpler statement of highly similar views. An ideal example is provided by an anonymous, twelfth-century commentary on Boethius' *Consolation of Philosophy*.[46] Commenting on the famous book iii,

[46] *Saec. Noni Auct. in Boetii Consolat. Philos. Comm.*, ed. E. T. Silk (Roma, 1935), now ascribed to the twelfth century; see P. Courcelle, *AHDLMA* 12 (1939), 36, 54, and E. T. Silk's rejoinder, *Mediaeval and Renaissance Studies* 3 (1954), 1-40.

meter 9, accepted throughout the Middle Ages as a synthesis of classical ideas on the structure of the cosmos, he offers the following explanation:

[*O qui perpetua mundum ratione gubernas* . . .][47] Before we explain this text, a few matters should be dealt with, so that what follows may be more rapidly assimilated. Those who have discoursed on the construction of the world (*de constitutione mundi*), either Christians or pagans . . . , have asserted that there are two worlds. One is called the archetype (*archetypum*), the other the sensible world. . . . They call the archetypal world the conception and mental image of the sensible world, which was in the divine mind before this world came to be. For before God created this sensible world corporeally, he saw it just as it is present now because he was conceiving it in his mind. Moreover, he saw everything—whatever has been made so far or is to be made in the future until the end of the world—as if, before the actual construction of the world, it were present and finished. The image of this entire cosmos was in the mind of God; the sensible world has been made after the pattern of its image. . . . This [same] image, which was thus in the divine mind, Plato calls *idea*, that is, form or image or figure. St. John the Evangelist calls it life, stating [1:3-4]: "[all things were made through him, and without him was not anything made] that was made. In him was life. . . ." Boethius, as well, in subsequent passages [i.e. book v], calls it the providence of God carrying out his will.

As we have made mention of the sensible world, let us inquire as well whose work it might be and how

---

[47] Boethius, *Consolatio Philosophiae*, iii, meter 9; *Saec. Noni Auct.*, pp. 155-59.

it was made. For every work is either the work of God, the work of nature, or the work of a craftsman (*artifex*) imitating nature. The work of God is just like *nous*, that is, the divine mind, [including] namely the word of the father and the world, the soul of the world, and that chaos which existed of old, the confusion of the elements, called *hyle*. . . . This sensible world is a work of God made from this matter called *hyle*, that is, the confused elements, of old called chaos, and from the form or idea in the divine mind, that is, the figure coming forth from the image and conception of the divine mind. . . .

Furthermore, it should be noted that all things that exist, have existed, or shall exist are either eternal, perpetual, or temporal. Those things are called eternal which exist before, with, and after the duration of time, that is, those things which never had an origin and will never have an end, such as God the father, the Good, *nous*, the divine mind, and the matter from which the world is made. Those things are called perpetual which are in existence with time and after time, that is, having a beginning but no end. In other words, these things began with and will end with time. . . . God the father, *nous*, and *hyle* are thus eternal; the world and the world soul are perpetual; . . . and all other things [like man and the beasts] are temporal because they had a beginning and will have an end and undergo change.

This quotation, a typical example of twelfth-century Christian Platonism (except in its reference to the eternity of matter), is undeniably close to Bernard's description of Noys in certain features. As in the *Cosmographia*, *nous* occupies a position in a hierarchy between God and the world. The hierarchy not only involves image/reality but also time/eternity. As in the *Cosmographia*, the real world to some extent reflects a divine exemplar and *nous* mediates this beneficent form from God. Yet Bernard's view of creation is a somewhat more co-operative effort, the duties being divided among many goddesses. For Bernard as well, the recreation of the cosmic order had to await the right moment in history when, according to Noys, the *cultus*, the cultivation or civilization, and the *facies*, the face or appearance of the world, could be reformed along rational lines, the *causae ad ordinem concurrentes*. While Bernard's view therefore is less complicated than the commentator's, both see *nous* as the *logos*, informing the world with God's design.

In conceiving Noys at once as the active spirit carrying out God's will and as the passive reflection of his design for the world, Bernard utilized chiefly two sources, Martianus and Chalcidius. From Martianus he drew not only the identification of *nous* with Minerva, but also the idea that a messenger of the gods carries out their will. In *De Nuptiis*, of course, this duty is assigned to Mercury. Jove, praising his virtues, states that he is

> . . . nostra ille fides, sermo, benignitas
> ac uerus Genius, fida recursio
> interpresque meae mentis, ὁ νοῦς sacer.[48]

> my very trust, discourse, good will, and true genius, the faithful recourse and interpreter of my mind, the holy *nous*.

Jove, in this address, assigns to Mercury approximately the same powers of omniscience that Bernard attributes to Noys later on.

[48] *De Nuptiis* i.92; ed. Dick-Préaux, p. 39. Cf. vi.567; p. 285, "sacer nus."

Secondly, Bernard drew from Chalcidius, as did many contemporary Platonists, the conception of *nous* as a metaphysical intermediary between God and the world. In a single chapter Chalcidius presents much of the relation between Noys and God in the *Cosmographia*:

> Everything that exists from the beginning, including the cosmos itself, is contained in and ruled by the highest God who is the *summum bonum*, beyond all substance and all nature . . . ; next, by providence, after him the highest of second place, which the Greeks call *nous*. [*Nous*] is an essence apprehensible to the mind which emulates the Good because of its tireless turning towards the highest God. For her a draught is taken from his good, and by it, not only is she herself beautified but all other things are honoured by their author. Therefore men call her Providence, the will of God, or, so to speak, the tutelary wisdom of all order. She is not so named, as some think, because she precedes future events in seeing or understanding them ahead, but because she understands the property of the divine mind, which is in fact the motion of her own mind.[49]

Here is not only the identification of *nous* with a female allegorical figure, the Providence of God, but also with

[49] *Comm.*, cap. 176; pp. 204-05: "Principio cuncta quae sunt et ipsum mundum contineri regique principaliter quidem a summo deo, qui est summum bonum ultra omnem substantiam omnemque naturam . . . ; deinde a prouidentia, quae est post illum summum secundae eminentiae, quem noyn Graeci uocant; est autem intelligibilis essentia aemulae bonitatis propter indefessam ad summum deum conuersionem, estque ei ex illo bonitatis haustus, quo tam ipsa ornatur quam cetera quae ipso auctore honestantur. Hanc igitur dei uoluntatem, tamquam sapientem tutelam rerum omnium, prouidentiam homines uocant, non, ut plerique aestimant, ideo dicam, quia praecurrit in uidendo atque intelligendo prouentus futuros, sed quid proprium diuinae mentis intellegere, qui est proprius mentis actus."

his wisdom, described in the same passage as "the eternal act of understanding God."[50]

Bernard, however, did not follow Chalcidius faithfully. The Platonist associations of *nous* outlined briefly above provide the foundation for the image of *Noys* in the *Cosmographia*, but two other features are also highly important. The first is a Stoic element. In the *Cosmographia*, Noys never appears on stage alone. She is virtually always accompanied by Natura. Yet the association of *nous/providentia* and *natura* is not derived from Chalcidius; it appears to be a survival of Stoicism. In Apuleius and in Cicero's *De Natura Deorum* ii, a different *providentia dei* is mentioned, the Stoic *pronoia* which, like Bernard's Noys, acts as the administrator of the cosmos.[51]

Secondly, Noys is related in an undefined way in the *Cosmographia* to astrology. In i.3, she is placed in the heavens with the other celestial deities and Bernard suggests that even her designs are written in the stars.[52] The right moment for the birth of the cosmos is the time when the heavenly bodies are in the correct position for the renewal of their courses. The *scientia* which Noys reflects is thus in part astrological prediction. (Later, Bernard harmonizes this idea with a partially astrological conception of God.)[53] In sum, Noys, as a member of the celestial host, is

[50] *Ibid.* 205: "est igitur mens dei intellegendi aeternus actus." Cf. Apuleius, *De Platone* ii.1.220; p. 104: "prima bona esse deum summum mentemque illam quam νοῦν idem vocat."

[51] E.g., Cicero, *De Natura Deorum* ii.29; ed. Mueller, p. 72: "Proximum est ut doceam deorum providentia mundum administrarari . . . ;" ii.30; p. 73: "Dico igitur providentia deorum mundum et omnes mundi partes et initio constitutas esse et omni tempore administrari."

[52] *Cos.* i.3.17-18: "Pura Throni legio quibus insidet ille profundus / spiritus et sensus mensque paterna Noys." The terms *spiritus et sensus* may be an allusion to Hermes' idea of celestial *genii* perceptible to the mind or the senses, discussed in Ch. IV.

[53] See Ch. IV.

a witness to God's plan for the world, a plan which is written in the stars and understandable through astrology.

These many-sided associations for Noys are perhaps embodied in the name Minerva. For Bernard, she is not only the traditional goddess of inventiveness, but queen of the arts, especially that of spinning. She thus presides over the weaving together of the cosmos into harmonious units. Bernard attempts to unite these different conceptions of *nous* in his second portrait of her powers in *Cosmographia* i.2.150-165. In this description, a parallel for which is found in an anonymous treatise on astrology, the *Liber . . . de VI Rerum Principiis*,[54] she is seen as the "fountain of light" and "the good of divine Good," her neoplatonic configurations, and as "the nursery of living things" and "the fullness of [God's] knowledge," as in Hermeticism. Her "knowledge," moreover, not only includes the design for the cosmos but whatever time, fate, and history will reveal, whatever angelic or human intelligence compre-

---

[54] T. Silverstein, *Modern Philology* 46 (1948-49), 96, states that Bernard knew Firmicus through the work, a claim he repeats in the introduction to his excellent edition of it, *AHDLMA* 22 (1956), 236: "It has been shown elsewhere by the present writer that the two books are undoubtedly connected, with the further assumption that Bernard was the debtor." Why make this assumption? First of all, the *Cosmographia* is definitely the earlier of the two works. It dates from the 1140s, while the *Liber* is a product of the next generation, even by Silverstein's own estimation. Secondly, Bernard's work had a large diffusion, even among his contemporaries; the *Liber Hermetis* is known in only four mss. Thirdly, both authors might well have read Firmicus independently. A codex of Paris, Bibl. Nat., lat. 17,867 consists of a twelfth-century copy of the *Matheseos* in single columns with light glossing in a late twelfth-century (?) hand, with some folios rewritten in a thirteenth-century hand. It is a French ms, as is the beautifully written copy of books i-iv in Paris, Bibl. Nat. lat. 7312, dating from the early thirteenth century.

hends,[55] i.e. astrological prediction. Thus for Bernard, the traditional figure of God's Providence is a rather complex literary allegory. Like his Natura, she is a composite idea, formed of many, not easily reconcilable, classical sources, and transformed in the poet's highly original imagination.

3. *Silva / Hyle*: Bernard's Materialism and Its Sources

The third partner in the opening scenes of the *Cosmographia* is matter itself. She is both allegorized in a poetic manner in i.1 and then, while retaining some of her allegorical features, presented more philosophically in i.2. The presentation of *hyle/silva* is one of the most elusive parts of the work, making heavy demands on even the erudite reader who is fully acquainted with Bernard's sources. One problem is that Bernard's view of prime matter does not appear to be wholly consistent throughout the *Cosmographia*. In spite of minor alterations, however, there are three themes which run through his entire discussion: one, that matter is a self-reproducing substance; two, that matter is an allegorical mystery, relating God and the

[55] *Cos.* i.2.152-67: "Ea igitur Noys summi et exsuperantissimi Dei est intellectus et ex ejus divinitate nata Natura; in qua vite viventis imagines, notiones eterne, mundus intelligibilis, rerum cognitio prefinita. Erat igitur videre velut in speculo tersiore quicquid generationi, quicquid operi Dei secretior destinaret affectus. Illic, in genere, in specie, in individuali singularitate conscripta, quicquid Yle, quicquid mundus, quicquid parturiunt elementa. Illic, exarata supremi digito dispunctoris textus temporis, fatalis series, dispositio seculorum; illic, lacrime pauperum fortuneque regum; illic, potentia militaris; illic philosophorum felicior disciplina; illic, quicquid angelus, quicquid ratio comprehendit humana; illic, quicquid celum sua complectitur curvatura. Quod igitur tale est, illud eternitati contiguum, idem Natura cum Deo nec substantia disparatum." Cf. Firmicus Maternus, *Matheseos* i.5.10-12; ed. Kroll and Skutsch, vol. i, p. 17, 3-8.

world; and three, that matter, in addition, is really the "stuff" of the world and of man, related directly to what is visible and tangible. Through a combination of these views, Bernard arrives at a position describable as a limited type of materialism. It has its roots in Stoic Hermeticism and Chalcidius, but it is presented with considerable originality. Let us look first at what Bernard actually says about matter, then at the *fontes* to which his ideas may be traced.

Bernard's Portrait of Matter

After the allegory of primal matter in the opening verses, the most thorough discussion of *silva/hyle* in the *Cosmographia* occurs just after Noys has finished explaining her powers to Natura and just before she sets about resolving the chaos of the four elements into a harmonious unit:

> Erat Yle nature vultus antiquissimus, generationis uterus indefessus, formarum prima subjectio, materia corporum, substantie fundamentum. Ea siquidem capacitas, nec terminis nec limitibus circumscripta, tantos sinus tantamque a principio continentiam explicavit quantam rerum universitas exposceret. Quodque varie et multiplices eternitatis seu materiam subjectumque obeunt qualitates, non turbari non potuit; quod ab omni natura tam multiformiter pulsaretur, stabilitatem bonumque tranquillitatis excussit. Frequens nec intercisa (*supp.* est) frequentatio naturarum: egredientium numerus ingredientibus locum pandit.
>
> Irrequieta est nec potuit Yle meminisse quando vel nascentium formis vel occidentium refluxionibus intermissius adiretur. Illud igitur inconsistens et convertibile hujus et illius conditionis qualitatis et forme cum proprie descriptionis judicium non expectet elabitur incognitum vultus vicarios alternando; et, quod

figurarum omnium susceptione convertitur, nullius sue forme signaculo specialiter insignitur. Verum quoquo pacto frenata est licentia discursandi, ut elementorum firmioribus inniteretur substantiis eisque quaternis velut inhereret materies inquieta.[56]

Hyle was the most ancient face of nature, the unwearied uterus of generation, the first representation of forms, the matter of bodies, and the foundation of substance. Her capacity, circumscribed by neither ends nor limits, poured forth from its source as great a bosom-full and contents as the universe asked for. Since the multiple, changing qualities of eternity were circling [her] material substratum all the time, she could not fail to be disturbed. For, since demands were being made so constantly from every [part of] nature, she had no recourse to the beneficial stability of peace. Nor was this repetitious process often interrupted. In fact, the number of things proceeding outward just made room for those coming in.

Being restless, Hyle could not recall when she was intermittently approached by the forms of things being born or the reflux of things dying. As a result, since the mutable or changeable [element] of this or that condition, form, or quality does not wait for the arrangement of its own limits, it slips out unrecognized, changing from one appearance to another; and, since it is changed by adopting forms indiscriminately, it is not stamped with the seal of the form which belongs to it. Nonetheless, license was bridled from running completely wild by whatever means [were available], so that restless matter was supported by the firmer substance of the four elements which clung to it like roots.

[56] *Cos.* i.2.47-69.

The first question to raise in regard to this portrait of matter is whether it supplements or provides a contrast to that presented by Natura in i.1. The solution to this problem, however, is not simple. While Bernard uses *hyle* and *silva* almost interchangeably, he also seems to imply a subtle distinction between them, as if they represented different aspects of prime matter. *Silva* seems to be synonymous with the concrete chaos of the primitive elements, while *hyle* is more abstract and mysterious, an indefinable substratum. Philosophically, this distinction corresponds roughly to two views of matter held in the early twelfth century: one, derived from Galen through Constantinus Africanus and other *medici*, asserted that matter was virtually identical to the four elements out of which it was composed; the other, derived in part from Chalcidius but ultimately from a number of ancient sources, held that matter was a substratum into which the elements inhered but remained separate from them. Views on the problem varied somewhat: Hermann of Carinthia, for instance, preferred the more physical approach,[57] while Bernard attempts to unite the two.

The difference between *silva* and *hyle*, however, is more profound than this. *Silva* is much more involved than *hyle* in the moral allegory through which a new and better universe is to be formed. In his descriptions, Bernard points out that *silva* is to be refined into a more cultivated visage for the world while *hyle* represents the eternal source of matter which reproduces itself. In i.1 it is *silva*, not *hyle*, which is associated with the image of a better form for *mundus*; it is she who is cut off from her own perfection and who longs to be reborn; it is she whom the infant cosmos thanks for being no worse off than it is. In i.2, a slightly different, though no less allegorical portrait of matter is

[57] See Lemay, *Abu Ma'shar*, 220. Abu Ma'shar, however, equates *medicus* with *physicus*; *Introductorium* i.5; f. b.2 recto.

found. *Hyle*, at least to some extent, is said to be more stable than *silva*. She rests motionless, though surrounded by motion, and passionless, neither good nor evil in herself. She is eternal, but owing to disorder she is unable to impress the correct seals on existential forms; thus they die in a confused, meaningless pattern. In associating one aspect of matter with good and evil, that is, order and disorder, while clearly dissociating another aspect of matter from any involvement in the moral question, Bernard is again combining different tendencies in Chalcidius. Finally, it is worth pointing out that *hyle* and *silva* are resonating, interdependent forms of the same reality. Just as the *vetus globus*, despite the continual warfare of the elements, remains battered but intact, so *hyle* is prevented from descending into complete chaos by the four elements that cling to her, as to *silva*, like roots.

The relation between *silva* and *hyle* in the *Cosmographia* is therefore more complicated than first appears. Bernard's conception of matter both as an allegory and as a philosophical principle is in fact a conflation of doctrines from different sources. In terms of earlier philosophical positions, these may be divided into Hermetic, Chalcidian, and Aristotelian *fontes*. In terms of their impact on Bernard's imagination, however, it is unwise to so divide them. From both the *Asclepius* and Chalcidius Bernard assimilates the position that matter is essentially a mystery, inexplicable in concrete, philosophical language, but he absorbs this idea as it is expressed in somewhat different ways. In the contrast between *silva* and *hyle*, he has also absorbed Chalcidius' view that matter may be considered before and after it has received properties. In the latter state, it is close to the Stoic notion that matter is the substance out of which all bodies are formed and in which all change takes place. Thus, while the *Timaeus* describes matter as a receptacle "in which" or "in whose bosom" forms make their appearance, Bernard, leaning towards Stoic views, uses the same metaphor but states that elements are formed "of matter and in matter."[58] In other words, Bernard seems to combine the allegorical mode of conceiving matter with a limited position of materialism, asserting at once that matter cannot, ultimately, be described, but that its role in the creative process is very large. Lastly, Bernard interrelates *silva* and *hyle* in another way through Aristotle, whose *Physics* he found imbedded in Chalcidius. In i.1 and 2, matter's longing for form reflects Aristotle in both ideas and expression. It is perhaps arguable that so eclectic a view could not have been made plausible except through allegory.

The Hermetic Element

To deal first with Hermeticism: Bernard derived his doctrines chiefly from the Latin *Asclepius*, which is the patristic translation of a lost Greek original. It was written in three parts by three different authors who reflected, to a large degree, different philosophic backgrounds.[59] The

---

[58] *Cos.* i.2.98; see Ch. III n. 2. Cf. M. McCrimmon, "The Classical Philosophical Sources," 131.

[59] See W. Scott, *Hermetica* i (Oxford, 1924), 49-81 and *Asc.* 291-92; on the diffusion of the text in the twelfth century, see *Asc.* 267-69, especially 267 n. 5. Throughout the Middle Ages, the Latin *Asclepius* was normally included in the philosophical works of Apuleius; see P. Thomas, *Apulei Opera*, vol. iii, pp. x-xii. Twelfth-century copies of the text are described briefly in *Asc.* 259-61, to which the following may be added: Berne, Bibl. Mun. 136, ff. 13-23; København, Univ. Lib., Fabricius 914, ff. 89-98; London, B.M. Add. 11,983, ff. 70v-84; Vatican, Ottoboni lat. 1516, ff. 69-83. There is a twelfth-century commentary on the *Asclepius*, the only one known to the author, in Vatican, Ottoboni lat. 811, ff. 160-67. Bernard's use of the *Asclepius* was noted briefly by R. B. Woolsey, *Traditio* 6 (1948), 340-44, and a line-by-line comparison was attempted by M. McCrimmon, "The Classical

major subject of the first part is man, of the second, the problem of evil, and of the third, a number of Hermetic topics arranged in no particular order. In spite of its internal contradictions, it was accepted throughout the Middle Ages as a unity. It was thought to be one of the most ancient sources of eastern wisdom.

The presentation of the problem of matter is largely Stoic, but it possesses one unusual feature and is placed in a Platonic context which accorded well with what Bernard found in Chalcidius. The unusual feature, and the one which obviously fascinated him, was the bisexuality of God and matter. Unlike some Hermetic astrologers, Bernard did not extend this principle throughout the solar system; however, going somewhat beyond even Hermes, he suggests that matter is capable of regenerating itself without the co-operation of God. In the *Asclepius*, God is conceived as "the One and the Many, infinitely full of the fertility of both sexes."[60] Ever pregnant with his own will, he is ever giving birth to what he wills. Possessing the latent forms for all existing things, his creative actions consist of an emanation from the One to the Many, from Identity to Difference.[61] In this mystic atmosphere, God reveals his powers.

According to Hermes, in the beginning there was only God, matter, and spirit.[62] Spirit was both in God and in

---

Philosophical Sources," 86-90. Yet Bernard's utilization of the text was established by von Bezold and, unknown to the above authors, scrupulously documented by André Vernet (1938).

[60] *Asc.*, cap. 20; p. 321: "Hic (= deus) ergo, solus ut omnia, utraque sexus fecunditate plenissimus, semper uoluntatis praegnans suae parit semper, quicquid uoluerit procreare." Cf. Firmicus, *Matheseos* v, *praefatio*; vol. ii, p. 2, line 20: [deus], "tu omnium pater pariter et mater."

[61] *Asc.* 2-3; p. 298.

[62] *Asc.* 14, p. 313; 20, pp. 320, 322.

matter but not in both in the same way. The qualities of matter may be summarized as follows:[63]

> Matter, so to speak the nature and spirit of the world, although it does not seem to be born from the beginning, nonetheless has in itself the power and nature of being born and of giving birth. For the beginnings of creativity are inherent in its property, which possesses, in itself, both the force and the substance of conceiving and giving birth. Matter, then, is the only thing which is generative without conceiving through another. . . . And thus, the material substance of the world,[64] although it is not born, yet contains within itself the latent properties of all things since through all these things it presents a highly fertile womb for conceiving. In sum, this is matter's chief property: it is capable of creating even though it is not created.

From this characterization of matter Bernard took not only the notion of autoreproduction but, more importantly, the

[63] In order, *Asc.* 14; pp. 313, 315 and *Asc.* 15; p. 314: "ὕλη autem uel mundi natura et spiritus quamuis nata non uideantur a principio, tamen in se nascendi procreandique uim possident atque naturam. Fecunditatis etenim initium in qualitate naturae est, quae et conceptus et partus in se possidet uim atque materiam. Haec itaque sine alieno conceptu est sola generabilis." "Sic ergo et mundus, quamuis natus non sit, in se tamen omnium naturas habet, utpote qui his omnibus ad concipiendum fecundissimos sinus praestet. Hoc est ergo totum qualitatis materiae, quae creabilis est, tametsi creata non est."

[64] *Asc.* 17; p. 315, equates *mundus* with matter: "ὕλη autem uel mundus." This was the basis of both Scott's and Festugière's translation of *mundus* consistently as matter. But is it not possible that here, as elsewhere, the translator is echoing popular Latin usage? *Mundanus*, by the fourth century, meant mundane, tangible, immediately at hand. Throughout the *Asclepius* the direct apprehension of the tangible world is very strong. Could not *mundus* then be "the mundane"?

metaphors of motherhood and birth that seemed to him to best express the elusive, creative aspects of substance. Thus, in the opening verses of the *Cosmographia*, matter's innate mysteries—both her capacity to reproduce and her relation to God—are presented in allegory. At least one medieval commentator on the *Cosmographia* realized this: he placed in the margin beside the opening stanzas: *biformis natura Yle.*[65] Bernard, moreover, could have found support for this view in other Hermetic writings available to him. Abu Ma'shar, recapitulating Hermes' astrological views, alludes to them,[66] as does Hugh de Santalla's translation of the *Liber de Secretis Hermetis Trismegisti*, a contemporary alchemical encyclopedia.[67] The latter work not only discusses the Hermetic conception of matter in a manner similar to the *Cosmographia*, but represents it graphically [Plate V].

[65] Paris, Bibl. Nat., lat. 6556, f. 79r. In the same MS there is a beautifully illustrated treatise entitled *De Quatuor Elementis et Cosmographia quedam Magistri Asaph Hebreij* (f. A, verso), ff. 1r-10rb, partially transcribed by L. Delisle, *Bibl. de l'Ecole des chartes* 54 (1893) 406-11; 587-88.

[66] *Introductorium*, v.4; f. [d.5] recto.

[67] Paris, Bibl. Nat., lat. 13,951; see F. Nau, *Revue de l'orient chrétien* 12 (1907), 99-106. A seventeenth-century copy of the same work is found in MS lat. 13,952. Written in elegant Latin and carefully corrected in its unique, twelfth-century version, the work is essentially a treatise on alchemy framed as an encyclopedia. An excellent blend of humanistic and scientific interests, it would seem, like the *Cosmographia* itself, to deny the distinction which Scott makes between religious and pseudo-scientific Hermetic literature; *Hermetica* i (1924), i. For a checklist of scientific works associated with Hermes, see F. J. Carmody, *Arabic Astronomical and Astrological Sciences in Latin Translation* (Berkeley and Los Angeles, 1956), 52-70; L. Thorndike and P. Kibre, *A Catalogue of Incipits of Mediaeval Scientific Writings in Latin* (New York, 1963), s.v. Hermes; on Arabic versions, see L. Massignon, in A.-J. Festugière, *La révélation d'Hermès Trismégiste* i (Paris, 1944), 384-400.

The Chalcidian Element

Bernard's major source on the problem of matter was Chalcidius, who takes a different view of matter's origin but nonetheless presents the entire problem in an allegorical context that harmonizes well with the *Asclepius*. The chapters of his *Commentary* on the *Timaeus* which deal with the subject explain only a small part of the original (*Tim.* 47E-53C), but they comprise the longest and most complicated discussion. The analysis as a whole may be divided into three parts: one, a paraphrase of *Timaeus* 47E-49A, occupying chapters 268 to 274; two, an historical and systematic exposition recapitulating the views of many ancient authorities, occupying chapters 275 to 320; and three, a paraphrase of *Timaeus* 49A-53C, including a summary of the previous discussion, occupying chapters 321 to 355. Bernard did not attempt to reproduce all the divergent views on matter reported by Chalcidius. In general, he modified or rejected the neoplatonic elements and emphasized the Stoic and Aristotelian ones. For the Stoic material, he drew on Chalcidius' critique of Plato; for the Aristotelian, a single quotation from the *Physics* which he clearly saw through his mentor's eyes.

The relevant part of the commentary begins at *Timaeus* 48E, the passage in which Plato is discussing the "mother-receptacle" in which a third kind of form, midway between matter and form, comes into being. Plato states that a fresh start must be made in the discourse, and Chalcidius, following him, suggests that the crux of the problem arises from the existence of corporeal forms and their relation to eternal or ideal forms. Referring to this aspect of existence, he employs the same metaphors as the *Asclepius*, but with a slightly different twist in meaning:

> Quae quidem corpora cum sola et per se ac sine suscipiente eadem essentia esse non possunt, quam modo

matrem, alias nutriculam, interdum totius generationis gremium, non numquam locum appellat quamque iuniores hylen, nos silvam uocamus. . . .[68]

For since this matter (or, these elements) cannot exist alone and through itself without someone sustaining it by means of the same essence, this [essence Plato] never calls "no place," but rather on one occasion "mother," on another "nurse," and on others "the womb of all generation." Younger [Platonists] call it *hyle*, while we use the term *silva*. . . .

Bernard, like Chalcidius, speaks often of a *gremium*, through whose fertility God's creativity and goodness are mediated. He interprets the metaphor, moreover, not in the sense of Plato's original, but as a simple circumlocution for creativity. Thus, by another route one arrives at Bernard's conception of matter both as a substance, with or without properties, and as an allegory.

Before turning to Bernard's actual use of Chalcidius' allegory of matter, however, it is perhaps worth recalling some features of *Silva/Hyle*'s appearance in the *Cosmographia* and comparing them with Chalcidius' attitude towards metaphor and myth.

In *Cosmographia* i.1-2, Silva represents matter in potential rather than in reality. What matter produces or what is produced in or from matter—the material products adorned with their appropriate forms in the diversity of the existing world—are not known at the beginning of the drama. They await fulfillment in the course of time and only represent corporeal realities when the creative act has

---

[68] *Comm.*, cap. 273; pp. 277-78. For Chalcidius, *corpora* mean "matter"; cf. *Tim.* 32C; p. 25, lines 11-12: "Igitur quattuor illa integra corpora . . . ad mundi continentiam sumpta sunt." On Chalcidius' use of Greek philosophical terms for matter, see J. R. O'Donnell, *MS* 7 (1945), 1-20.

concluded its initial work. Bernard, so to speak, has subtly introduced into the dramatic structure the philosophical dichotomy between *potentia activa* and *potentia passiva*. This may be seen not only in the two aspects of matter itself, represented as *hyle* and *silva*, but in the working out of matter's potential in the course of the drama. The *Cosmographia* consists, in large part, in realizing the possibilities inherent in matter and Bernard, through poetry, paints a dynamic picture of how this takes place. In the entire transformation of philosophical attributes into dramatic enactments, moreover, Bernard brings to perfection tendencies of mind easily discernible in Chalcidius.

Although a poor commentator in a purely philosophical sense, Chalcidius took a sincere interest in the problem of the communication of hard, cold facts in a scientific language. His rejection of Stoicism and his typically middle-Platonist absorption of Aristotle into Plato reflects, in part, his belief that indirect methods involving metaphors, similes, or allegory are often best for conveying the ultimate secrets of nature. In discussing the problem of the obscurity of philosophical discourse on one occasion, for instance, he says: "*multae quippe orationes uerae quidem sed obscurae.*"[69] The idea that a discourse could be true yet unclear or indirect obviously attracted his mind, as it did Bernard's. A little further on in the same chapter, he says that obscurity may be traced to the listener, the speaker, or the nature of the subject. In the case of Plato, it is clearly the last:

> For Timaeus, who is presenting the discourse, is not an unreliable speaker, nor is his audience slow-witted. Therefore the reason must be that the material itself is difficult and obscure. In fact, there is nothing more difficult to explain than matter. Whatever is said about

[69] *Ibid.* cap. 322; p. 317.

its essential characteristics, while in strict agreement with the truth, is not communicated openly or lucidly.[70]

On another occasion Chalcidius develops this approach to the verifiability of propositions about reality a little further. *Ratio*, he states, can never penetrate the ultimate obscurity of fundamental principles like matter:

> It is very difficult to obtain insight into the nature of matter and still more difficult to explain it to others. The difficulty with principles is that they cannot be explained by means of examples—indeed, there exists nothing which can be used as an example. Nor can they be illustrated by anything existing, since there is nothing which precedes a principle. The only result one can attain with this sort of problem is a vague and obscure notion. . . .[71]

Thus, when he finally turns to the problem of matter itself, he not only builds on Plato's ideas, but assumes that only an indirect, essentially literary rather than philosophical approach will be adequate. In doing so, he allows methods of description normally reserved for literary texts—for representations of reality—to be mixed freely with those intended for reality itself.

A good example of this sort of reasoning is provided by

[70] *Ibid.* 317-18: "Sed neque Timaeus, qui disserit, instabilis orator nec audientes tardi; restat, ut res ipsa difficilis et obscura sit. Nec silua quicquam difficilius ad explanandum; ergo cuncta quae de natura eius dicta sunt mera praedita ueritate sunt nec tamen aperte dilucideque intimata."

[71] *Ibid.* cap. 274; pp. 278-79, trans. J.C.M. van Winden, *Calcidius on Matter* (Leiden, 1959), 49. This sequence of thought may be compared to Martianus, *De Nuptiis* iii.221-22, where Martianus, in a dialogue with his muse, admits that nothing serious can be communicated without literary art; ed. Dick-Préaux, pp. 81-82.

a short digression on *potentia* itself, which occurs after a lengthy comparison of ancient authorities and acts as a prologue to the consolidation of his own views. Previous authors who have written on matter, he states, are agreed that qualities like shape and form are not innate characteristics of substance but are united with it afterwards. However, if such defining characteristics are absent at the time of description, they may be inferred indirectly since matter clearly possesses them *non effectu sed possibilitate*. Chalcidius then explains what is meant by potential:

> Possibility . . . may be understood in two senses: the one, when we say that in a seed the whole plan for the body's total perfection lies hidden within, and that the seed is the living creature in potential; the other, when, although it does not yet possess a plan for future growth, such is its nature that it can receive from the outside the plans for forms and qualities. In this sense we say that it is going to be what it is not as yet, like a formless mass of wax. . . .[72]

The point of this passage is not the metaphors of the seed and the wax impression. These are commonplaces and Bernard, in utilizing them, differs only slightly in their interpretation. The real similarity with Bernard arises from the way in which Chalcidius introduces the question. What he has said is applicable both to statements about reality and to reality itself. He is "so absorbed in this prob-

---

[72] *Comm.*, cap. 310; pp. 310-11: "Possibilitas autem gemina ratione intelligitur: una, ut cum dicimus in semine omnem totius corporis perfecti rationem intus latere semenque possibilitate animal est; altera, quod rationem quidem in se futurae generationis nondum habet, sed quia tale est natura, ut extrinsecus accipere possit rationes formarum et qualitatum, possibilitate dicimus fore quod nondum est, ut . . . ceraeue massa informis. . . ."

lem of the *possibilitas* that he forgets to say which kind of possibility belongs to matter."[73] In other words, the problem of the metaphor of the Platonic receptacle, as a literary discourse, is indistinguishable in his mind from the meaning which the metaphor is presumably illustrating.

Chalcidius' literary approach to scientific questions is what provides the subtle link between his commentary and the allegory of matter in the *Cosmographia*. His discussion of Plato's intentional obscurity, and similar discussions by numerous other commentators, not only of Plato but a variety of classical authors, legitimize Bernard's use of mythical allegory for portraying the ultimate secrets of the universe. In the discussion of *possibilitas* immediately above, both the metaphors themselves, the seed and the wax impression, and the modalities in which they are conceived, either as image/reality or *potentia activa/passiva*, are equally applicable to propositions about reality as to reality itself. In the *Cosmographia* this process is turned about. What is explained in commentary by Chalcidius is reformulated by Bernard into a new myth about Plato and Chalcidius. Viewed in this context, his allegory of *Silva/Hyle* is the isomorph, the logical inversion, of Chalcidius.

Bernard, however, did not follow Chalcidius on purely philosophical matters. This may be demonstrated by considering a later statement on the Platonic receptacle involving the metaphors of the seed and the wax impression:

> He calls it their receptacle not, as the Stoics think, because generated species begin to flourish from within the womb of matter, but because they come about from without, like images in wax. Yet he calls it their nurse with good reason because it bears someone else's child on its own shoulders. Indeed, it offers through these

[73] C. van Winden, *Calcidius on Matter*, 153.

services nothing more than something placed under [them].[74]

Bernard did not, of course, reject the Stoic position as did Chalcidius. Having found it expressed in the *Asclepius*, he assimilated it, somewhat eclectically, along with Chalcidius' images of the impressions of forms on matter. Other examples of Bernard's conscious adoption of Chalcidius' attitudes and expressions yet rejection of their factual content could easily be found.

The Aristotelian Element

Thus, in summary so far, Bernard appears to combine both an otherworldly and a this-worldly position in his view of matter. In retaining the mythical, allegorical framework, as presented by Chalcidius (and others), he committed himself in part to neoplatonism; in adapting Stoic or Hermetic notions to it, he took myth in a different direction. And in order to unite the two, he drew on Aristotle.

In a later description of Identity and Difference, Bernard attempted, not without ambiguity, to summarize this picture himself, stating:

Erant igitur duo rerum principia: unitas et diversum. Diversum longe retro antiquissimum; unitas non inceperat—simplex, intacta, solitaria, ex se, in se permanens, infinibilis et eterna. Unitas (*supp.* est) deus, diversum non aliud quam Yle eaque indigens forma.[75]

There were, then, two principles of universal order: unity and diversity. Most ancient diversity [is] a long

---

[74] *Comm.*, cap. 321; p. 317: "Quam quidem *receptaculum* eorum appellat, quia non ex gremio siluae generatae species florescunt, ut putant Stoici, sed extrinsecus obueniunt ut in cera signacula; *nutriculam* uero ideo quod alienos fetus uelut propriis humeris uehat; quippe nihil his praebet amplius praeter subiectionem" (my italics).

[75] *Cos.* ii.13.1-5.

way back. Unity had no beginning; [it was] simple, untouched, solitary, enduring out of itself and in itself, infinite and eternal. Unity is God; diversity is nothing else but matter needful of form.

The problem with this statement is its brevity and possible ambiguity. The language could equally describe a Stoic or neoplatonist theory of matter, or, as is more probable with Bernard, both at once.[76] No mention is made of dis-

[76] I add a query because there is clearly a difference between this rather more Pythagorean description and the more Stoic/Aristotelian approach of i.1-2. Some scholars have attempted to reconcile the two portraits; e.g. T. Silverstein, *Modern Philology* 46 (1948-49), 112-16. This description argues strongly for the influence of John Scottus and is similar to that of Thierry of Chartres, *De Septem Diebus et Sex Operum Distinctionibus*, ed. N. Haring, *AHDLMA* 22 (1956), cap. 36, p. 196: "Sed creatio numerorum rerum est creatio. Unitas igitur omnipotens est in rerum creatione, illud unice et simpliciter omnipotens est. Unitas igitur omnipotens." Diversity is accordingly synonymous with the creative differentiation from the One. Thierry cites similar passages to Bernard from the *Asclepius, ibid.*, cap. 26, p. 193, but, instead of developing them to harmonize with Stoic and Aristotelian doctrines, uses them to provide a metaphor of the fertility of the One. Another text which may well have influenced Bernard here is Hermann of Carinthia, *De Essentiis* i, ed. P. M. Alonso, *Hermann de Carintia, De Essentiis* (Comillas, 1946 = *Miscelánea Comillas* 5 [1946], 7-107), pp. 27-28: "Constat plane nichil genitum sine causa genetrice naturaque vetitutum ne quid sibi ipsi geniture sit origo seque ipsum efficiat. Sic igitur in omni generacione auctorem generantem causamque moventem intelligi necesse est. . . . Prima quidem una et simplex . . . antiquitate precedat. . . ." Yet Hermann's view as well, based on the primary and secondary heavenly motions in Abu Ma'shar, is quite different from Bernard's. The closest parallel to Bernard's union of Pythagorean, Aristotelian, and Hermetic notions is found, somewhat later, in Daniel of Morley, *Liber de Naturis*, ed. Sudhoff, p. 14: "Pitagoras uero et Aristoteles duo omnium principia dicebant, vnitatem id est deum, alteritatem id est naturam. Hanc enim ylen intelligebant. Pitagoras eam alteritatem uocabat, Aristoteles possibilitatem, quia ex

order, nor of the cultural images from i.1-2. Hyle, perhaps synonymous with *hyle/silva*, is nonetheless presented in recognizable terms: she is infinite and proceeds from the One to the Many.

One motif however is repeated from i.1-2. Matter's need for form is described by *indigens*, a term which provides a convenient introduction to Bernard's debt to Aristotle. Throughout the *Cosmographia* matter's need for formal amelioration is presented in Aristotelian language. Silva, for example, is said to be *carens*; her disorder is a *malitia, silvestris malignitas, malum silve, grossities, asperitas, rigor, grossitudo, inequalitas, silve contagio, malignans illuvies,* and *chaos*. While Hyle disposes of forms in a passive way, Silva actively begs for a new dress to relieve her ugliness and cure a certain moral sickness in the universe. Bernard's notion of evil is in fact synonymous with Silva's disorder and her condition is presented in effective, concrete images. The moral allegory in the *Cosmographia* is directly related to improving her condition, and it was this idea which Bernard drew, via Chalcidius, from Aristotle.

In his review of different theories of matter, Chalcidius does not neglect Aristotle. The passage that Bernard utilized, from *Physics* 192A, is contained in chapter 286, and in the following chapters Chalcidius attempts an exposition which Bernard clearly assimilated along with a corrupt version of the original.[77] Here is Aristotle in Chalcidius' text, followed by his explanation of it:

---

ea diuersarum rerum forma producta sit. . . . Forte est, qui me non predictis erroribus derogare, sed ipsis auctoribus estimet inuidere, ideo sicut ab inexpugnabili sententia magni Hermetis habeo, audacter, cum illo unum tantum principium esse concedo." But Daniel, writing a generation after Bernard, may have been influenced by him.

[77] For a comparison of texts, see C. van Winden, *Calcidius on Matter*, 82-92. A general summary of Chalcidius' view of matter is

[Aristotle]: It seems to us that matter should be distinguished from privation (*carentia*), inasmuch as matter is not something which exists by itself but rather accidentally, while privation is non-existing in the proper and absolute sense. . . . Matter in this sense is a mother for bodies (*mater corporum*) through her assistance in their formation, while the lack of being does not aid in their formation but actually impedes and resists it, to the extent that when form (*species*) is desirous of a divine reality, privation acts against it. To be precise, matter asks for form and amplification. The state of being desirous is in accordance with its very nature. . . . Only matter, furthermore, desires representation (*illustrationem*), in much the same way as the female desires the male, deformity, beauty. Finally, the deformity of matter is not due to nature but to accident. Matter becomes something and is reduced again in a definite manner. When it becomes something, it exists to a certain degree; when it is dissolved, it ceases to exist to the same degree. Destruction arises from individual privation. In this capacity, not by nature, matter is immortal and without generation, for it is particularly important that something more ancient should lie at the basis of

provided by Gregory, 190-93, while his tendency to platonize Aristotle's vocabulary is noted by O'Donnell, *MS* 7 (1945), 19. My use of Aristotle within Chalcidius is of course an assumption, but one which is supported by Bernard's extensive use of the commentator elsewhere. Yet one should not rule out the possibility, however remote, that Bernard knew other sources of Aristotle. A conception of *hyle* similar to Bernard's but more genuinely Aristotelian in language, for example, is found in Alkindi's *Liber de Quinque Essentiis*, in the *Sermo de Hyle*; ed. A. Nagy, *Beiträge* 2.5 (Münster, 1897), p. 33, lines 15-21: "Et est ut dicamus quod hyle est quod suscipit et non suscipitur, etc." The translation is attributed to Gerard of Cremona; Haskins, 56.

things being born, out of which they should be made to arrive at birth. Thus, it was necessary that matter should have existed before it was transformed into something. . . .

[Chalcidius]: Aristotle . . . is speaking of the beginnings of things and of the characteristics of matter, but as his discourse is somewhat obscure it would appear to require an exposition. He proposes a triple origin for all things: form, matter, and privation. He praises form as the same divinity as the highest God, resting on full and perfect good. . . . Matter [by contrast] desires cultivation and harmonious arrangement (*cultum ornatumque*), since it is not deformed on account of itself but because of need. Indeed, it is a disgrace (*turpitudo*) for matter to lack cultivation and form. . . . Consequently, we may state that badness (*malitiam*) and the beginning of evil (*initia malorum*) do not arise from matter but from privation. [Evil] is in fact the lack of cultivation and the disgrace of matter and indeed, as a result, its malevolence.[78]

If this citation from Aristotle and its accompanying commentary are considered as a unit in Bernard's imagination, then the picture of matter in *Cosmographia* i.1-2 is virtually complete. Aristotle's analysis, supplemented by Chalcidius' return to Platonic metaphors, provides Bernard with just the amount of flesh he needs to clothe his allegories with a little concrete philosophy. First of all, we have again the notion that matter is a "mother" for bodies. Secondly, towards the end of Chalcidius' commentary on the passage, the same visual metaphors (*turpitudo, malitia*) as Bernard uses in i.1 are contrasted with the cultivated and refined (*cultum ornatumque*) state of ordered matter.

---

[78] *Comm.* cap. 286-88; pp. 289-92.

Most importantly, a philosophic basis is provided for Bernard's view that creativity in general and the creation of the cosmos in particular must be understood largely in material terms. Matter is seen to be eternal but offering a variety of presentations. *Carentia* and *species*, the terms which Bernard uses in i.1-2, are invoked in order to express matter's primitive lack of but innate desire for *illustrationem*.

In sum, Bernard's sources appear to indicate that Natura's complaint in the *Cosmographia* is a more complex affair than would first appear. Mixing the metaphors from earlier verse cosmogonies, he first creates the impression of chaos, of impending cosmic revolution. Then, in imitation of Plato, he introduces the myth of the creation of the world and of man. Yet within this dramatic framework, he makes certain innovations which link him to the natural-philosophic speculations of his own day. First of all, it is a goddess called Nature, representing not only the regulatory forces in the universe but the spirit of rational inquiry into them, who calls for cosmic reform. Then it is Noys, a mysterious figure who represents God's providence and the new astrological predictability loosely associated with it, who brings down the plan for universal order. To these two allegorical personages he then adds a third, Matter herself. The reform of the cosmos, the subject of Natura's dialogue with Noys, is seen primarily in material terms. Matter, his most mysterious figure, provides the substratum from which the infantile *mundus* arises and clothes itself for presentation. As disorder is replaced by order, Matter gradually acquires the capacity to control the evil inherent in herself. In this way, Bernard introduces the idea of a moral allegory (i.e. the improvement of the cosmos and man) into his drama in primarily physical terms. Lastly, in comparison with his contemporaries, he strongly emphasizes the role of matter in the creative process. This view, an apparently conscious leaning towards Stoic as opposed to neoplatonic source material, is also linked in his mind to certain ill-defined images of cultural progress. While leading the reader on to the next act, Bernard has in fact laid the foundations for the most original aspects of his myth.

CHAPTER III

The Creation of the World

1. Ornatus Elementorum

AFTER Bernard has introduced Natura, Noys, and Silva/Hyle in the opening scene, the next act of the *Cosmographia* deals with the creation of the world. This unit, *grosso modo*, begins at i.2.78 and finishes at ii.3.13, when Noys, recapitulating her labors in another dialogue with Natura, turns to the problem of creating man. Within this part of the drama there are two further divisions: one, the actual creation of the cosmos and everything in it; two, an explanation of how the universe functions as a living organism and a mechanical fabrication.

If read one after the other, sections i.2, 3, and 4 also present an interesting transition in literary form. If i.1 and 2 are pure allegory, then i.3 is a type of encyclopedia, and i.4 is a commentary on what has taken place. There is also a noticeable change in Bernard's style. From the jagged verses of i.1, the reader proceeds through the turgid prose of i.2, only to emerge into the radiant, if somewhat redundant, elegiacs of i.3. Section i.4 returns to prose of exceptional complexity.

Broadly speaking, if one considers *Megacosmus* as a literary unit, there is still another type of transition at work: from mythologization to demythologization. This process, outlined above, is particularly evident throughout book one. The first act presents the mysterious allegory of matter and, following the creation of cosmic order in i.2 and 3, i.4 leads the reader back into the realm of the commentary, where allegory is replaced in part by exposition. It is difficult to account for this dialectical structure as anything but an aspect of Bernard's literary art. The dénouement of his dramatic myth is thus both the creation of the world and of man and the gradual desacralization of the mystery which creation represents.

If the thread of the story is taken up where it was left off in the above discussion of matter, then the remainder of i.2 and the whole of i.3 may be treated together. In these two sections, Bernard describes the resolution of chaos and the descent of the world-soul; then, after the *anima mundi* and *mundus* are united in marriage, the world's contents are unfolded in elegiac verse. In the first scene matter is organized along physical principles, fire, air, water, and earth each occupying positions relative to their densities. Fire, the most important element, rises to the top and forms a ring around the cosmos which is contiguous with the *aplanos*, the outermost rim. In the second scene, when the elements are arranged in harmony, the other components of the universe are unfolded before the reader's eyes. They include: the heavens and the nine orders of angels as well as pagan gods (Vernet, lines 1-30), the stars, constellations, and planets, including their astrological con-figurations (31-154), the four winds (155-58), the tradi-tional geographical divisions of the earth[1] (159-74), the mountains (175-200), the animals (201-34), the rivers (235-64), the trees appropriate to each region (265-84), the fruits (285-300), the spices (301-14), Nature's paradise among a group of paradises (315-52), domestic vegetables and flowers (353-414), fish (415-40), and birds (441-80).

---

[1] See, in general, M. Destombes, ed., *Mappemondes A.D. 1200-1500* (Amsterdam, 1964), which reproduces with only minor changes the classification of J. K. Wright, *The Geographical Lore of the Time of the Crusades*, 65-69. Illustrations of the principle types of twelfth-century maps are found in Destombes and in the older, but still useful, study of K. Miller, *Mappaemundi, die ältesten Weltkarten*, 6 vols. (Stuttgart, 1895-98).

Both in its range and detail, Bernard's encyclopedic description is more comprehensive than many of his contemporaries', including those in prose.

Cosmic Birth

To turn first to i.2, the metaphors employed throughout are understandably those of cosmic birth and marriage. Bernard first presents the way in which the *primordia rerum*, formerly bringing forth the forms, material configurations, and qualities of things in a chaotic state (i.e. i.1), now begin to reproduce harmoniously in accordance with the world's needs:

> Antiqui et primarii rigore generis expugnato in quos ductus Providentia (= Noys) voluit, materie secuta est tractabilis aptitudo, cumque quam fert Silva grossitiem elimatius expurgasset, ad eternas introspiciens notiones, germana et proximante similitudine rerum species reformavit. Yle cecitatis sub veterno que jacuerat obvoluta, vultus vestivit alios, idearum signaculis circumscripta. Mater igitur generum, ubi pregnationis sue gremium et ad parturiendum sinus fecunditatis exsolvit, ex ea et in ea factus est suus ortus essentiis, sua nativitas elementis.[2]

> When Silva's ancient and primary toughness had been driven out into the paths Noys wished, a malleable disposition of matter followed; and when she had expurgated more thoroughly the grossness that Silva bears, looking carefully at the eternal plans, she reformed the species of things by a faithful and approximate likeness. Hyle, who had been lying down, wrapped in the old cloak of blindness, put on other faces and was now surrounded by the seals of the

---

[2] *Cos.* i.2.89-99.

ideas. Then the mother of birth loosened her pregnant womb and opened her fertile sinus to give birth: from her and in her is made her own origin for essences, her own birth for the elements.

Here Bernard repeats motives from his early characterization of matter. The principles of order come about *ex consultis . . . Providentie secretioribus*.[3] Silva/Hyle is again portrayed as matter in the ordinary sense, whose innate toughness Noys beats out and refines, and, at the same time, as an allegory, the *mater generum*, who from herself and in herself creates the elemental forms of the universe. Hyle, as above, is the passive aspect of matter, whose long white hair, the result of neglect, is now shed for a newer, more youthful image. In other words, the old age of relative obscurity is yielding to one of clarity under the influence of the eternal ideas (or perhaps, as Bernard suggests, with the improvement of man's physical knowledge). Bernard thus unites again a directly apprehensible image with one of a learned, Platonic kind. In addition, in *reformavit*, he again suggests that the moral allegory, the process by which Natura is enlightened and the universe made more beautiful, is a type of renewal that is translated into physical terms.

After describing the harmonious union of the four elements by a knot, Bernard turns to the *anima mundi*, which is to be united with the newly reformed body of the world in marriage. First he describes how the world-soul descends from the heavens in fluctuations of mathematical and musical harmony:

Hujusce igitur sive vite sive lucis origine, vita jubarque rerum, endelichia (= anima mundi) quadam velut emanatione defluxit. Comparuit igitur exporrecte magnitudinis globus, terminate quidem continentie, sed

---

[3] i.2.86-87.

quam non oculis verum solo pervideas intellectu. Ejus admodum clara substantia liquentis fluidique fontis imaginem preferebat. . . . Unde fomes ille vivificus sic maneat ut perire non possit, cum speciatim singulis totus et integer refundatur.[4]

Then the world-soul, from the origin of life or of light, flowed down as if in a kind of emanation as the vitality and glory of the cosmos. In its descent it appeared as a globe of extended size and determined contents, but one which could not be seen with the eyes, only in the mind. Its quite clear substance presented the appearance of a liquid, flowing fountain. . . . From its place this living fire seems to endure in such a manner that it cannot perish, since, whole and unified, it is being poured out separately in individual [currents].

Endelichia, the world-soul, thus arises physically from a source near Noys herself,[5] and in his description of the descent, Bernard characteristically intermingles neoplatonic and Stoic metaphors. It is not clear, he states, whether the world-soul arises from Noys' creativity or from the living fire in the outermost rim of the cosmos (later identified in part with God). The descent to earth is a process of emanation; Bernard is here at his most Posidonian. The world-soul is considered to be one of the many life forces animating the living cosmos. Then, employing the familiar neoplatonic metaphor of the fountain[6] to portray Noys, he

---

[4] i.2.167-80.

[5] i.2.180-81: "endelichia, propinquis et contiguis ad Noym natalibus oriunda. . . ."

[6] The same image, used to portray the Good (Tugaton) or God, ii.5.23 ff, is discussed below in Ch. IV. It is a commonplace in medieval Latin poetry; cf. Alan of Lille, *Anticlaudianus*, i.97-106; ed. Bossuat, p. 60; vi.237-72; p. 148. A useful summary of neo-

touches on another of his favorite themes: the inability of such ultimate realities to be described except in images. *Endelichia* is immediately united with *mundus*, lest, through an imbalance of heat or liquid, a new cataclysm of the elements disturb the course of nature. Noys officiates at the ceremony as high-priest. The union itself, a delicate and proportionate fitting together of body and soul, is the only occasion in the *Cosmographia* when Bernard appears to share Thierry's delight in neopythagoreanism. In this heady atmosphere the world emerges for the first time full of life, truly, to echo Plato's term in a new context, a *sensilis mundus*.[7]

To anyone unfamiliar with other twelfth-century Platonist texts, Bernard's scheme of creation so far would appear highly complex. However, his individuality is best understood within a framework for cosmogenesis utilized in particular by Thierry and William of Conches. For instance, in his commentary on the *Timaeus*, William states:

Ut enim faber, volens aliquid fabricare, prius illud in mente disponit, postea quesita materia, iuxta mentem suam operatur, sic Creator, antequam aliquid crearet, in mente illud habuit, deinde opere illud adimplevit.[8]

For just as a craftsman, wishing to fashion something,

---

platonic images, upon which twelfth-century authors may have drawn, is John Scottus Eriugena, *Periphyseon* iii.4; *PL* 122, 632B-33A.

[7] For other texts on the *sensilis mundus*, see T. Gregory, *Platonismo medievale* (Roma, 1958), 87-91.

[8] *Glosae super Platonem*, ed. Jeauneau, cap. 32, p. 99 (= *Tim.* 27D). For parallels in Augustine and in William's other commentaries, see Jeauneau, p. 99 n. c. Chalcidius does not use *faber*, but translates δημιουργός as *opifexque et fabricator*; *Tim.* 29A, p. 21, line 16. It is worth noting as well that Chalcidius interprets rather than translates Plato's ὑπ' αἰτίου as "suum auctorem"; p. 21, line 11.

first arranges it in his mind, then, after seeking out the materials, creates it according to his mental image, so the creator, before creating anything, framed it in his mind, and afterwards filled it out as a work.

William's simple idea of the mental plan in the mind of God is paralleled by Bernard's conception of Noys, and both writers present the creator as a craftsman (not, it is worth noting, as the Aristotelian craftsman alone but also along the simple analogy of the mechanical arts). Yet in fundamental ways William's simile is also unsatisfactory as a characterization of Bernard's theory of creation. First of all, in the *Cosmographia*, God is known, *in actu*, through his vicegerents, the allegorical figures who personify physical forces. Secondly, according to Bernard, creation is not the imposition onto matter of an external design; it is the working out of the inherent potential in matter in accordance with a design. Thus, for Bernard, God is not only the external deity in whose beneficent name the act of creation is done. He is god-in-matter, informing the world directly through matter's latent creativity.

Cosmic Unfolding

More will be said about Bernard's relation to his contemporaries in Chapter V. To turn to the next stage of the drama, section i.3, the skeletal model presented in i.2 is now filled out by a comprehensive encyclopedia. The essential feature of this encyclopedic expansion is that it reveals, at once, both the totality of the cosmic order, that is, everything which is in it, and, at the same time, the relation and interdependence between the individual parts. In order to comprehend how Bernard has achieved this end, it is necessary to recall that his *Cosmographia* was also called *De Mundi Universitate*. The term *universitas* in this title is difficult to translate by a single English word. It can refer simply to the whole of the cosmos or, as is more likely the case, the structural-encyclopedic interrelationship between the parts.[9] The second alternative seems particularly appropriate if one recalls that Bernard may have taken this subtitle from the *De Mundo* of Apuleius, also a structural encyclopedia.[10] However verbose section i.3 may be at times, one never loses sight of Bernard's idea of the cosmos unfolding before the reader's eyes as the ordered completion of a pre-existing model.

Another way to approach i.3 is to consider the meaning of the phrase *ornatus elementorum*, the terms with which Bernard characterized section i.3 in his *Argumentum*.[11] *Ornatus* is an important concept in both Platonic philosophy and didactic poetry; it is one of the keys to the union of philosophy and rhetorical theory. Chalcidius, speaking in the first part of his *Commentary* of the work of Plato's Intelligence, calls it *exornatio mundi*. The term and its cognates are commonplaces in twelfth-century commentaries on the *Timaeus*; they refer to the structural differentiation of the cosmos.[12] In rhetorical poetry, *ornatus* has a slightly

[9] Chenu, 23-24, 26, 34.

[10] *De Mundo*, cap. 36; ed. Thomas, p. 172: "mundi universitas." Chalcidius employs *universitas* to translate Plato's τὰ ἄπαντα (*Tim.* 48B; p. 45, line 24), and throughout the *Commentary* uses the term and its affiliates; e.g., cap. 26; p. 77: "at uero cum de mundi, hoc est uniuersae rei, constitutione tractetur. . . ."

[11] Lines 32-33.

[12] For Chalcidius and the *Asclepius*, *ornamentum* = κόσμος. See Waszink, index greco-latinus, s.v., and *Asc.* 10; p. 308, lines 13-15. Bernard may also have had in mind Cicero, *De Natura Deorum* ii.51; ed. Mueller, p. 92: "Ut vero perpetuus mundi esset ornatus, magna adhibita cura est a providentia deorum [= Noys?], ut semper essent et bestiarum genera et arborum omniumque rerum, quae a terra stirpibus continerentur." This context would admirably fit *Cos.* i.3, as would, less colorfully, Apuleius, *De Mundo*, cap. 1; ed. Thomas, p. 137: "Mundus omnis societate caeli et terrae constat et eorum natura [= Natura?], quae utriusque sunt; vel sic: mundus est or-

different meaning, but one which is related to the above. It refers to the amplification in verse of the creative process; thus, late in the twelfth century, Peter Riga composed a poem not unlike *Cosmographia* i.3 in its content and entitled it *De Ornatu Mundi*.[13] In Bernard, *ornatus* is also an attempt to imitate the divine act of creation, to present it visually. Like the earlier Christian-Latin poets who versified Genesis, Bernard allows himself a certain latitude in filling out the details which are not found in Plato/Chalcidius. To do this, he employs a variety of classical and contemporary handbooks.

Bernard's section i.3, then, has two quite different functions: one, to fill out the skeletal model of the cosmos; two, to maintain, in spite of the diversity of the created universe, the pattern of a somewhat amplified but no less orderly model. In addition, Bernard has a third intention. He wishes the universe to appear before the reader in its real, living splendor.[14] There is as much interest in

---

nata ordinatio dei munere, deorum recta custodia." For Bernard, of course, *dei = deus*; he remains in this respect faithful to the monotheism of Genesis and Plato.

[13] *PL* 171, 1235-38. On *ornatus verborum* as one of the parts of the *artes poeticae* in the twelfth century, see the thorough but not very perceptive summary of E. de Bruyne, *Etudes d'esthétique médiévale*, II, *L'époque romane* (Bruges, 1946), especially pp. 258 ff., and vol. III, index, p. 394, s.v. A good specific example is furnished by Geoffroi de Vinsauf, *Documentum de modo et arte dictandi et versificandi* II, 3, 2: ed. E. Faral, *Les arts poétiques du XIIe et du XIIIe siècle* (Paris, 1924), 284-85: "Superficies enim verborum ornata, nisi sana et commendabili nobilitetur sententia, similis est picturae vili quae placet longius stanti, sed displicet proprius intuenti. Sic et ornatus verborum sine ornatu sententiarum audienti placet, diligenti intuenti displicet. Superficies autem verborum ornata cum ornatu sententiae similis est egregiae picturae, quae quidem, quando proprius inspicitur, tanto commendabilior invenitur. Unde dicit Horatius: Ut pictura, poesis . . . [*Ars poetica*, 362]."

[14] Cf. C. S. Lewis, *The Allegory of Love* (Oxford, 1938), 98.

the visual, tactile, and sensuous aspects of creation as in the architectural structure. The cosmogenesis is not simply the unfolding of a divine plan; it is a portrait of the universe as it suddenly bursts into life. One may even think of Bernard's polished elegiacs as an orchestral interlude—if a lengthy one—between two unusually complex prose passages, sections i.2 and 4. From this point of view, i.3 may be seen within Bernard's general framework for relating the otherworldly and the this-worldly. He would seem to be telling the reader once again that the world is not only the imitation of a divine exemplar; it is the reality itself, with the archetype latent in the empirical manifestation.

Yet can the critic judge i.3 to be wholly successful in this last respect? Elsewhere in the *Cosmographia*, Bernard expresses with clarity his delight in the real world, his existential conception of nature. In i.3, it is difficult to decide to what extent his description is the living universe and to what extent it is, like most earlier representations of nature in Latin poetry, an interposition between his own vision and the real world of the already existing portraits of earlier writers. In other words, it is difficult to know to what extent his description is reality, to what extent rhetoric. Although a gifted poet, Bernard was too consciously an imitator of previous classical models to have broken with one of their cardinal conventions: the indirect description of nature.[15] Nor was his literary imagination capable of reconstituting the whole of the natural order on its own, as had Lucretius. Bernard increases the difficulty of interpretation himself by drawing his material, at times, from the standard scientific authorities and, at others, from what appear to be raw empirical data.

Bernard's attempt to versify scientific *encyclopedica* in i.3 also draws attention to a larger issue in twelfth-century

[15] See in general E. R. Curtius, *Romanische Forschungen* 56 (1942), 219-56.

poetry. Is it not possible to see in his inability to find a formula for expressing the direct apprehension of nature in equally direct, sensuous images, the incapacity of a cultural form inherited in tradition to express contemporary sentiments, moods, or ideas? In any period of profound social and economic change, artistic conventions also undergo a metamorphosis. If one accepts the notion that during the twelfth century the attitude towards the natural universe changed from a Platonic-symbolic to what was, in part, an empirical, existential appreciation, then fewer conventions were less adequate for expressing the new sensibility than those of rhetorical Latin poetry. This is not to say that i.3 is not successful poetry by other criteria, simply that it is only partially successful by the theoretical criteria in other parts of the *Cosmographia*. And even if, by these criteria, i.3 is not a complete success, are not its failings those of a brilliant innovator?

The unfolding of creation in i.3 would then appear to be both a reality and, in rhetorical terms, an ideal. Within it, a number of features stand out in interest. One, mentioned above, is its comprehensiveness, which reflects the enormous range of Bernard's reading more opaquely than other parts of the *Cosmographia*. Clearly he did not content himself with the standard encyclopedias, but pored over herbals and medicinal treatises as well. Two aspects of the description however take precedent over others: one, an overt statement of the astrological construction of history; and two, the presentation of myths, not only in a cosmological context, but with an ease and sophistication which bears witness to Bernard's mastery of the classical tradition. Lastly, i.3, better than his proses, provides excellent examples of the playful ambiguity with which he was able to approach both classical and Christian traditions. The occasional *double entendre*, which must have provided considerable humor for his contemporaries, is used with full effectiveness.

A good example of perhaps all three of these characteristics is found in the opening lines of i.3. Here Bernard describes God among the gods, the stellar divinities, and the angels. While appearing to be related to astrology, God is not deprived of his omnipotence:

> In celo divina manus celique ministris
> omne creature primitiavit opus,
> celi forma teres, essentia purior ignis,
> motus circuitus, numina turba deûm,—
> dico deos quorum ante Deum presentia servit,
> quos tenet in vero lumine vera dies!
> Pacis enim locus etheree totoque tumultu
> aëris exceptus sepositusque sibi
> separat arcanas sedes. Super, immo superne,
> extramundanus creditur esse Deus. . . .
>
> Scribit enim celum stellis totumque figurat
> quod de fatali lege venire potest.
> Presignat qualique modo qualique tenore
> omnia sidereus secula motus agat.
> Prejacet in stellis series quam longior etas
> explicet et spatiis temporis ordo suis.[16]

In heaven and for the ministers of heaven the divine hand first outlines the whole work of creation, the smooth form of heaven, the purer essence of fire, the circular motion, and the multitudinous crowd of the gods. These are gods, I maintain, whose presence waits on God, whom true daylight holds in a true light. His region of ethereal peace, moreover, cut off from all the tumult of the air and set aside, divides off the hidden areas for itself [in the heavens]; above, in the very highest, resides God, it is believed,

---

[16] *Cos.* i.3.3-12; 33-38. Cf. Thorndike, *A History of Magic and Experimental Science*, vol. 2, 104-06.

beyond the cosmos. . . . The heavens, on the other hand, write by means of the stars and prefigure everything which is able to arise by means of the law of fate. They presignify by what mode or tenor the sidereal motion impels the passage of history. The order of events lies hidden in the stars; a longer and more ordered succession of time will explain it.

This view, it should be noted, is not a complete acquiescence to determinism such as is found in Abu Ma'shar's polemic against Christian cosmology.[17] It is a position in which God's effective power is translated into causal terms as Bernard understood them. As such, it harmonizes with the views he expressed in his *Mathematicus* and, if he wrote it, the *Experimentarius*.[18] *Extramundanus* is a key

[17] *Introductorium* v.5; f. [d.6 recto]: "[Christianus] ait ergo si factor omnium deus, cui seculorum omnium infinitas momentum est. Primo septem stellas in principatibus suis locatas, omnes eodem modo atque motu sese habere voluit; deinde transactis aliquot seculis tanquam penitens iam voluntatis prime eas relicto munere primo pariter alterari maluit que consequitur. An eius quod deinde facturus esset impotens erat, aut quod nature aptius primum nesciebat. . . . Quid ergo primum in principatibus suis locatas asserit, contra omnes Indos, Persas, Caldeos et Grecos astrologos est."

[18] E.g., *Le Mathematicus de Bernard Silvestris*, [ed. B. Hauréau], (Paris, 1895), p. 16 (= *PL* 171, 1366), describing the mother's consultation of an astrologer after the disappearance of her son:

> Spemque super dubiam quid fati volveret ordo
> certior esse volens consulit astrologum,
> qui poterat stellis superum deprendere curas,
> Parcarum mentem consiliumque Jovis,
> Naturae causas secretaque scire latentis,
> et quae fata, quibus legibus ire velint.

Cf. pp. 21-22. And is not the poem's ending, implying a certain ambiguity between fate and free will, entirely typical of Bernard? While Bernard's astronomical authorities are quite specific in their opinions, Bernard's type of ambiguity is reminiscent of Augustine, *De Beata Vita*, cap. 1.1; *PL* 32, 959: "Cum enim in hunc mundum,

term. It is derived from Apuleius, or possibly Martianus.[19] It indicates that God is placed beyond the universe which magnifies his spirit and suggests as well, as do Firmicus and Abu Ma'shar, that history is entirely predictable from the stars. To summarize Bernard's position: God stands outside the cosmos. His "ministers," who are also Plato's gods created by God, do all the work, and their number presumably includes both Christian angels and pagan mythological deities representing physical forces. The heavens reveal in their motions and changes the pattern of human cultural and social history. Thus the unfolding of creation, including Noys' part in it, is to be understood as the revelation of a pre-existing order.

In Bernard's ensuing description of the universe, myth, history, and geography are thrown together yet arranged in a delicate architectural model, continuing the initial image of a visual structure unfolding before the Creator. In this *universitas rerum*, no special place is given to Christian as opposed to pagan mythologies. For example, Christ and the presumably contemporary Pope are ranged among the heroes of antiquity:

> Exemplar specimenque Dei virguncula Christum
> parturit et verum secula numen habent.
> Munificens deitas Eugenum commodat orbi,
> donat et in solo munere cuncta semel.[20]

sive Deus, sive natura, sive necessitas, sive voluntas nostra, sive conjuncta horum aliqua, sive simul omnia (res enim multum obscura est, sed tamen a te (= Theodore) jam illustranda suscepta) veluti in quoddam procellosum salum nos quasi temere passimque projecerit."

[19] Martianus, *De Nuptiis*, ed. Dick-Préaux, index, s.v. *extramundanus*. On *ultramundanus* in Apuleius, see Ch. IV.

[20] *Cos.* i.3.53-56 (= Vernet, i.3.54-57). Lemay, *Abu Ma'shar*, p. 88 n. 16, notes that "the anticipation of the virgin birth of Christ through astrological knowledge" is derived from the *Introduc-*

A young maid gives birth to Christ, the exemplar and specimen of God, and history has its true guide. Beneficent deity provides Eugenius [III] for the world, giving everything at once in a single gift.

With a certain poetic dexterity, even audacity, Bernard puns on *virgo* and employs the overtly pagan *numen* to describe Christ's role in history. Other Christian references are treated in a similar way, but they are few in number, indicating either that Bernard was simply fonder of the classics or that, as the imitator of a classical literary form, he felt he should employ an appropriate content. Curtius thought that Bernard was consciously avoiding Christian details,[21] an interpretation which seems too limited. When he wishes to introduce one he can do so with wit and charm. For instance, among the historical events predicted for various rivers, he states:

Jordanisque sacer summoque futurus honore
nobilis auctoris tingere membra sui.[22]

And the holy Jordan shall have the highest honour to touch the members of its own noble creator.

Another example of Bernard's capacity to blend the mythical and the humorous may be observed in his handling of the well-worn topos of the *locus amoenus*, the description of a pleasant place or a paradise according to rhetorical rules.[23] In general, paradise was viewed in the Middle Ages either as a utopia, a past or future state, or as

---

torium vi.1. See as well the excellent note on this point by Silverstein, *Modern Philology* 46 (1948-49), 96 n. 27.

[21] *Europäische Literatur und lateinisches Mittelalter*, 119-20.

[22] *Cos.* i.3.245-46 (= Vernet, i.3.246-47).

[23] In general see E. R. Curtius, *Romanische Forschungen* 56 (1942), 244-45, and for bibliography L. Arbusow, *Colores Rhetorici* (Göttingen, 1948), 111-16.

a geographical location, the paradise which was denied to Adam and recorded in pagan legends. In ii.9 Bernard transforms this technique into a brilliant, creative poetic device; here, he is primarily concerned with enumerating the various locations which can be classified as paradises, including Eden. His catalogue occurs just after a list of spices; it is followed by a list of herbal and medicinal plants. As well as providing an example of his dexterity as a poet, his verses on paradise, if they are indeed his,[24] demonstrate what is best about his handling of mythical material throughout:

> At potius jacet Aurore vicinus et Euro
> telluris gremio floridiore locus,
> cui sol dulcis adhuc primo blanditur in ortu;
> cum primeva nihil flamma nocere potest,
> illic temperies, illic clementia celi
> floribus et vario gramine pregnat humum.
> Nutrit odora, parit species, pretiosa locorum,
> mundi delicias, angulus unus habet. . . .
> Inter felices silvas sinuosus oberrat
> inflexo totiens tramite rivus aque,
> arboribusque strepens et conflictata lapillis
> labitur in pronum murmure limpha fugax.
> Hos, reor, incoluit riguos pictosque recessus
> hospes, sed brevior hospite, primus homo.
> Hoc studio curante nemus Natura creavit,
> surgit fortuitis cetera silva locis.

[24] On the authenticity of the passage below, *Cos.* i.3.315-52 (= Vernet, i.3.317-54), Vernet notes in his thesis, p. 226 n. 1, that of the MSS collated for his edition, the prefatory *Argumentum* is found in 19, the dedicatory letter to Thierry in 26, the *Megacosmus* (whole or part) in 41, the *Microcosmus* in 34, and these controversial lines in only 7. Yet on the basis of textual evidence he presents a strong case for their authenticity, pp. 222-23.

Nascitur Aonium nemus oblectare poetas,
ad Paridis raptus Ida datura rates. . . .
Grandiloquis habitanda sophis, habitanda Platoni
frondet academici gratia multa loci. . . .
Briscelim sinus Armoricus, Turonia Vastem,
Ardaniam silvam gallicus orbis habet.

There is a region bordering Aurora in the East where
the earth presents a more flowering bosom. The sweet
sun shines on it as it did on the first day and the old
flame can do no harm [there]. The temperate clime
and tranquil skies make the ground swell with flowers and with grass of all kinds, bringing forth aromas
and spices. One corner [of the world] thus possesses
the precious things of [all other] regions, [all the]
pleasures of the world [at once]. . . .

A winding rivulet wanders ever among these happy
glades with a never-failing course, murmuring with
the trees, lapping over the pebbles, ever falling in
downward flight. In these humid, picturesque forests,
I think, dwelt the first man, a guest, but briefer than
a guest.

Natura created this wood with studious care; other
woods arise in fortuitous places. Helicon is born to
please the poets, Ida about to donate an oar to the rape
of Paris. . . . To provide a home for eloquent sophists,
a home for Plato, leafy boughs burst forth with the
manifold grace of an academy. The Gallic orbit [too]
has woods [like] the Ardennes: Brittany has the
Brocéliande, Tours the desolate [Gastine Touran-
gelle].

This description, consisting of details from the Bible, contemporary philosophy, classical mythology, and local geography, is identifiable as a *locus amoenus* through its tag-line,

"At potius iacet. . . ."[25] In his way, Bernard is continuing the tradition of the Christian-Latin poets of the fourth and fifth centuries, who employed the topos to portray the garden of Eden and thus to effect, in Christian poetry, a counterpart to the descriptive capacities of the classical poets. Curtius has pointed out that the tradition of the *locus amoenus* is a continuous one; yet the innovations of various poets, which he tended to overlook, are often as important as the similarities.[26] For example, the ninth-century poet Theodulf of Orléans left a brief description of paradise that unites classical and Christian material in a manner which furnishes, so to speak, a perfect archetype of the period's artistic sensibilities, while, in the eleventh century, Peter Damian employs the same topos in his brilliant rhythm on paradise, uniting Plotinan and Augustinian images in a highly individualistic manner.[27] Bernard's *locus amoenus* also presents certain innovations. One of them is a new freedom in dealing with Christian and classical material. While his description contains the standard details of the spice garden of the East, it suggests in a perhaps deliberately ambiguous manner that Adam's stay in paradise, like other historical events, was predictable from the stars and took place in the continuum of cultural history which embraces many other "myths." Adam, he states, may have resided in paradise for a time. Assuming that *reor* is intentional, Bernard also suggests that his stay was as much myth as history. Adam, a brief guest in paradise, was forced to leave, and Eden, as a result, joined a series of utopian landscapes down to those of the France of his own day. Is

[25] See the discussion of *Cos.* ii.9 in Ch. IV.

[26] *Europäische Literatur*, 189-213; but see now Peter Dronke, *Poetic Individuality in the Middle Ages* (Oxford, 1970), 1-32.

[27] Theodulf's poem is found in *MGH, Poetae*, i, p. 573; Peter Damian's in M. Lokrantz, ed., *L'opera poetica di S. Pier Damiani* (Uppsala, 1964), 80-83.

Bernard in fact suggesting that the *primus homo*, like other mythical heroes, had his golden age, which succeeded in time to others? The playful optimism of i.3 does not preclude such an interpretation, especially in view of Bernard's notion of periodic cosmic reform. What seems, in sum, to have found a union in Bernard's imagination is his own inquisitive spirit and the rhetoric which had served Latin poetry so long.

2. Physics, Motion, and Time

Cosmographia i.4 consists of an explanation of the animated hierarchy of the universe, both the physical principles by which it runs and the problems of motion, time, and eternity. Although short in length (128 lines), it is Bernard's most complex prose and central to the understanding of the way in which he relates the skeletal and encyclopedic structures. As mentioned above, the section plays only a small role in the allegorical drama. If i.1, 2, and 3 develop from pure allegory to *encyclopedica*, i.4, while not abandoning allegory altogether, transforms the presumably omniscient viewpoint of i.3 into a still more abstract discussion, related in part to i.2 but wider in its implications.

Section i.4 really explains how the *universitas* is run, beginning with the role of heat and light in all generative processes (5-21), and working from these physical principles to God's relation to matter (25-61), matter's relation to eternity (61-84), and eternity's relation to time (97-120). The prose concludes with a mystical invocation of the descent of being through various levels of creation: Noys, pregnant with the divine will, gives birth to the other informing principles, the world-soul, Nature, and fate. Throughout, Bernard's language and meaning are difficult, making it necessary to translate important parts of his discourse with a commentary. When this has been done, it is possible to analyse his argument in terms of its source material.

Fire and Heat

The argument of i.4 begins essentially where i.2 left off, with *mundus* fully created as a living being, a union of Silva's material offspring and the *anima mundi* which descends from the heavens. The form of the world is a globe, and each of the elements within it occupies a place according to its physical properties. Fire, being lightest, goes to the top, forming a band around the upper regions of the cosmos. For Bernard, fire is an *ignita substantia*, provided by the heavens for the nourishment of all life below. Here is his reasoning:

> Quicquid enim ad essentiam sui generis promotione succedit, ex celo tanquam ex Deo vite subsistentie sue causas suscipit et naturam. Unde enim stelle irrequieto circumferruntur excursu, nisi quia ethereum fomitem imbiberunt? Unde terrestre, unde equoreum, unde aerivagum genus se suis vestigiis emoverent, si non de celo motus vivificos insumpsissent? Ignis namque ethereus, sociabilis et maritus, gremio telluris conjugis affusus generationem rerum publicam, quam de calore suo producit ad vitam, eam inferioribus elementis commodat nutriendam. Spiritu animantium de convexis celestibus evocato, Terra corporibus prebet operam nutriendis et a nutricationis officio non desistit adusque naturalibus satisfecerit incrementis.[28]

For whatever rises to existence by the advancement of its own kind receives the causes and nature of its subsistence from the heavens, so to speak, from the God of life. For how are the stars made to trace their

[28] *Cos.* i.4.5-18.

tireless courses unless they have drunk of the ethereal heat? How would earthly, marine, or flying kinds of animals move on their courses if they had not taken on vivifying motions from the heavens? For ethereal Fire, [like] a bridegroom eager to unite, pours forth into the womb of Earth, his bride, the universal generation of things, which it brings to life from its own heat and provides for the nourishment of the lower elements. After the spirit of living things has thus been called forth from the starry vault, Earth gives her attention to the nurture of the bodies. She does not cease from her duties as nurse until she has made sufficient provision for natural growth.

This statement is half allegorical, half analytic. In it, Bernard states that generation, growth, and other natural processes constitute a hierarchy. The activity of creation is repeated at every level of the universe. The process begins with God's manifestation as heat, as fire. Here Bernard recapitulates in fanciful language the simple Stoic notion that fire is both an element and a vital force. Cicero summarized this particular idea as follows:

It is a law of nature that all things capable of nurture and growth contain within them a supply of heat without which their nurture and growth would not be possible; for everything of a hot, fiery nature supplies its own source of motion and activity, but that which is nourished and grows possesses a definite and uniform motion. And as long as this motion remains with us, so long sensation and life remain. . . . Every living thing therefore, whether animal or vegetable, owes its vitality to the heat contained within it. From this it must be inferred that this element of heat possesses in itself a vital force that pervades the whole world.[29]

[29] *De Natura Deorum* ii.9.23-24; translated (with minor punctua-

In Cicero's terms, a large role is assigned to motion, which impels heat as a force and which is the visible sign of its having acted on a body, animal or vegetable. Bernard also makes motion an important component of his hierarchy of creative forces emanating from heat. Yet his interpretation is somewhat different. First of all, he emphasizes that heat moves in a natural cycle, proceeding outward from heaven and returning to heaven. Secondly, in discussing the role of motion in this process, he is somewhat wider in its application. Motion is not only related to the elemental copulation of fire and earth, but gives birth to time from the bosom of eternity. A little further in i.4, in fact, he states that the *ignita substantia*,[30] in its circular motion, not only gives birth to the *generatorum sobolem multiformem*,[31] the multiform offspring of those things produced, but adds:

> Ex eo incipientis vite primordio cum volvente celo de motu quoque siderum substantia temporis nasceretur, que successerunt secula simplici eternitatis initiata principio cum sua numerus varietate suscepit.[32]

> In addition, when the substance of time was born from the beginning of primordial life through the motion of the revolving heavens and, as well, of the stars, number, with its variety, gave rise to the centuries which followed and which were initiated from the simple principle of eternity.

The important point is that the cyclical physiology of the cosmos, including the motion which governs heat's actions

---

tion changes) by H. Rackham, *Cicero, De Natura Deorum, Academica* (London/New York [Loeb], 1933), pp. 147, 149. On Stoic fire in the Middle Ages, see, in general, E. Edsman, *Ignis Divinus* (Lund, 1949) and Gregory, 124.

[30] *Cos.* i.4.2.   [31] i.4.1.   [32] i.4.21-24.

and the relation of time to eternity, is the unifying element. What Bernard has said in fact amounts to this: creation consists of the work of fire, motion, and natural laws; and number, the Many descending in emanation from the One, results as well from celestial mechanics, and "history" is the byproduct. It is interesting to note that while Bernard is perhaps alone among his contemporaries in insisting that nature possesses an historical development—a Hermetic initiation—he also adds the view, common among astrologers, that history itself is a secondary category of reality whose meaning is foretold in heavenly motion.

Light

The next stage of the argument deals with light. Bernard sees divine light as God's wisdom, the living image of eternity, determining the eternity of matter and of the elements:

> Rerum porro universitas, mundus, nec invalida senectute decrepitus, nec supremo est obitu dissolvendus, cum de opifice causaque operis—utrisque sempiternis —de materia formaque materie—utrisque perpetuis— ratio cesserit permanendi. Usia namque primaria, eviterna perseveratio, fecunda pluralitatis simplicitas, una est, sola est, ex se vel in se tota natura Dei. . . .

> Ex ea igitur luce inaccessibili splendor radiatus emicuit, imago nescio dicam an vultus Patris imagine consignatus. Hec est Dei sapientia vivis eternitatis fomitibus vel nutrita vel genita. De sapientia consilium, voluntas de consilio nascitur, de divina mundi molitio voluntate. Porro Dei voluntas omnis est bonitas. Dei ergo vel voluntas vel bonitas summi Patris est ejusque mentis in eadem operatione consensus. Quisnam ergo mundo et eternitati ejus audeat derogare, ad cujus continentiam causas eternas videat

convenisse? Dei quidem de voluntate consensum, de sapientia consilium, de omnipotentia causas pariter et effectum, de stabilitate, de eternitate sibi mundus conscire presumit, quod gradatim firmeque, dispositis causarum sibi succedentium ordinibus, mundus sensilis integrascit. Precedit Yle, Natura sequitur elementans; elementanti Nature elementa, elementis elementata conveniunt; sic principia principiis, sed a principe, principio coheserunt.[33]

The whole universe, the cosmos, neither is made decrepit with old age nor can be dissolved in final death, since its plan for permanent existence was drawn from the maker and cause of the work—both sempiternal—and from the substance and form of the material—both perpetual. Material being, moreover, is the primary, enduring principle, a fertile simplicity in multiplicity. It is unitary, unique and the whole nature of God is either from it or in it. . . .

From this inaccessible light [of Usia], a radiating splendor shone forth: I don't know whether I should call it an image of the Father or a face impressed [with his image]. This is the wisdom of God, nourished or brought forth from the living flames of eternity. From wisdom counsel is born, from counsel, the will to act, from divine volition, the activity of the world. For every wish of God is goodness. In other words, the will of God or the goodness of the highest Father is an accord of his mind in one and the same operation. Who, then, perceiving the eternal causes which contribute towards this result, might deprecate his world and his eternity? Indeed, the cosmos presumes to be aware of the consent of God by means of his will, his counsel by means of his

[33] i.4.25-52.

wisdom, his causes as well as effects by means of his omnipotence, stability and eternity, since the world, being a living creature, renews itself gradually and firmly by an arranged order of causal sequences. Matter precedes; elementing Nature follows; the elements for elementing Nature come together as those things produced by the elements (*elementata*).[34] Thus principles are united with principles but from the first Principle.

In this passage the *universitas rerum*, the material world, is eternal, but its eternity depends upon an intimate relation to God. Creation, as in i.2, arises from two principles, the One and Matter. The term *usia*, employed here as a synonym for matter as in the *Asclepius*,[35] also describes the resonance between matter, as a principle of being, and God. Again referring indirectly to the mysterious nature of matter, Bernard states that it is *nutrita* or *genita* from the living flames (or burning bush ?) of eternity in which God makes his presence known. God, for Bernard, is not known directly either through his causes or effects. He

---

[34] On *elementatum*, see T. Silverstein, *MS* 16 (1954), 156-62. Lemay, *Abu Ma'shar*, p. 99 n. 1 and Appendix II, suggests that John of Seville used the term to render "compound bodies" from Arabic; cf., *ibid.* 264-68. The translation would then be: ". . . Natura brings together the commixtures or semi-corporal bodies." This seems far too technical for Bernard, whose view is closer to that of Daniel of Morley; see the discussion in Ch. V, n. 111.

[35] W. Scott, *Hermetica* iii ,115: οὐσία = ὕλη, and presumably therefore Bernard's *usia* = *hyle/silva*. The problem however is not so simple. John Scottus used *ousia* throughout the *Periphyseon* to mean "being" and Bernard's sense seems closer to that. As Bernard clearly employs *silva* and *hyle* to denote aspects of matter, could he not be specifying here that aspect of it which directly reflects life-forces? Cf. Apuleius, *De Platone* i.6; p. 88: "οὐσίας, quas essentias dicimus, duas esse ait, per quas cuncta gignantur mundusque ipse; quarum una cogitatione sola concipitur, altera sensibus subici potest."

is described in metaphors, like matter itself; his existence is inferred indirectly through the results of his actions. In this sense, *usia*, his material being, gives birth to or nourishes his wisdom, embodied in Noys. From his wisdom, counsel, synonymous with the plan (*ratio*) necessary for the cosmic order, is born, and from the divine counsel springs the activity (*molitio*) through which the world is brought into being. The world, moreover, a *sensilis mundus*, is aware of God's intention, since his order is translated down through the cosmic hierarchy and appears as a series of natural laws. The process does not stop with emanation downwards: the world responds to God's goodness in terms of physical principles responding to stimuli. The world, thus, is a *sensilis mundus* in two senses: one, in which there is interposed between the creator and the created, the One and the Many, a group of laws for motion and nourishment; two, in which, at every stage of the creative process, the type of creativity is consistent with the types of components involved.

Creativity

The third stage of Bernard's argument states, in effect, that the life-giving principle of the cosmos is life itself. God, transfusing his goodness through the various levels of creation, animates the *sensilis mundus*:

> Rerum incolumitas vitaque mundi causis quidem principalibus et antiquis, spiritu, sensu, agitatione, ordinatione consistit. Vivit Noys, vivunt exemplaria: sine vita non viveret rerum species eviterna. Prejacebat Yle, prejacebat in materia, prejacebat in spiritu vivacitatis eterne. Nec enim credibile est sapientem opificem insensate materie nec viventis originis fundamina prelocasse. Mundus quidem est animal, verum sine anima substantiam non invenias animalis. De terra porro

pleraque consurgunt, sed sine vegetatione non stirpea, non plantaria, non cetera compubescunt. Ex mentis igitur vita, silve spiritu, anima mundi, mundialium vegetatione rerum universitas coalescit. In Deo, in Noy scientia est, in celo ratio, in sideribus intellectus. In magno vero animali cognitio viget, viget et sensus, causarum precedentium fomitibus enutritus. . . . Mundus enim (*supp.* est) quiddam continuum. . . .[36]

The sound condition and vitality of the cosmos consist in ancient, first causes mediated by spirit, sense, motion and order. Noys is living; the exemplars are alive. Without life, the eternal impressions of divine forms would not endure. Hyle was set down first: its existence was prearranged in matter and in the spirit (πνεῦμα?) of eternal life; for it is not credible that the wise creator put in their place the foundations of insensate matter and not their living origin. Indeed, the cosmos is a living creature; moreover, you, as *animal*, couldn't find its substance without an *anima*! A great many things arise from the earth, but without a life-giving principle neither shrubs nor young trees nor anything else grows to maturity. For this reason, by the life-giving principle from the divine mind (= Noys), by the spirit in matter, and by the soul of the world, the whole of the mundane world quickens with life by means of its animating activity. In God, in Noys, is the knowledge; in the heavens, the design; in the stars, foreknowledge. Moreover, in the great living being (= the cosmos), there is a growing perception and an increasing awareness, nourished by the warmth of the preceding events. . . . For the cosmic order is a kind of continuum. . . .

[36] *Cos.* i.4.61-79.

In addition to matter and order, then, a third principle of creation is creativity itself. In his blending of Platonic and Hermetic ideas in the above passage, Bernard carefully subordinates the abstract to the concrete, the purely philosophical to the tangibly biological. Matter, as stated elsewhere, is eternal, and soul is seen as the life-producing principle in matter. This relation, moreover, extends through the whole of the created order; and the cosmos, through a sympathetic understanding of the causes which motivate it, comes to understand the very processes which brought it into being. Rather like Natura herself, the cosmos is initiated into the secrets of the world as the world comes into being.

The idea of a sentient cosmos, animated by astrological and biological laws and forces, is what unites the encyclopedic account of the universe in i.3 with the explanation of it in i.4. In i.3, the catalogue of all created things, written beforehand in the stars, unfolds before the reader as if the entire continuum had been brought to life suddenly by the emanating *spiritus vivacitatis eterne*: it is Plato's Intelligence, working out its own Necessity. In addition to spirit, the living cosmos displays sense, motion, and order. The *sensilis mundus* of Plato, moreover, is interpreted by analogy with the senses in man, an adaptation of his views common in Stoic medical theory, which Bernard may have found in Constantinus' translation of Galen. The cosmos, so to speak, senses life in its very being. And these life-forces themselves act as a principle of renewal. Echoing Firmicus Maternus' language of cosmic reform,[37] Bernard says that the ordered *agitatio*, a union of the spirit of life with the material component of the world, comprises the motion by which the *sensilis mundus* renews itself by an

[37] *Cos.* i.4.48-49: "mundus sensilis integrascit." Cf. Firmicus, *Matheseos* iii.1.9; ed. Kroll & Skutch, vol. i, p. 94: "apocatastasis id est redintegratio."

arranged sequence of natural causes. Bernard thus introduces another conception of cosmic reform along physical principles: the moral allegory involves the response of the world to natural laws. Bernard seems to be stating, in fact, that the cosmos, like man, only comes to "understand" itself in a process of change in which it is a wilful contributor, for, as the world springs to life in i.2, 3, and 4, it acquires a certain degree of control over itself. Beginning from the One, renewal results in the unfolding of a new world animated by laws and conscious of its relation to them.

Time and Eternity

In the next state of the argument, the world and time are related to eternity:

Equeva namque generatione mundus et tempus . . . eorum imagines propinquas et simillimas emulantur. Ex mundo intelligibili mundus sensilis perfectus natus est ex perfecto. Plenus erat qui genuit plenumque constituit plenitudo. Sicut enim integrascit ex integro, pulcrescit ex pulcro, sic exemplari suo eternatur eterno.

Ab eternitate tempus initians in eternitatis resolvitur gremium longiore circuitu fatigatum. De unitate ad numerum, de stabilitate digreditur ad momentum. Momenta temporis presentia instantia, excursus preteriti, expectatio est futuri. Has itaque vias itu semper redituque continuat, cumque easdem totiens totiensque itineribus eternitatis evolverit ab illis nitens et promovens nec digreditur nec recedit quodque ubi finiunt inde renascuntur, relinquitur ad ambiguum. . . . Ea ipsa in se revertendi necessitate, et tempus in eternitate consistere et eternitas in tempore visa est commoveri. . . . Eternitas igitur, sed et eternitatis imago tempus, in moderando mundo curam et operam partiuntur. . . .

Mundus igitur tempore, sed tempus ordine dispensatur. Sicut enim divine semper voluntatis est pregnans, sic exemplis eternarum quas gestat imaginum Noys endelichiam, endelichia Naturam, Natura imarmenen quid mundo debeat informavit. Substantiam animis endelichia subministrat, habitaculum anime corpus artifex Natura de initiorum materiis et qualitate componit, imarmene, que continuatio temporis est sed ad ordinem constituta, disponit, texit et retexit que complectitur universa.[38]

The world and time, by their simultaneous birth . . . emulate each other's approximate and similar images. The world as a sentient creature was born from the intelligible world (i.e. the copy from the original), perfection from perfection. He who gave birth to it was full, and its plenitude comprises his fullness. For, just as [the world] gradually becomes unified from unity and made beautiful from beauty, it is eternalized for its exemplar by its own eternity.

Time, beginning from eternity, returns to the bosom of eternity after being tired out by a longer route. From unity it divides into number, from stability into movement. The momentary instants of present time, the running out of the past, are the expectation of the future. Therefore [time] continues on its route by eternally tracing and retracing its courses. As often as it traverses the same routes, it revolves around the paths left by eternity, and it neither digresses nor withdraws from them as it strives and proceeds. Where they finish and whence they are renewed are left ambiguous. . . . By this same necessity of returning into itself, time is both seen to consist in eternity and eternity to be moved in time. . . . Eternity, then, and time,

[38] *Cos.* i.4.91-128.

the image of eternity, share each other's care and la-
bour in guiding the universe.

Thus the cosmos is regulated by time but time by
order. For since Noys, by bearing the divine exemplars, is pregnant with the divine will, she informs the
world-soul, the world-soul Natura, and Natura fate,
concerning what ought to be done for the cosmos. The
world-soul gives [individual] souls their substance,
Natura the craftsman fashions the bodily home of the
soul from matter and the quality of first things, and
fate, the continuity of time addressed towards order,
arranges, weaves, and reweaves everything which she
embraces.

In summing up his metaphysical discussion, Bernard attempts to relate his hierarchical emanation of life-forces
to the Platonic notion that time is the moving image of
eternity. Without abandoning his biological metaphors—
indeed, by an extension of their meaning—he tries to relate
time to eternity, not only as an image to reality, but as a
process of birth emanating from God. *Mundus*, whose
eternity is reflected in *hyle*, thus possesses the same origin
as time. This origin, however, is not a statement about
God's creation of the world and time; it is a metaphor for
the continuous and cyclical revolutions by which time emanates from eternity and returns to its source and by which
the cosmos, along analogous principles, is periodically renewed from its source. The *gremium* from which both derive their being is the same womb which, transferred to
lower levels of the creative process, permits reproduction.
To the classical problem of time/eternity, Bernard has a
Platonic response, but one which is placed in the context of
the Stoic-Hermetic hierarchy as he understood it. Thus,
God's *usia*, that by which he manifests himself, is both
eternity-in-time and time-in-eternity: God is both the One

and the Many. While Bernard, as noted above, seems to rest undecided on the issue of what his hierarchy of descent actually is, he summarizes his position as follows: God, as matter/spirit, is represented by his messenger and wisdom Noys, who bears both his good will and plan for the world. Informing the world-soul, Noys provides the life-giving forces through which Natura implements her laws. The descent of the world-soul is thus related to Natura's initiation into the secrets of the universe. Natura, with ineluctable necessity, governs fate,[39] which disposes orderly events in the succession of time. God's being, manifested both in a spiritual or rational and in a material way, thus informs the cosmos continually but indirectly. No longer primarily an anthropomorphic deity, He is manifested in the creativity of the world.

The Sources: Plato and Hermeticism

The extension of the biological metaphors and their union with the classical Platonic problems of motion and time provide a useful clue to the type of source material which Bernard has brought together in i.4. In general, he has united Stoic theories of elemental change with a Platonist (or neoplatonist) theory of motion and time.

[39] On *heimarmene*, see Scott, *Hermetica* iii, 246-48. For Bernard, as in the *Asclepius*, fate is a god; cf. *Asc.* 39; p. 350: "Haec itaque est aut effectrix rerum aut deus summus aut ab ipso deo qui secundus effectus est deus aut omnium caelestium terrenarumque rerum firmata diuinis legibus disciplina. Haec itaque εἱμαρμένη est necessitas ambae sibi inuicem indiuiduo conexae sunt glutino, quarum prior εἱμαρμένη rerum omnium initia parit; necessitas uero cogit ad effectum quae ex illius primordiis pendent. Has ordo consequitur, id est textus et dispositio temporis rerum perficiendarum." Cf. Apuleius, *De Mundo*, cap. 28; pp. 174-75. Cf. F. von Bezold, *Das Fortleben der antiken Götter*, 79-81; *idem, Aus Mittelalter und Renaissance* (München/Berlin, 1918), 165-95.

The use of such apparently irreconcilable sources immediately raises the question of the validity of attempting to unite them in a single work. Of course it may be argued that many of Bernard's own sources, like Firmicus Maternus, do just this. Quite aside from that, however, it would appear that Bernard's union of these differing world views was consistent with his overall design. For Bernard, God, the earth, and man are locked in a divine rite. This rite is his "religion" of nature. The cosmogony, in this sense, is the working out of the dramatic and narrative possibilities of a syncretistic world view. Just as Bernard's chief allegorical personifications, Natura, Noys, and Matter, cannot be reduced to the philosophical notions which lie behind them without distorting their meanings, the myth of the *Cosmographia* as a whole often interweaves opposing ideas into a religious or symbolic unity. There are, of course, contradictory notions. For example, Bernard seems capable of embracing an Aristotelian conception of matter and a Platonic understanding of the relation between time and eternity. Again, he suggests that nature has a natural history and yet, at the same time, that it is governed by eternal, universal laws. He will divide the work of creation between two goddesses in i.1-2 and introduce in book two a number of *genii* who appear to usurp their functions. Yet there are a number of unifying ideas as well. The most important is the consistent denial of the omnipotence of God in the traditional sense and the replacement of this view by a division of powers among subordinates who represent aspects of his creative activity. From this it follows that there is a certain logical opposition between the otherworldly God and the infraworldly operation of his forces as natural laws. Within the scope of nature's new role as a mediator of forces between God and the world, there is also the growth of the spirit of rational inquiry into the secrets of the universe. Despite his diverse source material, these ideas help to unify the mystic rite of creation.

To return to the source material of i.4, Bernard, in general, derived his Stoic theory from Cicero, Seneca, and Constantinus, mediating them through the *Asclepius* and Chalcidius. As in i.1-2, it is the latter sources which provide a great deal of the substance of Bernard's argument. Before examining this debt in detail, however, some attention might be addressed in particular to Bernard's use of Stoic physics.

In Thierry of Chartres and Bernard, Stoic physics as such is not distinguishable from general physical theory. The sources available to them on this subject, like Constantinus and the *Asclepius*, contained large doses of Stoicism absorbed in relation to the two major sciences, medicine and astronomy. Stoicism did not appear, as in antiquity, as a separate system in itself. Moreover, Stoicism's strong identification with a scientific physical theory in late antiquity insured that throughout the Middle Ages, when original sources of all kinds were greatly reduced in scope, new ideas about cosmic order often began with developments of themes familiar to Stoicism. Thus many of the features which Sambursky[40] has isolated in Stoic physics— activity and passivity in the elements, the *pneuma*, mixing, tension, causality, divination, the subordination of time to nature, and the propagation of a state through a cosmic continuum—may be isolated as well in the *Cosmographia*, providing an excellent example of the continuity of Stoic theory. Yet it would be imprudent to argue from this evidence alone that Bernard presents a modified Stoic world-

---

[40] *Physics of the Stoics* (London, 1959). A thorough review of the influence of Stoicism on late Latin poetry is in preparation by Dr. M. Lapidge.

view. In the first place, only fragments of the original Stoic *Weltanschauung* are available; still less must have been accessible to medieval authors who knew little or no Greek. Secondly, if the structure of Bernard's myth is to be appreciated in its full originality, the tendency to reduce the *Cosmographia* to its various scientific and philosophical sources must not be carried beyond a reasonable degree. As in the case of Bernard's debt to the classical poets, the Latin Plato, and Chalcidius, perhaps it is wisest to employ the metaphor of Bernard of Chartres: "standing on the shoulders of the giants."

Many of the major Stoic notions in i.4 may in fact be traced to a single source, the Latin *Asclepius*. On at least two occasions in this work a Stoic theory of elemental change is outlined. The Stoic conceptions, however, are presented in a contaminated form, and so Bernard adopted them. Nonetheless, the emphasis is the same in both, and even Bernard's accretions from non-Stoic sources like Chalcidius do not change the overall tone of his discussion. Fundamental to both works is the notion of unity and diversity. In the *Asclepius*, Eros, invoking God's love for the cosmos while describing, quasi-scientifically, how it functions as an ordered continuum, makes the following statement:

> De caelo cuncta in terram et in aquam et in aëra. Ignis solum, quod sursum uersus fertur, uiuificum; quod deorsum, ei deseruiens. At uero quicquid de alto descendit generans est; quod sursum uersus emanat, nutriens. Terra, sola in se ipsa consistens, omnium est receptrix, omniumque generum, quae accepit, restitutrix. Hoc ergo totum, sicut meministi, quod est omnium uel omnia. Anima et mundus, a natura conprehensa, agitantur ita, omnium multiformi imaginum qualitate uariata. . . . Totus itaque quibus formatus

est mundus elementa sunt quattuor: ignis, aqua, terra, aer. Mundus unus, anima una, et deus unus.[41]

Everything is borne from the heavens to the earth, both into water and into air. Fire alone is a vital force because it is borne back on high; what is below is subservient to it. But whatever descends from on high generates life; whatever emanates back to the heavens nourishes it. Earth, consisting of itself alone, is the receptacle of all life and the restorer of all the created things it receives. This [latter state] is the All, as you will recall, since all things belong to it or because it consists of all things. The soul and the matter of the world, embraced by nature, are thus put into motion, varied by the different qualities of all kinds of images. The entire material world, thus formed by this process, contains four elements: fire, water, earth, and air. The material cosmos is one; the soul is one; God is one.

Bernard drew a number of essential features of his description of physical processes from this passage but developed the argument somewhat beyond the original. As in i.4, fire is the vivifying element, the *ignis ethereus*. Bernard's metaphor of growth, however, is that of sexual reproduction. By analogy with man, he sees the life-forces of the universe engaging in reproduction at every level. In addition, his phrasing of the eternal resonance between God and matter is somewhat different from the *Asclepius*. Bernard uses the scholastic terms *essentia*, *promotio*, and *subsistentia*, while the *Asclepius* attempts to convey the sense of Greek participles in *generans* (γενετικόν) and *nutriens* (θρεπτικόν). Allowing for such differences, however, the basic ideas are the same. For Bernard, creation

[41] *Asc.* 2; p. 298, with slight changes in punctuation. On the translation of *mundus*, see Ch. II, n. 64.

is not the act of an anthropomorphic God, but the transformation of the One—the united spiritual and material aspects of deity—into the Many, the descent of creative processes in emanation.

Bernard also echoes the *Asclepius* in other important respects. Hermes states that the cosmos is identical with matter and spirit, the two essential components of the world, in one of their manifestations. The perpetual movement of nature brings into being the multiform diversity of the created world. The cosmos does not only magnify God's glory; it exists in a perpetual state of symbiosis with deity. Earth is thus both the *receptrix* and the *restitutrix* of the created world. While Bernard, elsewhere, appears to retain a neoplatonic conception of God,[42] here he presents him in a Stoic relationship with matter. As in the *Asclepius*, God represents the descent of life-forces through heat from the One to the Many.

Significant traces of the Asclepian relationship between matter, the heavens, nature, and creation are also found in the *Cosmographia*. For instance, Hermes states:

> Caelum ergo, sensibilis deus, administrator est omnium corporum, quorum augmenta detrimentaque sol et luna sortiti sunt. Caeli uero et ipsius animae et omnium quae mundo insunt, ipse gubernator est, qui est effector, deus. A supradictis enim omnibus, quorum idem gubernator deus omnium, frequentatio fertur influens per mundum et per animam omnium generum et omnium specierum per rerum naturam. Mundus autem praeparatus est a deo receptaculum omniformium specierum; natura autem per species imaginans mundum per quattuor elementa ad caelum usque perducit cuncta dei uisibus placitura.[43]

---

[42] *Cos.* ii.5, discussed in Ch. IV.
[43] *Asc.* 3; p. 299.

Heaven, then, a god perceptible to sense, is the administrator of all bodies, whose growth and decay the sun and moon arrange. But God himself, the creator, is governor of the heavens, of their soul, and of all things which are in the world. For, from each of these things of which God is the governor a continual flux and reflux, flowing down, is borne through the world, through the soul of all genera and species, through the nature of all things. Furthermore, the cosmos [in its material aspect] is prepared by God to be the receptacle of all kinds of forms; and Nature, fixing the image of the material world through the forms by means of the four elements, extends up to heaven all created things so that they may be pleasing in the sight of God.

This passage, with its perhaps deliberate reminiscence of the Bible or of the *Timaeus* in the last lines,[44] contains several motives from i.2, 3, and 4. As in i.3, the heavens represent natural forces mediating between God and the world; the stars themselves are gods. Bernard seems to have preferred the formulation of this idea in the *Asclepius* rather than in Pliny, whose atheism he implicitly rejects. At the same time, in i.2, the dynamic union of the elements and the graphic language with which it is portrayed owe more to Pliny.

The term *frequentatio*, employed in i.2, is also a key

---

[44] Cf. *Cos.* i.2.127-28: "Bona vidit que fecisset omnia Deique visibus placitura." Gilson, *AHDLMA* 3 (1928), 11-13, thought that Bernard was echoing Genesis, but a similar statement occurs in *Timaeus* 29D-E. Scott, *Hermetica* i, 11-12, points out that phrases like this one, which Bernard lifted from his source, may be indebted originally to Genesis although not to Christianity; for a detailed comparison of texts, see C. H. Dodd, *The Bible and the Greeks* (London, 1935), and the important discussion in Gregory, 98-99.

to a central notion: emanation. It is not clear whether Bernard derived his conception of emanation from the *Asclepius*, Macrobius, or John Scottus, or perhaps from a combination of all three. From the *Asclepius*, with its debt to Stoicism, Bernard drew the idea of a type of emanation in which part of Natura's role as *artifex* lay in mediating life-forces. In doing so, Bernard was of course reviving a view frequently found in middle Platonism. The *Asclepius*, in fact, was reflecting a weak form of the relationship between nature and God which was given its classic statement by Philo Judaeus. Bernard found confirmation for it in Apuleius and Chalcidius, not to mention Constantinus and Abu Ma'shar.

In his conception of the *sensilis mundus* using biology as his basis, then, Bernard appears to have developed certain tendencies in Stoic physical and medical theory as he found them in the *Asclepius* with supporting views from Cicero, Seneca, and the *medici*. These ideas he transformed and enriched through his own originality. And, as a poet, he united the whole into a harmonious, imaginative reflection of what he thought the world was.

Something similar may be said of Bernard's defence of the eternity of the world in i.4. Here the selection of sources was somewhat wider, including Macrobius and, to a greater degree, Chalcidius. But the overall pattern, particularly the way in which creativity is related to time/eternity, is again derived from the *Asclepius*.

In spite of his deliberate vagueness on a controversial question, Bernard suggests overwhelmingly in i.4 that, as a natural philosopher, he believed the world, in its essential aspects, to be eternal. Bernard's use of current philosophical vocabulary for defining the question at i.4.25 ff. (*sempiternus . . . perpetuus*) suggests that he was anything but ill-informed on contemporary positions in the debate in his own time,[45] and, in spite of the superficial sophistication of his arguments, his position is stated in a reasonably straightforward manner. Bernard's argument proceeds in two stages. At i.4.25 ff., he states that the permanence of the world rests on four factors: the creator, the causes of creation, matter, and form.[46] All of these are eternal, although in different respects, and it is this thesis which he undertakes to defend at i.4.87 ff. The latter stage consists of the superimposition of three different arguments. The world is said to be eternal (1) because of God's will, (2) because of matter's self-reproducing forces, and (3) because the world is made in the image of an eternal design. Of these latter arguments, (1) and (3) clearly come from Plato-Chalcidius, while (2) is an extension of ideas in the *Asclepius*.

The problem of time/eternity is treated in *Asclepius* 30-32; it was here that Bernard found a suitable format for adapting Plato-Chalcidius to a theory of cosmic physiology. At *Cosmographia* i.4.61-63, recapitulating his argument somewhat in advance, Bernard states that the sound condition and life of the cosmos depend upon spirit, sense, motion, and order. While the first three factors may be drawn from *Asclepius* 6, the fourth, as well as the argument for defending them in a scheme of eternal, cosmic renewal, is taken from *Asclepius* 30. This text is not only central for understanding why, in Hermes' words, "in ipsa . . . aeternitatis uiuacitate mundus agitatur"[47] (in this very capacity for life in eternity the world is put into motion). It also provides a summary of other aspects of cosmic

---

[45] For a general summary of positions, see T. Gregory, *Platonismo medievale*, 77-96.

[46] I have benefitted in this section from the excellent analysis of M. McCrimmon, "The Classical Philosophical Sources," 115-19.

[47] *Asc.* 30; p. 337.

change which Bernard has mentioned throughout *Mega-cosmus*:

> The cosmos is itself the dispenser of life to all things below. . . . The movement of the cosmos moreover consists of a twofold action. Life is infused into the cosmos from without by eternity, and the cosmos infuses life into all things which are in it, distributing them all by fixed and predetermined relations of number and time in accordance with the operation of the sun and the movements of the stars. The process of time is wholly determined by divine laws; the passage of time on earth moreover is marked by the changing states of the atmosphere and the variations of heat and cold, while that of celestial time is marked by the return of the heavenly bodies to their former positions as they move in their periodic revolutions. The cosmos is the receptacle for time (*receptaculum temporis*); and it is by the progress and movement of time that life is maintained in the cosmos. The process of time is regulated by order; and time in its ordered course renews all things (*innouationem omnium rerum . . . faciunt*) in the cosmos by alternation. All things are subject to this process; nothing remains unchanged. . . .[48]

As in *Cosmographia* i.4, the passage of time is seen as a continuous process involving both seasonal and cosmic renewal. Into the statement that life is brought to the cosmic *animal* from without by eternity, Bernard introduces Plato's argument that time is the moving image of eternity. But he does not stop there. For him, as for the *Asclepius*, divine laws, reflecting God's will, perpetuate

[48] *Ibid.* pp. 337-38, trans. (with my changes) by W. Scott, *Hermetica* i, 349.

ordered motion in the universe and all change, including temporal change, operates within a type of space-time, which Hermes expresses by adopting the Platonic term *receptaculum*.

In order to understand precisely how Bernard has utilized this idea, however, it is necessary to return to Plato's notion of reform in the cosmos. At *Timaeus* 37D-39D, it will be recalled, Plato summarizes the doctrine of the *sensilis mundus* and states that the heavenly bodies imitate eternity through a perpetual cycle of days, months, and years. In addition to this seasonal alternation, there is a *perfectus annus*, at which time all the planets return to their respective positions and begin the cycle again. The Stoics, adapting this idea, argued that all things, not just heavenly bodies, return to their original states. Chalcidius, aware of the Stoic position, attempts a reconciliation of the two, stating that

> quem quidem motum et quam designationem non est putandum labem dissolutionemque afferre mundo, quin potius recreationem et quasi nouellam uiriditatem positam in auspicio motus noui.[49]

> this very motion and rearrangement should not be thought to bring about the destruction and dissolution of the cosmos but rather its recreation and, so to speak, its renewed vigor placed under the auspices of a new motion.

The notion of cyclical renewal in the cosmos, a combination of Platonic and natural-philosophic conceptions, is highly similar in Chalcidius and the *Asclepius*. Especially important in both schemes is the modification of the inexorability of all processes of change in classical Stoicism so as to admit a greater number of principles affecting re-

[49] *Comm.*, cap. 118; pp. 163-64.

newal. The governing powers in Chalcidius are God, providence, and fate; in the *Asclepius*, matter/spirit (the manifestation of God), nature, and fate. By combining both
hierarchies, one arrives at the position summarized in the
closing lines of i.4: God, Noys, the world-soul, Nature,
and fate, interrelated, as in both sources, by time/eternity.

Paradoxically, while Bernard appears to have explicitly
rejected a classically Stoic type of cosmic renewal, he has
nonetheless gone considerably beyond Chalcidius and the
Asclepius and reintroduced into his scheme a new relationship between determinism and free will. For Bernard, as
for Abu Ma'shar, causal forces rule the universe in an inexorable fashion, and these forces are controlled directly by
the movements of the stars. What redeems Bernard's world
from complete and senseless mechanism is not only the
humanistic alternative of free will but the idea of progress.
In the *Cosmographia* the reform of the cosmos is directly
linked to scientific progress, and it is this information, foretold in the stars, which accounts for Bernard's unusual
combination of determinism and optimism. In Chalcidius
and the *Asclepius*, the periodic dissolution and reconstitu-
tion do not constitute a progressive amelioration of the
world. Like Plato, they state that at the appropriate time
a natural cycle is completed and, when the planets regain
their former positions, the course of events begins again.
Throughout *Megacosmus*, in contrast, the creation of the
world is related to its improvement. Natura asks Noys to
remake the cosmos in the image of a better form in order
to relieve, so far as possible, the disordered state of Matter,
which is identified with evil. In addition, Bernard, perhaps
reasoning by analogy from man, refers on more than one
occasion to the self-sufficiency of the *sensilis mundus*. Like
a healthy man, the cosmos is well constructed so that its
internal regulators of health, like the four humors, may
respond to external necessities and prevent illness. Thus,

instead of making the health and stability of the cosmos dependent on free will and God as in Chalcidius, Bernard deliberately de-emphasizes free will and God's direct action in the world in order to indicate that the cosmos, and later man, by incorporating natural laws into their fabric, resist the defects of their former states. Bernard's argument for the eternity of the world is in fact dependent on the notion that the cosmos, once created as perfect as possible, reproduces its ordered perfection *ad infinitum*. He argues from cosmic physiology and symbiosis to time's imitation of eternity, to number's ordered descent from the One. Bernard thus subtly incorporates into the structure of his myth the concept of progress, related on the one hand to renewal and on the other to the conquest of ignorance through science. His optimism suggests that, in view of the progress of civilization and learning in his own time, his own epoch was not only a type of *perfectus annus*, but the moment when God was stamping the design of the cosmos with a new form.

CHAPTER IV

The Creation of Man

1. The Heavenly Journey

ALTHOUGH entitled *Microcosmus*, suggesting a comprehensive, formal parallel with *Megacosmus*, the second part of the *Cosmographia* really treats two interrelated themes: the celestial journey which Natura takes under the guidance of Urania, queen of the heavens, and the formation of man which Natura, Urania, and a third goddess, Physis, undertake in the presence of Noys. In general, ii.3-9 deals with the first topic, ii.9-14 with the second, and the opening scene of the second act consists of a recapitulation of book one. At Noys' request, Natura leaves the earth to seek out Urania (ii.3.36 ff.), Martianus' muse of the heavens, and, after encountering some difficulties, is introduced to her by another celestial deity called Pantomorphos. Urania then guides Natura back to earth through the solar system, beginning at the palace of Tugaton, where God or the Good resides, and progressing through the planetary spheres. At ii.9, they arrive in a paradise called Granusion, where they find Physis seated between her two daughters, Theory and Practice. Noys then arrives on the scene and delivers a discourse on the dignity of man. The three goddesses, Natura, Urania, and Physis are each assigned official duties in his creation. Man emerges as a microcosm of the universal order, and the description of his five senses—which is really a hymn in praise of man—concludes the book.

The two major themes of *Microcosmus* are clearly parts of a whole. Natura's trip through the heavens is a continuation of her education into the secrets of the universe, while the descent of Urania and Natura provides an allegory for the descent of the soul into the body. In general, *Cosmographia* two is also less overtly philosophical than one; it is more literary, allegorical, and mythical. Macrobius and Martianus Capella, together with other astrological writings, play a larger role than in book one: the theme of emanation is modelled on the former, while the dramatic ascent of an earthly abstraction into the heavens is developed along lines originating in *De Nuptiis* i-ii. In book two, the originality of Bernard's presentation of Natura is also more evident. She plays a larger role than in book one, and the role is somewhat changed. Some of her regulatory powers are taken over by Physis, while she herself becomes more closely identified with rational curiosity, with human nature inquiring into the causes of the universal order. On one occasion there is even a fleeting identification with the author. Another way of stating these differences is to say that in book two the myth as opposed to the model predominates, that *Microcosmus* is a type of *Bildungsroman*, equally encyclopedic but less abstract than book one. The process of education however is continuous: in book one, Natura learns about the elements and primordial creation; in two, about the elements and how man is made. Book two thus completes Bernard's scheme of a universal science which unites medicine and astronomy with more general physical and philosophical principles.

The opening scenes of the heavenly journey, a *mélange* of educational dialogue and science fiction, set the tone for the whole book. Natura, setting off at Noys' bidding, enters *anastros*, a region contiguous with the ether, but she cannot find Urania. Using the parallels and *colures* as guides, she wanders for a while among the stars, arriving finally at the *aplanos*, the outermost rim of the firmament. There she meets Pantomorphos, who introduces her to Urania, the *regina siderea*. Unlike Martianus' muse of the same name,

Urania is gifted in the art of prediction; she therefore knows beforehand that Natura is on her way.[1] In ii.4, she tells Natura not to fear the heavens; she was created by Noys for Natura's companionship and instruction. In one of the several speeches in praise of man in *Microcosmus*, she then outlines briefly her role in his formation. It will be difficult for her to leave her astral duties and undertake a journey into the lower world, a region for which she is physically ill-equipped. As her primary duty is to look after the education of the soul as it descends to earth, the *anima humana* will be a "guest" in man and to that degree he a "guest" on earth. The purpose of her descent is to acquaint the soul with its celestial origin:

> Mens humana mihi tractus ducenda per omnes
> etherios, ut sit prudentior
> Parcarum leges et ineluctabile fatum
> fortuneque vices variabilis,
> que sit in arbitrio res libera, quidve necesse,
> quid cadat ambiguis sub casibus. . . .[2]

The human soul is to be led by me through all the ethereal tracts so that it might better know the law of fate, the inexorable nature of destiny, and the undependable changes of fortune; [so that it might better know] which actions take place with free will, which by necessity, and what falls under ambiguous cases.

While man's knowledge of the heavens will never be comprehensive, Urania concludes, he will know what he does know through his senses and his reflection on what they provide. Throughout this episode, the reader, follow-

---

[1] *Cos.* ii.3.103-07 [Pantomorphos]: "Adsistricem indigentemque celi Uraniam, quam queritas, eam adspice te propter assistere sideribus inhiantem reditusque stellarum et anfractus temporarios sub numerum et ad certas observationis regulas colligentem."

[2] ii.4.31-36.

ing Natura's point of view, experiences a dramatic initiation into the secrets of the heavens. The Natura who, in book one, asked permission to record Noys' discourse,[3] now presents herself as a novice before Urania. It is important to note as well that Urania is not identical with Martianus Capella's muse of the same name. She represents astrology, the new astrology making its appearance in Bernard's time, and Natura's search for her among the stars thus has a deeper meaning. In *De Nuptiis*, Urania's powers are presented within the context of neoplatonic astronomy.[4] Urania presides over the musical harmony of the physical bonds of the universe as reflected in the heavens. In Bernard, Urania is primarily concerned with causality and prediction. She has not lost her neoplatonic associations, but she now has a new role as well. She is a sister-goddess to Natura, presiding over the heavens in the same way that Natura, through fate, governs the lower world.[5] Throughout the *Cosmographia*, moreover, the neoplatonic astronomy of Martianus and Macrobius, while not subjected to direct criticism, is subtly reinforced

---

[3] i.1.17: ". . . consilii si rite tui secreta recordor."

[4] Urania's verses on behalf of Philology's ascent reflect her spirit precisely; *De Nuptiis* ii.118; ed. Dick-Préaux, p. 50:

> Sidereos coetus et culmina sacra polorum
> nil iam coniciens numine fisa uide;
> olim disquirens nexos quid torqueat orbes,
> nunc praesul causas raptibus ipsa dabis.
> Quae circos textura liget, quae nexio cludat,
> ambiat et quantos orbita curua globos,
> sidereos cursus quid cogat quidue retardet,
> quis Lunam flammet uel minuat radius,
> qui caelum stellet fomes et quanta reuoluat,
> quae sit cura deis uel modus aspicies.

These lines may be compared to the accuracy with which Urania's powers are reflected by Pantomorphos; ii.3.103-07, cited above in n. 1.

[5] *Cos.* ii.4.17-18.

through astrology. One may thus think of Natura's journey, in which after "no little delay,"[6] the queen of the heavens (Abu Ma'shar's queen of the predictive sciences) was found, as an allegory of the way in which Bernard was recently exposed to the new astronomy through the translations of Hermann of Carinthia. Natura would seem to represent the *ratio* of the author, seeking out the true nature of the heavens. Pantomorphos' somewhat lofty introduction for Urania would also make sense in this context. Astrology was a dangerous discipline, which John of Salisbury, among others, had spoken out against. Bernard could not be too bold in introducing it.

The Celestial Elements

Pantomorphos (or Omniformis) is the most unusual figure in the opening scene. In introducing him, and in describing the relation between the outer heavens and God, Bernard's chief source was the *Asclepius*. In the notion of *aplanos*, however, he seems closer to his own contemporaries. Twelfth-century commentators on Plato who took an interest in astronomy did not neglect the *aplanos*,[7] and

---

[6] ii.3.69-70: "Ad huius rei spectaculum mora consumpta est aliquanta, et que quaeritur non inventa."

[7] E.g., *Glosulae Abrincences*, MS Avranches 226, ff. 67v-81r. The problem of the *aplanos* is treated on f. 69. For a description of the *Glosulae*, see R. Klibansky, *The Continuity of the Platonic Tradition during the Middle Ages* (London, 1950), p. 52. A full list of the contents, including highly interesting and hitherto unpublished works, is provided by C. Leonardi, *I codici di Marziano Capella*, 2-3, and E. Jeauneau, *Guillaume de Conches, Glosae super Platonem*, 33-37. On the term *aplanos*, see the interesting note of T. Silverstein, *Classical Philology* 47-48 (1952-53), 86 n. 24. In addition to the use of the term in Milo's *De Mundi Philosophia*, which Silverstein notes, there is a lengthy discussion in Daniel of Morley, *Liber de Naturis* . . . , ed. Sudhoff, p. 35: "Speras igitur non decem, ut quidam (i.e. Platonici) numerant, sed octo esse, ut in libro Alphragani docemur, ipsa ueritas testatur. Prima quidem

Bernard's brief discussion recalls the treatment in particular of Adelard of Bath. In *De Eodem et Diverso*, Adelard merely reiterates Macrobius' notion that the *aplanos* is the fixed outer layer of the firmament.[8] In the *Questiones Naturales* he takes up the question again in a discussion of heavenly motion. Chapters 69-76 of this work reveal a position not unlike Bernard's, and the manner in which the inquisitive uncle leads on the orthodox nephew would appear to be a more direct way of confronting problems which Bernard preferred to leave to allegory. Adelard states that the power which produces heavenly motion is really the *aplanetici corporis conversio*.[9] This leads however to another question: is *aplanos* "alive"? The question is answered ambiguously in the last chapter of the *Questiones*. The nephew, growing warm to the scent of heresy, wants to know exactly what *aplanos* is, "qui universa formata sinu continet"[10] (which contains everything which has been formed in its womb). Some philosophers maintain that it is inanimate while others—alluding to Pliny—"dare to call it God."[11] In his reply, the uncle carefully sidesteps controversy by declaring that the real problem is one of terminology:

---

et propinquior terre est spera lune, secunda mercurii, tercia ueneris, quarta solis, quinta martis, sexta iouis, septima saturni, octaua stellarum fixarum quam greci aplanon quasi sine errore uocant. Aplanos uero hiis circulis distinctus est, quorum primus, arabice almustakim, latine equinoccialis nuncupatur. . . ."

[8] *De Eodem* . . . , ed. H. Willner, p. 32, line 2. On Bernard's relation to Adelard, see F. Bliemetzrieder, *Adelhard von Bath* (München, 1935), 229-35; on Adelard's possible use of Cicero's *De Natura Deorum*, see T. Silverstein, *art. cit.*, 82-86.

[9] *Questiones Naturales*, cap. 74; ed. M. Müller, *Beiträge* xxxi.2 (Münster, 1934), p. 67, lines 7-8.

[10] *Ibid.* 76; p. 68, 10.

[11] *Ibid.* 76; p. 68, 18-19: "Quidem . . . deum vocare ausi sunt."

If one considers a god as a living creature, both rational and immortal, then it must be conceded that *aplanos* is a divinity in this sense. But if an inquiry is made into the nature of God from whom—being uncomposed, unformed, immutable, and infinite—everything which is created derives its entire causes, then, in this sense, it should be intolerable to speak of the outermost sphere as a god.[12]

This statement is similar to Bernard's earlier idea that God manifests himself through the heavens by the *ignis ethereus*. And, like Adelard, Bernard appears to have two conceptions of God at once: one, as the diffused life-force, familiar to Stoic sources, which repeats and reproduces itself at every level of creation; two, as a neoplatonic abstraction, the One or the Good, from whose will the Many descend in emanation.

A similar union of Stoic and neoplatonic ideas appears to be embodied in Pantomorphos. Bernard describes him as follows:

Hoc igitur in loco Pantomorpho persona deus venerabili et decrepite sub imagine senectutis occurrit. Illic Oyarses idem erat et genius in artem et officium pictoris et figurantis addictus. . . . Oyarses igitur circuli quem Pantomorphon Grecia, Latinitas nominat Omniformem, formas rebus omnes omnibus et associat et adscribit.[13]

Then, in the region of Pantomorphos, this god appears as a personage in the venerable figure of old age. Here

---

[12] *Ibid.* 76; p. 68, 31-35: "De deo enim animali rationali, immortali, si quaeritur, hoc modo aplanon deum esse concedendum est. De Deo vero, a quo universalis rerum causa, incomposito, informi, immutabili, infinito si investigatur, hoc modo extimam sphaeram deum dici abominandum est."

[13] *Cos.* ii.3.89-100.

indeed was a celestial deity, a *genius* talented in both the art and the office of drawing and of configuring. . . . The Greeks therefore name this deity by the sphere of Pantomorphos, which is called 'all-form' in Latin, since here he brings together all forms and assigns them to individuals.

Elsewhere Bernard speaks of the Oyarses (pl.) as celestial *genii* who incorporate and transfer God's wisdom and life-forces from above. In both places he appears to be drawing not only on Censorinus[14] but on *Asclepius* 19, where a similar theory of the role of *genii* somewhat obscurely outlined. Hermes says that there are many kinds of gods, some apprehensible to the mind, others to the senses. Those understandable to the mind, called "rulers of material things," preside over areas of the universe. Gods perceptible to sense are their subordinates. As *usia* in the *Asclepius* is a synonym for matter, the Ousiarchs (= οὐσιάρχης, Bernard's Oyarses) are "those who make all things throughout the sensible world, working one through another, each pouring light into the thing he makes."[15] Hermes then gives some examples: Zeus, ruler of heaven, and Pantomorphos, ruler of the Decans, that is, the thirty-six fixed stars of the horoscope, which Bernard outlined in detail

[14] *De Die Natali*, cap. 3; ed. F. Hultsch (Leipzig, 1867), 5: "Genius est deus, cuius in tutela ut quisque natus est vivit. Hic sive quod ut genamur curat, sive quod una genitur nobiscum, sive etiam quod nos genitos suscipit ac tutatur, certe a genendo genius appellatur." There is a twelfth-century copy of the *De Die Natali* (beginning at ch. 4) in B.M. MS Harleian 3969. Bernard may of course have taken his demonology from Apuleius' *De Platone* or *De Deo Socratis*, bound, incidentally, in the same MS. On Bernard's *genii*, see as well Thorndike, *A History of Magic and Experimental Science*, vol. 2, 103-04.

[15] *Asc.* 19; 318, 19-21: "hi . . . qui per sensibilem naturam conficiunt omnia, alter per alterum, unusquisque opus suum inluminans"; trans. W. Scott, *Hermetica* i, 325.

in i.3. Hermes includes the seven spheres who have as their Ousiarch "Fortune or Destiny, who changes all things according to the law of natural growth, working with a fixity which is immutable and yet which is varied with everlasting movement."[16] Bernard incorporates Hermes' view, though not exactly, into the *Cosmographia*. His world is also peopled with celestial and earthly spirits, operating numinously between the two worlds.

The exact manner in which Pantomorphos represents physical principles in Hermetic cosmology has been admirably summed up by Walter Scott:

> [Pantomorphos], the ruler of the outermost sphere, 'bestows life on all things' employing the visible οὐρανός [from Aristotle's *De Caelo*] as his agent or instrument. . . . The function of the god is to transmit to the material world copies of the ideal forms of the several kinds or traces of living beings, these copies (the "generic forms") being as yet unmodified by the differences which distinguish one individual from another of the same race. If so, he must transmit them, not directly to the world below, but to the οὐσιάρχης next beneath him, to be modified by individual differences, before they can be imposed upon the matter of which individual bodies consist; for the generic form never finds material embodiment until it has been thus differentiated. On the other hand, in terms of the Stoic doctrine of πνεῦμα, it might be said that the function of the first οὐσιάρχης consists in the constant emission of vitalizing fire from the material substance of the highest heaven, and that this vitalizing element passes down through the lower spheres of heaven, and

---

[16] *Ibid.* 19; p. 319, 7-9: ". . . quam fortunam dicunt aut Εἵμαρ μένην, quibus inmutantur omnia lege naturae stabilitateque firmissima, sempiterna agitatione uariata"; trans. W. Scott, *loc. cit.*

entering the air, combines with it to form πνεῦμα, by which life is conveyed into the bodies of men and beasts on earth.[17]

While Bernard, as a poet rather than a philosopher, may have had a somewhat less exact idea of this process than described above, he appears to have united both conceptions, not only in Pantomorphos but, what is more unusual, in God.

This fact emerges from the next stage of the heavenly journey. Proceeding through the spheres in pursuit of their "sacred and religious task,"[18] Urania and Natura approach the residing place of God. Tugaton, as Bernard calls the place, is seen directly through the eyes of Natura in ii.5, then explained at length by Urania in ii.7. The initial description is an allegory of the neoplatonic Good, derived from Chalcidius and, above all, from Macrobius, but presented in a spatial architecture found in neither. God's "palace" is called the *summi et superessentialis . . . sacrarium*;[19] Bernard thus repeats the notion that God is located outside the universe. The *mansiones* of the other celestial divinities are located near his; they are pictured looking

---

[17] *Hermetica* iii, 109; cf., 121. MS Bodl. Laud. Misc. 515, fol. 200v, contains the following gloss, which I cite from Vernet's Appendix IV, p. 496: "*Pantomorpho*, vel Oyarses, idem quod genius deus scilicet illius circuli, secundum Tholomeum, dictus Pantomorpho, id est pictor, unde post dicit: *in officium pictoris addictus*; forme enim que sunt in inferioribus partibus superioribus formis obediunt. In lingua chaldea dictus Oyarses, id est 'potestas deputata,' quia naturalis rerum potestas erat ei a supremo Deo deputata. Item deus dicitur genius a 'generacione,' quia secundum motum illius circuli provenit omnium rerum naturalis generacio. Et notandum quod deus ille nichil aliud est quam naturalis exsecucio eorum que proveniunt per operacionem superiorum."

[18] *Cos.* ii.5.5-6: ". . . sanctum . . . et religiosum opus. . . ."

[19] ii.5.10.

up in God's direction for a reflection of his wisdom, assenting to his will in nods.[20] Tugaton itself is presented as the *tabernaculum* from which an "infinite and eternal" beam of light radiates forth, confusing the sight of the viewer.[21] This image is followed by another which is equally well known in neoplatonism: the triune fountain, whose beams pour forth with equal clarity and then turn back upon themselves.[22] After these fleeting images—and so intentionally presented with dramatic realism by Bernard— the two goddesses say a prayer and, *comitato vestigio*, descend into the ether. The reader must wait until ii.7 for an explanation of what he has seen. At this point Bernard brings the discussion back to the relation between *caelum* and *deus* and effectively summarizes his entire argument. (It is worth noting that ii.7 bears, in some respects, to ii. 3-6 the same demythologizing relationship as the explanatory i.4 does to i.3 in *Megacosmus*.) Here, in part, is his description:

> Celum, ether, äer, tellus, quaterna quidem regio universam mundi continentiam circumcludunt. Celum simplex est, una eademque quantitate continuum nec qualitatibus disparatum. Binam etheris, binam item aeris, trinamque telluris partitionem cognoveris. Suum numen, suos habent angelos et principaliter singuli et

[20] There seems, in fact, to be a hierarchy; ii.5.15-23: "Contingentes invicem mansiones et linea continuationis annexas uniformis pervadit spiritus qui vires sufficit universis, verumtamen non uniformiter a spiritu suscipiunt uniformi: qui enim propiores ad consessum divinitatis adsistunt, nudatis ostensisque interdum consiliis, internam adusque mentem proprius deducuntur; ceteri, pro qualitate distantie decisum nec adeo integrum retinent contemplatum gustantque parcius divinitatis notitiam et scientiam futurorum." With characteristic ambiguity, Bernard does not tell the reader which "gods" are closest to God.

[21] ii.5.23-26.   [22] ii.5.26-35.

subdivisio singulorum. Celum ipsum Deo plenum
est. . . .

Deus . . . divine licet majestatis caligine abscondatur
incognitus, de suorum tamen vestigiis operum perspicuus innotescit. . . . Sua celo animalia (*supp.* sunt)
ignes siderei, hujus generis animal rationale quidem
nec morte dissolvitur nec afficitur passione. . . . In sub-
limiori igitur fastigio, si quid celo sublimius, tabernaculum Tugaton suprema divinitas collocavit, quem
circumsistunt obeuntque vicinius agmina ignite flam-
mantisque nature perlucida, ex pyr spiritus et creata
pariter et vocata. Ea, propter infatigabilem et per-
petuam ad Deum conversionem, membra vel divinitatis partes specie similitudinis estimantur: non enim
verum est quippiam in divinitate dividuum. Illi ergo
ex proximitate Deo convertuntur plurimo et de Mente
(= Noys) ejus excipiunt futurorum arcana, que in
fatum mundi publicum per inferiores mundi spiritus
ineffugibili necessitate constituunt proventura. Qui,
quia eterne beatitudinis visione perfruuntur, ab omni
distrahentis cure sollicitudine feriati in pace Dei, que
omnem sensum superat, conquiescunt.[23]

The region which surrounds the entire contents of
the cosmos is divided into four parts: the heavens, the
ether, the air, and the earth. The heavens are unified;
they consist of a continuum of one and the same
quantity, not differing in quality. You might know as
well that ether is divided into two parts, the air in
two and the earth into three regions. The heavens
possess their guide, their messengers; they are both
one kind in principle and divided into individuals.
[For] the heavens are full of God. . . .

[23] ii.7.10-53.

God . . . , being unknowable, is free to remain hidden in the splendour of his divine mist, but, becoming manifest, he is made known by his traces in all his works. . . . His living beings in the heavens are the starry fires. These living, rational beings belong to the genus of creatures who are neither destroyed in death nor influenced by passion. . . . In the loftiest heights, if anything could be higher than heaven, the supreme divinity places the tabernacle of Tugaton. Very lucid streams of ignited or flaming nature, both created and, equally, called after the fire of spirit (*pneuma?*), surround and enwrap it rather closely. This [living fire], on account of its unwearied and perpetual turning towards God, is thought to be the members or parts of divinity through the beauty of its likeness; for it is true that not a single thing is divided in divinity. Thus, these [members] are converted to God by their proximity to him and receive from his Mind the secrets of future events, which they establish as about to happen to the public fate of the world by means of ineluctable necessity through the agency of the lower spirits of the world. Since [these celestial beings] enjoy the vision of eternal beatitude, they benefit from a perpetual holiday, far from any sollicitude or distracting care and rest tranquil in the peace of God which surpasses every sense.

The simplest way to understand this synthesis is to regard it as a continuation of the theogony of i.2, 3, and 4, with certain fundamental notions clarified in the preceding discussion of the Oyarses. For Bernard, God is both outside the world and in the world: outside, in the sense that abstractions, representing philosophic or scientific powers, carry out his will and implement his design; inside, in the sense that, as the cosmos is a living continuum, it is really divine substance which informs it and from which its creativity derives. Accordingly, each of the divisions of the heavens, and presumably of the earth, is governed by its own *angeli, genii,* or *numina,* which mediate all generated things including the ungenerated life-force itself. In this sense the heavens are literally full of God; but God is not quite subsumed into the heavens. Here, as elsewhere, Bernard maintains a delicate balance between this- and otherworldliness, between delight in the existing world and respect for its deeper, symbolic meaning. His portrait of deity also fulfils perfectly Macrobius' dictum that the highest mysteries should not be disclosed openly but in images. The choice of images however leaves no doubt as to Bernard's meaning: the *ignis divinus* from i.2 and 4 is now juxtaposed with neoplatonic images of the paradise to which souls return after their sojourn in the body.

But is there not as well another meaning for God lurking just beneath the surface of Bernard's two dominant images, the Stoic and the neoplatonic? In i.2, Noys is described as the *intellectus* of the *exsuperantissimus Deus*[24] in the very passage, heavily indebted to Firmicus Maternus, in which her astrological associations are established. In an excellent article, Franz Cumont has demonstrated that the phrase *extramundanus* or *exsuperantissimus deus* itself has astrological associations.[25] In the *De Platone* of Apuleius, which was used by Bernard,[26] the idea implies demonology;[27] in the *De Mundo*, trinitarian images very

[24] i.2.152.

[25] *Archiv für Religionswissenschaft* 9 (1906), 323-36.

[26] See in general M. McCrimmon, "The Classical Philosophical Sources," 65-66, 83-84.

[27] *De Platone* i.12; p. 96: "Et primam quidem providentiam esse summi exsuperantissimique deorum omnium, qui non solum deos caelicolas ordinavit, quod ad tutelam et decus per omnia mundi mem-

like those of Bernard are employed, not to illustrate a neoplatonic relationship between heavenly abstractions, but an astrological one between physical forces.[28] Commenting on both works of Apuleius, Cumont states:

[Apuleius] divides the heavenly powers into three classes: the lowest is formed from the local *genii*, or, to employ the Greek term, the "demons;" the second from the inhabitants of the sky (*caelicoli*), in particular the stars; finally, above the planets and the fixed stars resides the god, "alone and unique, ultramundane and incorporeal, the father and architect of this divine world." Although the qualities of the supreme being are Platonic, the rest of Apuleius' development reveals another influence entirely: it is inspired by the sidereal theories of the astrologers.[29]

It is difficult to avoid the idea—even though Bernard nowhere expresses it directly—that God plays an important role in an astrological conception of universal order. First of all, the two other essential elements which Cumont mentions are found in book two. The stars and planets, as in i.3, are divine, and the local *genii* are also described in ii.7.[30] Furthermore, the apparently neoplatonic trinitarian

---

bra dispersit, sed natura etiam mortales eos, qui praestarent sapientia ceteris terrenis animantibus. . . ." Cf. *De Mundo*, cap. 31; p. 167, line 21: "exuperantissimis"; cap. 27, p. 163, lines 11-12: "summus atque exuperantissimus divum."

[28] *De Platone* i, cap. 11; p. 95: "Deorum trinas nuncupat species quarum est prima unus et solus ille ultramundanus, incorporeus quem patrem et architectum huius divini orbis superius ostendimus."

[29] *Art. cit.*, 330 (my trans.).

[30] *Cos.* ii.7.110-16: "Telluros qui terram incolunt, sic habeto. Ubi terra delectabilior nunc herboso cacumine tergoque montium picturato, nunc fluviis hilarescit, nunc silvarum viriditate vestitur, illic Silvani, Panes et Nerei innocua conversatione etatis evolvunt

relationship of ii.5 and 7 is also susceptible in part to an astrological interpretation. Cumont continues:

Following the oriental astrologers, the divine world is a trinity; it is both one and triple. It is composed of the non-decomposable, fixed stars, the planets divided into seven, and the earth starting from the [orbit of] the moon. Each of these lower worlds receives from the upper world a portion of its power and participates in its energy; and the source of all force and all virtue resides in the highest sphere, single and indivisible, which rules the movements of all the other parts of the universe.[31]

This statement is very close to the Stoic/Asclepian doctrine of the emanation of creative forces from the One to the Many, from the *aplanos* contiguous with deity to the earth. It is worth adding, in this context, that Bernard nowhere makes specific mention of the Christian Trinity.[32] While his adaptation of Apuleius may not be exact, it is reasonable to propose that beneath the two more overt images in which God appears, there is a third, an astrological construction which harmonizes well with Bernard's other scientific views. After all, he could hardly delegate astrology as queen of the sciences without appending her forces to God.

The Descent

To return to ii.5, from the palace of Tugaton on the outer rim of the heavens, Natura and Urania begin their

---

tempore longioris: elementali quadam puritate compositi, sero tamen obeunt in tempore dissolvendi." The Oyarses is of course Pluto.

[31] *Art. cit.*, 330-31 (my trans.).

[32] Cf. T. Silverstein, *Modern Philology* 46 (1948-49), 108-09, whose interpretation begs the question.

descent towards the earth. As stated above, this part of the *Cosmographia* is an allegory of the descent of the soul from the One, drawn chiefly from Macrobius, *Commentary* i.11-12. Bernard found there the doctrine of reminiscence, which Urania mentions in her opening speech, and the notion that the soul only rests temporarily in the body, after which it returns to its celestial home.[33] In creating an allegory out of Macrobius' straightforward presentation of the question, however, Bernard has considerably altered the original. If his descent of the soul may be considered a continuation of the doctrine of the *anima mundi* from i.2, then its meeting place in Macrobius is perhaps the following statement on the first influx of matter into the pure soul:

> Anima ergo cum trahitur ad corpus in hac prima sui productione silvestrem tumultum id est ὕλην influentem sibi incipit experiri.[34]

> When the soul is drawn towards the body in its first procession, it begins to experience a material tumult, that is, *hyle* flowing into itself.

In ii.5, Bernard has omitted the initial entrance of the soul into the planetary spheres perhaps because he feels the *anima* is created totally by natural forces, but he adheres to the outline of the descent of the soul which Macrobius presents in partial translation from Plotinus. From Saturn, the human soul receives *ratiocinatio* and *intelligentia*, the theoretical sciences; from Jupiter, *vis agendi*, the practical; from Mars, *animositatis ardor*, bellicosity; from the sun—whose role Bernard thought particularly important—*sentiendi et opinandi natura*, the nature of sensing and of imagining; from Venus, *desiderii . . . motus*, appetite; from Mercury, *pronuntiandi et interpretandi [natura]*, the power

---

[33] ii.4.1-14; 21-26.   [34] *Comm.* i.12.7; p. 49.

to speak and to interpret; and lastly, in the lunar sphere, φυτικός . . . , *id est natura plantandi et augendi corpora*, the vegetative soul, which he considerably reinterprets.[35] These doctrines are all reproduced and somewhat transformed in the *Cosmographia*.

Bernard's originality in this respect may perhaps best be appreciated in his portrayal of Saturn and Jupiter. The relation between the theoretical and practical sciences which they represent becomes transformed in ii.9 into one of the central elements in the formation of man. Bernard begins his description of Saturn with the traditional details, but then he proceeds to something quite different:

> Quotquot illi filios uxor fecundissima peperisset, interceptis vite primordiis, recens editos devorabat. Parturienti sedulus excubator non torpuit consideratione, non relanguit misericordia, ut quandoque parceret vel sexui vel decori. Natura senis crudelitatem exhorruit et, ne sanctos oculos fedo violaret obtutu, faciem suam virginea pavitatione devertit. Fuit seni unde malum, unde sevitiam exerceret. Si quandoque defuit quem voraret, crudus adhuc nec citra vires emeritus, insumpto falcis acumine, quicquid pulcrum, quicquid florigerum demetebat: rosas et lilia et cetera olerum genera, sicut nasci non sustinet, non sustinet et florere.[36]

[35] *Ibid.* i.12.14-15; p. 50.

[36] *Cos.* ii.5.48-64. Cf. Bernard's *Experimentarius*, ed. M. Brini Savorelli, *Rivista critica della storia della filosofia* 14 (1959), p. 309: "Saturnus itaque est homo fuscus et paucos pilos in barba habet; non est pulcher, operatur inique, gravis piger non ridet, et iracundias quasi semper habet in calcaneo, color eius est glaucus, pectus subtile, capilli sunt ei asperi, fetida vestimenta sunt ei, et nigra libencius amat quam alia." A somewhat longer description is presented on pp. 311-12, but Saturn is nowhere given the individuality he has in the *Cosmographia*.

However many sons [Saturn's] most prolific wife bore him, he would cut off their life at the beginning and immediately devour them. He kept a careful guard for what was being produced, neither growing sleepy through contemplation nor weak through pity, so as [not] to spare sex or beauty at any time. Natura was horrified at the cruelty of the old man. Lest he violate her sacred eyes by uniting them with his (*lit.* by a union of the eye), she turned away her face with virginal fear. She was to the old man [the source] from which he might exhaust his evil, his fierceness. If and when there was a lack of someone to devour— for he was blood-stained but not yet worn out in strength—he would take up his sharp scythe and reap whatever was beautiful, whatever was in bloom: roses, lilies, and so forth, and all kinds of vegetables. For as he could not bear them to be born, he could not bear them to flower.

The normal interpretation of this passage would simply see Saturn limiting the effects of excessive growth or speculation. But Bernard here goes considerably beyond descriptions of Saturn in classical mythology and astrological handbooks. In her study of Bernard's source material, Miss McCrimmon felt that there was possibly a topical reference.[37] While the argument must be stated most hypothetically, it is a fact that certain aspects of this satire on Saturn seem to point to a contemporary target: Bernard of Clairvaux. Saint Bernard's *De Consideratione*, to which Silvester may be alluding, was written between 1149 and 1152,[38] reasonably close to the time the *Cosmo-*

[37] "The Classical Philosophical Sources," 190 n. 7.
[38] Manitius-Lehmann, *Geschichte der lat. Literatur des Mittelalters* iii, 124. Bernard may also be parodying Bernard of Clairvaux

graphia was being finished. While Bernard did not, so far as we know, fashion his allegorical figures in the image of real persons from his own day, he was a clever satirist who was not afraid to show the mirror to the foibles of his contemporaries. The opposition between the love of *ornamentum*, represented by works like his, and the asceticism of the Cistercians, is well known. Even if Saturn is not Bernard of Clairvaux, a deeper meaning for the passage is suggested. If Natura, at this point, represents not only the regulatory forces in the universe but also a combination of theory and practice, then she would seem to be recoiling from the excess of theory. In this sense, Bernard may simply be trying to defend the simple, the practical, in short, the *joie de vivre* which he so often displays elsewhere and, at the same time, to be acknowledging a certain fear of censorship. This would perhaps be suggested by Natura's statement that, in spite of Saturn's ugliness, "she felt the old man should be revered."[39] Bernard's dedication of the *Cosmographia* to Thierry of Chartres (often, incidentally, an opponent of St. Bernard) may be a related factor.

There are, of course, other hints throughout the *Cosmographia* that Bernard valued freedom of thought and expression highly. One is the manner in which he playfully invokes Christian ideas in a pagan context. Clearly, for him, there was only one religion, which included both humanisms. Nor is it merely his own contemporaries whom he criticizes for vagueness. In ii.5, for instance, he states that Tugaton is the residence of the supreme divinity, *si*

---

in another place. Compare *De Consideratione* ii.3; *PL* 182, 745C: "Noveris licet omnia mysteria, noveris lata terra, alta coeli, profunda maris"; with *Cos.* ii.10.37-39: "Aërios tractus, tenebrosa Ditis,/ alta poli, terra lata, profunda maris/viderit. . . ." Bernard also calls his man *pontifex*; ii.10.50.

[39] *Cos.* ii.5.67-70: "Ex contemplatu operum durum licet adiudicet et in posterum, ex eo tamen Natura senem credidit venerandum. . . ."

theologis fidem prebeas argumentis.[40] A perhaps better example is furnished by the ensuing description of Jupiter. As in the case of Saturn, Bernard again goes beyond the source material in painting a portrait that he felt was poetically convincing. In contrast with Saturn, Jupiter is a figure much more to Natura's fancy:

Hujus regionis Oyarses adeo presens, adeo benivolus, ut eum Latinitas Jovem nominaret a 'juvando', fidesque est quam certissima per omnia mundi membra indulgentiarum Jovis beneficia permeare. . . . In consistorio suo Jupiter regia prenitebat majestate; manum quidem sceptratus dexteram, de sinistra suspenderat momentanam, ad cujus equilibritatem nunc hominum nunc res superum pensitaret.[41]

The genius of this region is so ready, so benevolent that he is called in Latin Jove from "helping." The belief is very certain that, through all the limbs of the cosmic organism, Jove sends forth the benefits of his indulgences. . . . In his counsel-chamber, Jove was glorious in regal majesty. His right hand was sceptered and from his left hung a pair of scales in which he balanced now the acts of men, now of gods.

[40] ii.5.10-11, where *theologis* refers not to contemporary theologians but to ancient authorities; F.J.E. Raby, *A History of Secular Latin Poetry in the Middle Ages*, vol. 2 (Oxford, 1957), 10 n. 2. The commentator here is very probably Macrobius, whom Bernard, with access to more modern astronomical theory, perhaps regarded as being outmoded. A good example of his more accurate views occurs in his description of the *colures*, the circles intersecting the tropics and the equator and passing through the poles. At *Cos.* i.3.61-72, Bernard indicates that he knows of the precession of the equinoxes, i.e. the fact that the *colures* do not return to their starting points. Bernard's account may be compared to Macobius, *Comm.* i.15.14; pp. 62-63. The progressive nature of celestial change is of course important for Bernard's metaphysics.

[41] *Cos.* ii.5.71-89.

In addition to the expected classical description of Jove, Bernard thus presents him as a secular regent or a beneficent pope, presumably balancing with his indulgences the excesses of Saturn. A topical reference beneath the traditional elements would also help to explain Natura's attraction for him. Only with great difficulty does she regain her stability and continue towards Mars. It is worth recalling, at this point, that Eugenius III, the only pope specifically mentioned in the *Cosmographia*, was in northern France in 1147-48 for the trial of Gilbert Porreta.[42]

In presenting the planetary deities who govern various qualities and conditions, not only in unborn souls, but on the earth and in the lives of men, Bernard has drawn considerably on astrology. His portraits bear a resemblance to the miniatures in the 1506 edition of Abu Ma'shar that were based on medieval prototypes. In particular, Bernard is indebted to Abu Ma'shar for his outline of the role of the sun and the moon, the two "planets" whose physical effects were recognized by late antique astronomers like Posidonius and were thus subjects of continuing interest. For Bernard, there is no Oyarses in the heavens more important than the sun: it is "illustrior lumine, presentior viribus, augustior majestate" (more noble by its light, more present by its forces, more august by its majesty); it is "mens mundi, rerum fomes sensificus, virtus siderum mundanusque oculus"[43] (the mind of the cosmos, the fire giving sense to things, the force and worldly eye of the stars). Bernard's conception of the sun's powers is drawn from a combination of medical and astrological theory. From medicine he draws the metaphor of the sun as the eye of the world, an idea which is paralleled in ii.14 by the sense of vision in the *minor mundus*, man. The general context

[42] R. L. Poole, *Eng. Hist. Rev.* 35 (1920), 341-42; E. Faral, *SMed* 9 (1936), 71.
[43] *Cos.* ii.5.133-35.

of the sun's physical powers, however, is drawn from astrology. In the *Introductorium* iv.5, Abu Ma'shar describes the sun as "omnis rerum generationis pater . . . universalis"[44] (the universal father of all generation of things), adding later that "universis itaque totius mundi calor . . . solis est"[45] (the heat of the sun thus permeates everything in the entire cosmos). Elsewhere he states that the sun takes precedent over the other stars since, as a god among gods, it is, in a sense, the creator of all things by tempering nature through heat. It acts like an efficient cause:

> For just as fire is a cause of burning by virtue of its innate powers, so the sun, the divine light, the universal author of light and heat, the divinity governing the natural composition of things, exists as an efficient cause endowed with a definite power.[46]

For this reason God created the sun as the second power among his celestial "ministers," the planetary divinities. The sun holds dominion "in nature temperie rerumque compositione"[47] (in the tempering of nature and the com-

[44] f. d.1 verso.

[45] *Introductorium* v.4; f. [d.5 recto].

[46] *Ibid.* iii.3; f. [b.8 recto]: "Ut enim ignis propria virtute vrit causa exustionis est: sic divinum lumen sol lucis et caloris universalis auctor naturalis rerum compositionis divinitus data virtute efficiens causa existit."

[47] *Ibid.* iii.4; f. [b.9 recto]. Daniel of Morley summarizes the astrological theory of the sun's effects as follows in the *Liber de Naturis*, ed. Sudhoff, p. 33: "Enumeratis diuersis solis et lune effectibus, sciendum est, quod non sine causa sol in medio mundi positus est, quia, si sol usque ad applaneticam speram sublimatus esset, uel usque ad lunarem orbem humiliatus, tunc uel inde frigore uel hinc calore nimio mundus stare non posset. Quamobrem prouidus auctor omnium deus solem, tanquam uniuersalem corporee substantie fomitem, in media mundi regione medium locauit, iussitque eum moueri. Quia non fuit necessarium, ut calor esset super faciem terre

position of things), while the moon holds power over the movement of the sea, the status of bodies and the flowering and ripening of earthly things. Bernard's interest in the lunar powers is clearly demonstrated in the next stage of the drama which takes place at Granusion, within the moon's orbit.

Before turning to this new episode some general features of Bernard's treatment of the neoplatonic descent may be summarized. In general Bernard has incorporated Macrobius' schema without committing himself to the otherworldliness it implies. In Plotinus, in Macrobius, and, to a lesser degree, in John Scottus, the descent of the soul is a type of death: from eternity to time, from the One to the Many, from simplicity to diversity, the human soul is said to descend into its tomb, the body. In Macrobius, as in Augustine, the soul, once it is on earth, forgets its celestial origins, which it may win back in part through the practice of virtue. In Augustine this is synonymous with the practice of the Christian life, including the liberal arts. Something of the dynamics which such a view could inspire may be seen in Alan of Lille's *Anticlaudianus*, in which the seven liberal arts of Martianus Capella are transformed into a physical vehicle for bringing about the return of man's soul to its pristine unity with God. Between Macrobius, Martianus, and John Scottus certain neoplatonic assumptions are held in common, while in Bernard, neoplatonism here, as in i.4, tends to be balanced by philosophical naturalism and astrology. For him, the descent of the soul does not result in a state of relative degradation which must await reunion with a state of grace. On the contrary, even though man's body is formed from the leftovers of the divine, man will reflect his divine origin di-

---

uno et eodem modo semper, quoniam habentia uitam aliquando frigore, aliquando calore, aliquando temperie opus habent."

rectly through the operation of his mind and his senses. For this reason, Urania displays a certain ambivalence throughout the descent. On the one hand she is apprehensive about her survival and relevance to the earthly world; on the other, she is pleased at the prospect of the creation of man and realizes that his earthly embodiment, rather than his divine origin, is the object of creation. The descent is therefore an initiation not only for the soul but also for Natura who is about to represent *humana natura*. Man will be the glory of the universe not chiefly in the pursuit of virtue, which is entirely omitted from the astrological programming of the soul, but through his physical composition. These facts emerge clearly in the next act of the cosmic drama.

2. *Granusion*, *Physis*, and Man

Man's Creation

This act begins at ii.9, when Urania and Natura, descending through the lunar sphere, enter a region where the fluid substance of the four elements appears to be changing its shape continuously. Horrified at the "congenital inconstancy," the two goddesses attempt to reach an island of peace and calm, a still-flowering "bosom" of the earth which runs out between the warring elements.[48] This place

---

[48] *Cos.* ii.9.1-14: "Ventum erat inter colloquendum ubi aer inferior Eoliis fratribus regio decertata nunc rigescens, nunc adestuans, verberata sepe grandinibus collisis, sepe nubibus intonatur. De cujus inequalitate Urania constupuit, que nihil insueverat in diversa traducibile vel discrepans a tranquillo. Videt lubricam elementi substantiam ad omnes contrarietatis incurrentias convertibili qualitate mutari, nunc offendi pluviis ex Oceano comparatis, nunc densari nebulis quas terra parturit crassiores. Que quidem omnia quantum obvia consuetudini, tantum egra animo, tantum contraria visioni. Illis innatam regionibus inconstantiam abhorrentes elementorum excursis interstitiis, jam florentis terre gremio consistere contendebant."

is called Granusion. It is a paradise not in a moral or geographical but in a physical sense. Its invention, and the creation of man which takes place there, are, along with the portrait of chaos in i.1-2, Bernard's most brilliant syntheses of poetry and philosophy.

In Granusion—so named by Bernard because it causes all kinds of living things to mature[49]—the four elements out of which the cosmos is made are held in perfect balance.[50] This harmony is unattainable elsewhere, and Bernard suggests as well that Granusion is not really part of the created order brought into being by Noys but a permanent model of physical perfection from which the earth generates inferior copies. Here the sun shines with especial tenderness, both making the meadows grow green and the innate fertility of matter reproduce.[51] The image of self-reproducing fertility is carried throughout the description; Bernard not only tries to unite physical properties and astrological influences, but also includes a good deal of medical theory:

> Quicquid occurrit morbis, quicquid sanitatem conciliat, quicquid deliciosos voluptate sensus irritat, plantas, herbas, odoramenta, species in diversa mortalium commoda sinus abditus subministrat. Hec in mundo sola est, ut opinor, exceptata particula, que de elemento-

[49] ii.9.15-19: "Is quidem de recentis puerique Solis teneritudine feliciorem aeris temperiem consecutus et virescit ad gratiam et germinat ad fecunditatem. Nomen loco Granusion, quia graminum diversitatibus perpetuo compubescit." C. S. Lewis, *The Discarded Image* (Cambridge, 1964), 59-60, underestimates the force of astrology in Bernard's Granusion.

[50] ii.9.22-25.

[51] ii.9.45-48: "His quidem giris et anfractibus suos hactenus differebat effectus, ut humoris materiam graminibus sufficeret universis."

rum intensione nihil in se suscipiens plenam consum-
matamque temperiem adepta est confiteri.[52]

The hidden womb supplies for the various conven-
iences of man whatever restores health, whatever
arouses the pleasurable senses with desire—plants,
herbs, odors, and spices. The place, in my opinion, is
unique: although it has limited the particles, and while
it takes nothing unto itself from the tension of the elements [as a result of limiting and ordering them], it
is fit to proclaim a full and consummate temperate-
ness.

Granusion is thus like a healthy organism through whose
senses a perfect harmony is maintained between itself and
the outside world. By a union of neoplatonic and Stoic
metaphors, Bernard suggests that the *locus* is, in some sense,
both the One at its stage of descent from the Many, and,
at the same time, the union of the elements which is free
from "tension." The medical metaphors are later utilized
in the description of man's sensorial psychology, since he is
to be made in Granusion. In thus reworking the topos of
paradise, Bernard appears as well to be presenting an ideal
of perfection which is not a lost utopia but an earthly, physical reality.

As Urania is now beginning to pass out of her realm,
Natura takes over the role of guide. She suggests that they
change direction, since Physis, for whom they are search-
ing, is to be found in the region. As Natura and Urania
actually approach Granusion in search of Physis, the *locus
amoenus* appears to swell in anticipation like an expectant
mother and a blooming garden at once. Bernard presents
the sequence in lines modelled on Martianus' description

[52] ii.9.19-25.

of the approach of Apollo, Mercury, and the Muses to the throne of Jove:[53]

Locus utique suapte perspicuus speciem pulcritudinis amplioris adjecit, quippe matrem generationis, Naturam, presenserat adventare. De nature igitur gremio fecunditate concepta derepente tellus intumuit et confortatis cespitibus, vis occulta subrepsit.[54]

The place, bright of its own virtue, added an appearance of greater beauty [to itself], for it had sensed in advance that Natura, the mother of growth, was on her way. As a consequence, the earth swells suddenly with a fertility conceived from the womb of *natura* (i.e. Natura = *natura*) and a hidden strength steals into the enriched ground.

Continuing the sensorial metaphors and adding to them the notion of astral prediction, Bernard sees Granusion, sensing its very life-forces arrive, grow fertile at their arrival. Reiterating the role of Natura in the hierarchy of governing forces at the end of i.4, Bernard conceives her as a mediating genius between the heavens and the earth. As in the *Asclepius*, the earth also plays a creative role. Putting on a festive face for Natura's arrival, the woods of Helicon's daughters pour forth their perfumes and oriental spices fill the air. A stream flows through the *locus amoenus*: "sweet to listen to, it was even sweeter to see . . .

---

[53] *De Nuptiis* i.27; ed. Dick-Préaux, p. 19: "Tum uero conspiceres totius mundi gaudia conuenire. Nam et Tellus floribus luminata, quippe ueris deum conspexerat subuolare Mercurium, et Apolline conspicato aëria Temperies sudis tractibus renidebat. Superi autem globi orbesque septemplices suauius cuiusdam melodiae harmonicis tinnitibus concinebant ac sono ultra solitum dulciore, quippe Musas aduentare praesensarant. . . ."

[54] *Cos.* ii.9.30-34.

as if, putting aside corporality, it had transformed itself into a virtually pure element."[55] Completing his parody of the earthly paradise, Bernard substitutes for the angels guarding the gateway to Eden the simple heat of the sun, which, girding the entrance and working through the moist, shady soil of the forest, produces all kinds of flowers and pleasant odors.[56] Combining the virtues of the sun and the moon, paradise is ever-young and ever-new for Bernard, because man, who is to be made there, is not created merely to fall into sin. Not so much created as creating, his paradise reflects the spirit of natural, spontaneous generation in matter itself, awaiting the guiding hand of the creator.

Granusion is, so to speak, the stage upon which the drama of man's creation is to be enacted. In rhetorical terms, Granusion is also a type of earthly paradise. Bernard indicates this by introducing it with the tag-line, *Granusion locus est eoum ad cardinem secretior in reducto.*[57] This type of introduction, as noted earlier, recalls the poetic descriptions of the garden of Eden composed by Christian-Latin poets in the fourth and fifth centuries A.D.[58] With the

[55] ii.9.39-44: "Erat rivus oriundis ex alto cursibus in plana precipitans non ut tumultus violentos incuteret, verum auribus amico murmure blandiretur. Blandus auditu, blandior fuerat visione etheree liquidum puritatis excedens, tanquam corporalitate deposita ad purum fere transierat elementum."

[56] ii.9.47-52: "Totam loci continentiam utrobique silva lateraliter circumplectens geminato commodo et temperebat solibus et communes arcebat ingressus. Claudentes intra terminos agebat calor ethereus in humecto, ut ibi flores varii, ibi odoramenta, ibi seges aromatum cresceret vel injussa."

[57] ii.9.14-15.

[58] E.g., Lactantius, *De Ave Phoenice*, line 1; *CSEL* 27, part 2, fasc. 2 (1893), p. 135: "Est locus in primo felix oriente remotus. . . ." C. Marius Victor, *Alethia* i.224; *CSEL* 16, part 1 (1888), p. 372: "Eoos aperit felix qua terra recessus. . . ." A number of examples are gathered in A. Graf, *Miti, leggende e superstizioni del medio evo* (Torino, 1925), Appendix I.

exception of *The Phoenix* attributed to Lactantius,[59] however, none of these utopian landscapes combines rhetoric and philosophy as effectively as Bernard in his prose poem on Granusion. One reason for this is the breadth of Bernard's source material. He has built into his *locus amoenus* an unusually large number of philosophical and astrological ideas.

The major classical source for Granusion is Chalcidius. In chapter 129 of the *Commentary*, Plato's translator briefly summarizes the theory of the *demones* from the *Epinomis* and states that there are five regions of the cosmos which are, in his words, *capaces animalium habentes*. The first three, fire, ether, and air, were described in the descent of Urania and Natura. The fourth has the nature "humectae substantiae, quam Graeci hygran usian appellant, quae humecta substantia aer[e] est crassior . . ."[60] (of a moist substance, which the Greeks call "liquid being" [= Granusion], since a fluid substance is denser than air). Influenced by this notion, Bernard developed his Granusion into both a type of paradise in the neoplatonic sense, representing unity in diversity, and into a place of intense fertility, uniting the powers of the sun, the moon, and the four elements, providing an appropriate astrological cradle for the creation of man.

The idea of Granusion which Bernard presents poetically in ii.9 is not without parallels among his contemporaries. In a MS of the British Museum, Cotton Galba E.iv, a recently edited treatise on the four elements describes the region of the *humecta substantia* as follows:

> Beneath the moon begins the region of pure air, in which the poets place the Manes. From the air begins

[59] See Stock, *Classica et Mediaevalia* 26, fasc. 1-2 (1965), 246-57.
[60] p. 172.

a region which is called the moist substance and it continues down to the earth. It is called the *humecta substantia* suitably because the highest point of this airy region terminates the ascent of wet clouds. In the summit of this moist substance there are contrary winds and from the vehemence of their conflict they create a flame which, through the protracted constriction of the winds, now imitates a serpent, now a rod, now a stripe—something which is in accord with the motion of the winds. . . .[61]

This description possesses an added relevance for understanding the *Cosmographia* in that it occurs in a twelfth-century manuscript containing the *Premnon Physicon* of Nemesius of Emesia and the *Questiones Naturales* of Adelard of Bath,[62] two documents that Bernard would surely have known. An earlier, anonymous treatise in the same manuscript (ff. 187-189v) is not dissimilar to the *Cosmographia* in its sources. It cites Seneca, Macrobius, the *Timaeus*, and Aristotle's *Physics*. Like the *Cosmographia*, this collection of scientific treatises "belong[s] to the epoch when Aristotelian science was coming in through Arabic channels but had not yet been fully absorbed."[63]

In Granusion, Physis makes her first appearance in the drama. She is described as "clinging to her daughters,

[61] Cotton Galba E.iv, f. 189; ed. R. C. Dales, *Isis* 56 (1965), 189: "Sub luna incipit purus aer in quo poete Manes esse finxerunt. Ab illo aere incipit regio que dicitur humecta substantia et durat usque ad terram. Humecta substantia dicitur ideo quia summitas illius aeris terminat ascensum humidorum nubium. In summitate huius humecte substantie contrarii venti sunt et ex vehementia conflictus flammam creant que constrictione ventorum protracta nunc imitatur serpentem, nunc virgam, nunc clavam quod pro qualitate motus ventorum accidit. . . ." William of Conches' interpretation is different; see *Glosae super Platonem*, cap. cx, ed. Jeauneau, pp. 199-201.

[62] Haskins, 93 n. 63.   [63] Haskins, 95.

Theory and Practice."[64] (Bernard uses the phrase *individuo . . . consortio*, by which he may mean that Theory and Practice, while separated in the division of the sciences, act in concert under Physis' direction.) In contrast to Natura, who mediates life-forces from above, often in the abstract, Physis' powers are directly related to the human sciences. It is she who

> naturarum omnium origines, proprietates, potentias, effectus, postremo universam omnemque Aristotelis categoriam, materiam cogitationis, effecerat. Sumptis a suprema divinitate principiis, per genera, per species, per individua, Naturam et quicquid eo nomine continetur indeflexo vestigio sequebatur.[65]

had brought about the origin of all essential qualities, their properties, potencies, effects, and, in addition, the entire list of Aristotle's categories, the material for serious contemplation. For, taking her principles from the supreme divinity, she followed Natura and whatever comes under her name through genera, species and individuals.

In the hierarchical descent of being in which an adaptation is made of divine life-forces at each stage, Physis thus represents the mediation of Natura's powers directly on earth. However, this is not all she represents. First, Physis brings medicinal remedies to heal the unruly changes in human nature as a result of the stars: she thus completes Bernard's idea of a universal science. Secondly, Physis corresponds to the vegetative aspect of the soul described by Macrobius as the last stage in the descent to earth. Thirdly, and most importantly, Physis appears to

---

[64] *Cos.* ii.9.52-54: "Eo igitur in loco Physin residere super aspiciunt, Theorice et Practice individuo filiarum consortio coherentem."
[65] ii.9.55-60.

be the Aristotelian craftsman. Unlike Aristotle, Bernard places her in a hierarchy in which her powers are not predominant. Yet, within a larger context Physis may be seen as the completion of Bernard's idea of mechanical, physical forces operating in the cosmos. Bernard has not just employed the idea of *natura artifex* at the earthly level; he has adapted it to all levels including the resonance of life-forces with God. The way in which the upper levels of the cosmos redeploy life-forces is drawn on the analogy of Physis' work lower down. At the earthly level, Bernard has merely made the notion more explicit by placing it in the context of the human sciences of his time.

Certain parallels, for instance, may be observed between the activity of Urania and Physis. Urania, the muse of the heavens, is normally engaged in predicting the effects of changes in the motions of the stars. Her astrological interests are essentially scientific and Bernard's portrayal of them reveals more than an amateur interest in how astrology actually works. Physis, operating at the earthly level, is in charge of physical or medical forces. Thus the parallel between astronomy and medicine in the formation of a universal science is again emphasized. Like Urania, however, Physis does not merely reflect the powers she controls in a passive way. In the process of inquiring into physical causes, she seems, like Urania, to be attempting to relate theory to practice, even conducting "experiments":

> Verum id disquisitiori pertractabat ingenio, ut elementa, partes mundi primarie, partesque partium, in his, ex his et per hec que generant, causis physicalibus deservirent.[66]

[66] ii.9.71-74. *Pertracto,* to touch or explore, seems to have acquired the sense "to observe empirically." Cf. Daniel of Morley, *Liber de Naturis,* ed. Sudhoff, p. 31: "His ad hunc modum petractatis, sciendum est, quod Ptholomeus . . ." etc.

Physis, moreover, was making observations with a more inventive skill, so that the elements, the parts of the cosmos and the atomistic particles of the parts might be subject to the physical causes which she brought forth in them, from them, and through them.

Physis' inquiry, lastly, covers a wide range, including lapidary medicine (*de lapidibus remediales etiam . . . effectus*)[67] and, on the arrival of Urania and Natura, the possible medical applications of poisons.

Physis is thus an important allegorical figure in the cosmic drama: she is, in fact, virtually a summary of the progress of physical science in Bernard's day. Her arrival at the climax of the *Cosmographia* could have many meanings. André Vernet sees in the list of her interests not only a reference to the *Categories*, known throughout the Middle Ages, but to other Aristotelian works being introduced in the 1140s,[68] works which caused considerable excitement even among authors who had not yet been able to gain access to their doctrines.[69] Another possibility is that Bernard himself, aware of the progress which science was making, allowed Natura's powers to be usurped somewhat by those of Physis, just as, in his time, the Platonic notion of nature was being replaced or supplemented by the Aristotelian. In such an interpretation it is possible to add that Physis is much less mythical and more scientific than Natura. If Natura vaguely represents natural forces and human nature, Physis represents the exact sciences, the mechanical arts, and the new rational faith in causality. Thus Physis is not only Natura's earthly helper: she is the agency through which Natura's forces are transferred down to a

---

[67] ii.9.74-76.   [68] Vernet, 364.

[69] See L. Minio-Paluello, *L'Occidente e l'Islam nell'alto medioevo*, vol. 2 (Spoleto, 1965), 603-37; bibliography, 637. A more detailed bibliography is provided in G. Lacombe *et al.*, *Aristoteles Latinus*, *Codices* (Roma/Cambridge/Bruges, 1939-61).

different level of theory and practice, one in which empirical generalizations are to be employed for the material improvement of the world. Lastly, among the sciences which she represents, Physis is predominantly interested in the mechanical arts. This aspect of her activities becomes clearer when the creation of man takes place. When the three goddesses are assembled, Noys appears on the scene and delivers a speech outlining the design for man which she has brought down from the creator. It is no surprise at this point that Bernard conceives man as a microcosm: the idea, foreshadowed in *Megacosmus*, was widespread in his sources and virtually a commonplace among twelfth-century Platonists.[70] In Bernard, man is both a faithful reflective image of the *megacosmus*, containing all the components of the *universitas mundi*, and, as in the theological interpretation of John Scottus, an *officina*,[71] a workshop, in which the laws and principles of the greater world are continually being reproduced. That is to say, while Bernard reiterates from Genesis and the *Timaeus* the idea that man was the chief object of creation,

[70] The literature on *homo microcosmus* is now quite large. The most important background study is perhaps K. Reinhardt, *Posidonios* (München, 1921), 343-422. Recent scholarship is conveniently summarized by E. Jeauneau, *Jean Scot, homélie sur le prologue de Jean* (Paris, 1969), 336-38. Among the most useful studies are: R. Allers, *Traditio* 2 (1944), 319-407; H. Schipperges, in P. Wilpert, ed., *Antike und Orient im Mittelalter, Miscellanea Medievalia I* (Köln/Berlin, 1962), 129-53 and, more generally, Chenu, 34-43. Illustrations of the theme in German and Austrian MSS only are found in F. Saxl, *SB Heidelberg, philos.-hist. kl., Jahr 1925-26* (Heidelberg, 1927), 40-49 and plates XI-XIII. The recent study of F. Rico, *El pequeño mundo del hombre* (Madrid, 1970), summarizes past studies accurately, pp. 11-45, but, oddly, omits any reference to Bernard Silvester.

[71] *Lit.* ἐργαστήριον. The theme however is not a prominent one in Eriugena in a naturalistic sense; see Jeauneau, *Jean Scot*, for a brief but illuminating discussion.

like Macrobius, Scottus, and the Porretani in the 1140s, he places him in an ordered hierarchy. Through his *continuitas* man not only culminates the structural differentiation from the One, but acquires a value and dignity that depends largely on his physical makeup, his innate capacity to understand the world around him through the natural laws which govern both it and him. Although a popular theme in the period, *homo microcosmus* was interpreted in highly different ways. It appears in a literary and theological context in Alan of Lille and Godfrey of St. Victor[72] and in a political framework in John of Salisbury. It is transformed into a uniquely brilliant vision by Hildegard of Bingen.[73] In Bernard, the emphasis is on the natural-scientific parallels between the world and man, and these lead him to ideas about man's secular and religious life.

Noys' speech to the assembled goddesses in ii.10 is both the climax of the *Cosmographia* and a summary of Bernard's microcosmic theory in highly poetic language:

Sensilis hic mundus, mundi melioris imago,
  ut plenus plenis partibus esse queat,
effigies cognata deis et sancta meorum
  et felix operum clausula fiet homo. . . .

Mentem de celo, corpus trahet ex elementis,
  ut terras habitet corpore, mente polum.
Mens, corpus, diversa licet, jungentur ad unum,
  ut sacra complacitum nexio reddat opus.

[72] On Alan of Lille, see *Anticlaudianus* ix.380-426, where man emerges as a microcosm of the virtues and the seven liberal arts; on Godfrey, see Ph. Delhaye, *Le microcosmus de Godefroy de St-Victor* (Lille/Gembloux, 1951), 144-49, where comparisons with Bernard are made.

[73] See H. Liebeschütz, *Das allegorische Weltbild der heilige Hildegard von Bingen* (Leipzig/Berlin, 1930), 86-107, whose sources, in my opinion, take us too far from what the abbess can be expected to have read.

Divus erit, terrenus erit, curabit utrumque
   consiliis mundum, religione deos.
Naturis poterit sic respondere duabus
   et sic principiis congruus esse suis.
Ut divina colat, pariter terrena capessat
   et gemine curam sedulitatis agat,
cum superis commune bonum rationis habebit:
   distrahet a superis linea parva hominem.
Bruta patenter habent tardos animalis sensus,
   cernua dejectis vultibus ora ferunt,
sed majestatem mentis testante figura,
   tollet homo sanctum solus ad astra caput,
ut celi leges indeflexosque meatus
   exemplar vite possit habere sue. . . .

Viderit in lucem mersas caligine causas,
   ut Natura nihil occuluisse queat. . . .

Omnia subjiciat, terras regat, imperet orbi:
   primatem rebus pontificemque dedi.
Sed cum nutarit, numeris in fine solutis,
   machina corporee collabefacta domus,
ethera scandet homo, jam non incognitus hospes
   preveniens stelle signa locumque sue.[74]

Let man, this sensible world, the image of a better
world, [be created in such a way] that, by containing
all things, he may be able to exist for each (*lit.* he may
be full of all full parts). Let man be made an imitation
related to the gods, a holy and happy conclusion to my
works. . . . He shall draw his mind from the heavens,
his body from the elements, so that he shall inhabit
earthly regions with his body, the stars with his mind.
Mind and body, though different, shall be united in
one in such a way that the sacred bond [between them]

[74] *Cos.* ii.10.9-54.

will produce a pleasing work of art. He shall be godly and earthly: he shall show his devotion for the world with his counsel, for the gods with his religion. Thus he shall be able to react with two natures [at once], and thus he shall be balanced through his own principles (or, fitted to his own beginnings). That he might tend to divine responsibilities and at the same time manage earthly problems—that he might look after this double responsibility—he shall have the advantage of reason in common with the gods. [Indeed], a thin line shall separate man from the higher orders. While brute animals clearly have slow senses and bear their heads towards the earth from downturned faces, man, with a figure bearing witness to the dignity of his mind, shall alone raise his sacred head towards the stars in order that he may know the laws of the heavens and their unending courses, and take them as an exemplar for his life. . . . He shall see the causes which have been immersed in mist as in a clear light, so that Natura can hide nothing from him. . . . Let him subdue all things, reign over the earth, rule the world. Lo, I have presented you with the primate and the pontifex of the universe. And when the frail machine, his corporeal home, falls at last through the destruction of its harmony, man shall rise to the ethereal heights. Now no longer an unknown guest, he shall [re]ascend to the sign and position of his own star.

Noys' speech is perhaps the most brilliant poetic synthesis in the *Cosmographia*. The opening lines (of the cited portion) restate three of the most important themes: man, the microcosm, as a *sensilis mundus*; man, who like the greater world, repeats the process of the One and the Many; and man, who as the *felix . . . clausula* of creation is, in the moral allegory, "the image of a better world." The praise for man is largely drawn from *Asclepius* 6 and 8 where man's place in creation is described in identical terms.[75] Yet Bernard has broadened considerably the application of the ideas. More emphasis is placed on man's role as creator rather than as the object of creation. Bernard sees him guiding both nature, whose secrets he himself unlocks, and the world, whose "lord" he is through his physical superiority of the other beasts. In addition, he has altered somewhat an important statement in *Asclepius* 8 on man's practical activities. Hermes says that mortal things not only include the two elements, earth and water, which Nature has placed under man's government, but everything which man makes in or out of these, including agriculture, navigation, and social relations:

> quae pars terrena mundi artium disciplinarumque cognitione atque usu seruatur, sine quibus mundum deus noluit esse perfectum.[76]

> This earthly part of the world is preserved by the knowledge and use of arts and disciplines, without which God would not have wished the world to be completed.

[75] In particular, *Asc.* 6; pp. 301-02: "Propter haec [= mentem humanam (*Asc.* 5, 9-15)] o Asclepi, magnum miraculum est homo, animal adorandum atque honorandum. . . . O hominum quanto est natura temperata felicius! Diis cognata diuinitate coniunctus est. Partem sui, qua terrenus est, intra se despicit; cetera omnia quibus se necessarium esse caelesti dispositione cognoscit, nexu secum caritatis adstringit; suspicit caelum. Sic ergo feliciore loco medietatis est positus, ut, quae infra se sunt, diligat, ipse a se superioribus diligatur. Colit terram, elementis uelocitate miscetur, acumine mentis maris profunda descendit. Omnia illi licent: non caelum uidetur altissimum; quasi e proximo enim animi sagacitate metitur. Intentionem animi eius nulla aëris caligo confundit; non densitas terrae operam eius inpendit; non aquae altitudo profunda despectum eius obtundit. Omnia idem est et ubique idem est."

[76] *Asc.* 8; p. 306.

Only one part of this statement really finds an echo in Bernard: he sees man, using the arts and sciences inherent in his nature, to become the religious and secular head of the world. But man does this within the context of his physical rapport with the outside world, as outlined in another important text from the same work:

> ... effecit ut sit ipse et mundus uterque ornamento sibi, ut ex hac hominis diuina conpositione mundus, Graece rectius κόσμος, dictus esse uideatur. Is nouit se, nouit et mundum, scilicet et meminerit, quid partibus conueniat suis, quae sibi utenda, quibus sibi inseruiendum sit, recognoscat. ...[77]

> [God] has arranged that man and the world are both well designed orders for each other, so that the world, more correctly in Greek "the order," may be seen to have been named after the divine construction of man. Man knows himself and knows the world, that is, he recalls what is fitting for his role and recognizes what he is to use and what is to render him service.

As in the *Asclepius*, *mundus* and *homo* are the two "images" of deity. Bernard sees the world often by analogy with man, its ornament. At the same time he includes the astrological idea that man's soul, ultimately, will return to its own star, a deliberate parody of neoplatonic astronomy and soul-theory. In Bernard, in fact, there is more attention paid to the notion of a return of the soul to its origins than in the *Asclepius*, and an even more emphatic celebration of man's physical nature. Bernard's positive attitude towards the visible and tangible world, clearly revealed in his *ornatus elementorum* in i.3, is strongly echoed in his praise of man as the chief glory of creation.

[77] *Asc.* 10; p. 308.

In ii.11, the goddesses begin the work of making man. His soul is formed by connecting the world-soul to the edifice of virtue; his body, as in Plato, from the remnants of pre-existing matter, by Physis. The bringing together (*concretio*) of both by Natura takes place according to an order already existing in the heavens. Noys then briefly assigns to each goddess a particular area of control over man. "To Urania," she says, "I present the mirror of providence, to Natura, the table of fate, and to Physis . . . the book of memory."[78] These three aspects of the microcosm are then described in some detail, reflecting Bernard's intense interest in the symmetry between the cosmos and man. Each of the three, providence, fate, and memory, reflect in their way what each reflected in *Megacosmus.* The *speculum providentie,* as in i.2, mirrors the eternal ideas, ancient and future forms, the divine fire, the planets, the constellations and even the "friendship of the elements, the mediator entwined in itself."[79] The *tabula fati,* as in i.4, represents *heimarmene,* the *genius* which carries out Natura's wishes in time. Presenting its functions in colourful terms, Bernard sees there not only the *miraculum opificis* in bringing about order from chaos but also the history of the world from the first man, not omitting that of the common people, whose humility was often "trod under foot."[80] Physis,

[78] *Cos.* ii.11.16-18: "Providentie speculum Uranie, tabulam fati Nature, et tibi, Physi, librum recordationis exhibeo."

[79] ii.11.32-33: ". . . elementorum amicitia mediator et complectibilis ex se, in se concidens et mutuus internexus." The things which the mirror of Providence reveals (ii.11.19-44) are comparable to those attributed to Noys (i.4.61-73). Their extension into man would be part of the *linea continuationis* (i.4.78) binding all forces in a hierarchy. Their association with Urania in ii.11 strengthens Bernard's astrological associations for Noys in i.4.

[80] ii.11.59-74: ". . . naturalia et que temporis sunt porrectiore spatio tenebantur. Illic cause unde antiquissimus tumultus in silva

for whom there is no direct equivalent in *Megacosmus*, is given the *liber recordationis*, which, according to Bernard, "is nothing other . . . than an object which takes events unto itself." In judging the sense impressions recorded on the *tabula rasa*, "the intellect often compels the memory by verifiable reason, more often by probable guesses."[81] By assigning three different functions to these goddesses, moreover, Bernard gives the *Cosmographia* a new dimension. Urania, who looks after human souls and sees to their descent, appropriately receives the mirror of providence in which the eternal ideas, imprinted on the souls like wax impressions, are found. Fate, a general principle of causality in both the *Asclepius* and Bernard, mediates the laws of Natura on earth and in man. Physis, preoccupied with terrestial causes and effects as well as the mechanical arts, receives the book of memory which Bernard, possibly following Cicero,[82] conceived as a mechanical function.

Before turning to the last stage of man's creation, it is perhaps worthwhile to call to mind one other source for Bernard's idea of *homo microcosmus*. The prologue to Firmicus Maternus, book three, summarizes in a single paragraph many of the essential features of Bernard's conception:

> Scire itaque nos principe in loco oportet . . . quod ad imaginem speciemque mundi formam hominis ac statum totamque substantiam deus ille fabricator hominis

---

miraculumque opificis, quod in tanto rerum divortio pax inventa. . . . Fatalem igitur mater generationis tabulam cum fidelius inspexisset, que tantas inter species latitabat humanitas, vix reperta. Primum inter hominum, quem pagina designabat, ab occipitis regione longa longis historiis fatorum series sequebatur. In ea namque fortuna, calcata plebis humilitas. . . ."

[81] ii.11.86-89: "Liber enim recordationis non aliud quam qui de rebus se ingerit et compellat memoriam intellectus, ratione sepe veridica, sed probabili sepius conjectura."

[82] See F. Yates, *The Art of Memory* (London, 1966), 1-21.

natura monstrante perfecerit. Nam corpus hominis ut mundi ex quattuor elementorum commixtione composuit, ignis scilicet et aquae, aëris et terrae, ut omnium istorum coniunctio temperata animal ad formam divinae imitationis ornaret, et ita hominem artificio divinae fabricationis composuit, ut in parvo corpore omnem elementorum vim atque substantiam natura cogente conferret, ut divino illi spiritui, qui ad sustentationem mortalis corporis ex caelesti mente descendit, licet fragile sed tamen simile mundo pararet hospitium. Hac ex causa hominem quasi minorem quendam mundum stellae quinque, Sol etiam et Luna ignita ac sempiterna agitatione sustentant, ut animal, quod ad imitationem mundi factum est, simili divinitatis substantia gubernetur.[83]

It is necessary to know then in the first place that, with Natura showing the way (or, as Natura shows), God, the fabricator of man, created his form, his condition and his entire material frame in the image and likeness of the cosmos. For he made the body of man just as of the world from the mixing together of the four elements, namely of fire, water, air, and earth, in order that the harmonious union of all these might adorn the living being in the form of a divine imitation; and so he formed man through the craftsmanship of a divine fabrication in such a way that, with Natura acting as co-ordinator, he combined in this little body all the force and substance of the elements, so that a hospice which was perishable yet nonetheless similar to the world might be prepared for that divine spirit which descends from the celestial mind for the sus-

[83] *Matheseos* iii, *prooemium* 2-3; ed. Kroll and Skutsch, i, 90-91. Cf. Daniel of Morley, *Liber de Naturis*, ed. Sudhoff, p. 12: ". . . operante natura. . . ."

tenance of the mortal frame. The five stars, the sun, and the moon on this account support man, [who is] so to speak a kind of little world, by their fiery and sempiternal motion, so that this living being which is made in the image of the world, might be ruled by a substance similar to divinity.

This passage, one of the most beautiful praises for man's dignity in the late Latin period, admirably sums up some of the essential features of Bernard's image of man throughout book two. Firmicus subtly introduces the Christian phrase *ad imaginem speciemque*, not only to indicate man's theological relation to God, but his physical relation to the world.[84] As in Bernard, Natura calls for the formation of man and "shows the way." Yet it is God's plan that is brought down to Noys for his creation. In *commixtio*, Firmicus refers to the Stoic mixing of the elements which Bernard later drew from him or from Constantinus; in *coniunctio*, very probably to the doctrine of "sympathy" associated with Posidonius. And in employing *ornare* to describe man's relation to divinity, he effectively summarizes the Chalcidian and Asclepian notions. *Fabricatio* here, as well, points in Bernard's direction, yet it is still Plato's idea based upon mixture rather than the twelfth-century notion, which has possibly contemporary roots in the mechanical arts. As in Bernard, the soul descends for a time into the perishable body, and the astrological forces, represented by the stars, guide man with the same *ignita ac sempiterna agitatione* as they do the world.[85] (The

---

[84] On this subject see G. Ladner, *The Idea of Reform* (Cambridge, Mass., 1959), 83-107.

[85] Cf. *Mathematicus*, ed. Hauréau, p. 18 (= *PL* 171, 1368A-B). When the youth Patricida reveals for the first time his gifts, chief among them is a knowledge of the stars:

phrase itself, in fact, is reminiscent of Bernard's explanation of cosmic physics in 1.4.) Firmicus is on the whole more neoplatonic than Bernard; but granting this slight difference, he expresses ideas identical to his later admirer. In ii.12-14, Physis, now commanding the stage, completes the drama of man's creation. Bernard skilfully weaves together the physiology of the brain and the senses from Constantinus' *Pantegni* and *Liber de Oculis* with the human psychology of Chalcidius, and frames the whole in a praise for man's sensorial nature which may be indebted to obscure Hermetic sources.[86] In ii.12, not Bernard's smooth-

---

> Novit enim quam sideribus, quam primitus orbi
> sementem dederit materiamque Deus;
> quae fuit in rebus ratio, quae causa creandis,
> quos habeant nexus, quas elementa vices;
> et numeri quo fonte fluant, qua lege ligentur,
> quo sibi conveniant schemate dispositi. . . .

[86] A. S. Ferguson, *Hermetica* iv (1936), xlvi, mentions a lost Hermetic book, *Hermetis de Mundo et Caelo,* cited by Bradwardine in *De Causa Dei.* Similar passages are found in *Cos.* i.4.157ff. Silverstein, *Modern Philology* 46 (1948-49), 96 n. 25, assumes that this book was the *Liber . . . de VI Principiis,* but, as stated above, there is virtually no evidence for this. There are in fact closer parallels in Hugh de Santalla's translation of the *Liber de Secretis . . . Hermetis Trismegisti* in MS Paris, Bibl. Nat. lat. 13,951. This work contains a long eulogy in praise of man (ff. 22r et seq.) and concludes, as does the *Cosmographia,* with a description of the senses. The work may also have been cited by Bernard's friend, Hermann of Carinthia; *De Essentiis,* ed. Alonso, part 2, p. 77: ". . . sic Apollonius in Secretis naturae. . . ." (The possibility is discussed by Alonso, p. 77 n. 14.) Yet too many conclusions should not be drawn from such superficial parallels. The above mentioned subjects were not limited to Hermetic treatises. For instance, the late twelfth-century *Microcosmographica* attributed to William of Reims in MS Trier, Stadtbib. 1041 deals successively with the relation of man's body to the elements (ff. 14v-22r), then turns to the senses: sight (23v-26v), touch (28r), hearing (29r), smell (30r), and

est meter stylistically, Physis appears to reiterate the complaint which Noys made about matter's imperfectibility in i.2. She perceives a certain latent fault (*macula*) in the *turbida materies* of matter, the plastic stuff out of which man's body is to be formed:

> Sunt mala que soleant etiam cum corpore nasci
> Physis et illa timet.[87]

For these are the evils which may normally be born with the body, and Physis fears them.

Man, claims Physis, is to be reformed (*reformandum*) to the extent of the physical limitations of matter and the conditions laid down for his existence in the stars, for the one will provide the constitution (*machina*) and the other the makeup of his soul.[88] In ii.13, Bernard reiterates the theme of identity and difference; then, under Natura's direction, Physis moulds a stable structure (*aedificatio*) for man from the *reliquias elementorum*. Bernard's conception of man's original imperfection is thus essentially Platonic: inasmuch as man is made from the elements not needed for the formation of the cosmos, he is made in its physical image in a slightly inferior way.

The analogy with the greater world is predictably the overriding metaphor throughout ii.13-14 and here, as in i.3, Bernard displays his talent for putting into *Kunstprosa*

---

taste (30v). The treatise is also notable for its interest in astrology. And would Bernard not have had at his disposal that most obvious source, Cicero, *De Natura Deorum* ii.51-64, where man's physiology results from the joint labors of Providence and Nature?

[87] *Cos.* ii.12.49-50. On *reformare* in this physical sense, cf. William of Conches, *Glosae super Platonem*, cap. 72; ed. Jeauneau, p. 147: "Sed huius discordie est reconciliatio quia quantum de uno elemento in uno tempore consumitur, tantum de alio in idem *reformatur*. . . ."

[88] ii.12.53-62.

and elegiac verse the scientific thoughts of others. A typical example of his use of Chalcidius is provided by the analogy between the triune division of the earth and the similar makeup of the body. Physis, Bernard says, knows that no error will be committed in making man, the little world, if she takes the greater world as her model. Therefore, in his "subtle contrivance" Physis places "the heaven" on top, ether and air in the middle, and earth on the bottom. From man's head, his "divinity" governs and gives orders. Angelic powers, his nerves, correspond to the *genii* who carry out God's orders in the cosmos. And thus "earth," his lower parts, are sensibly governed. Here are the two passages, Chalcidius and Bernard, side by side:

[Chalcidius:]
Certe hominis membra sequuntur ordinationem mundani corporis; quare, si mundus animaque mundi huius sunt ordinationis, ut summitas quidem sit dimensa caelestibus hisque subiecta, diuinis potestatibus quae appellantur angeli et daemones, ⟨in⟩ terra uero terrestribus; et imperant quidem caelestia, exequuntur uero angelicae potestates, reguntur porro terrena, prima summum locum obtinentia, secunda medietatem, ea uero quae subiecta sunt imum; consequenter etiam in natura hominis est quiddam regale, est aliud quoque in medio

[Bernard:]
In minore mundo, homine, Physis intelligit non errandum, si majoris mundi similitudinem sibi sumpserit in exemplum. In illo subtili mundani corporis apparatu

positum, est tertium in imo: summum quod imperat, medium quod agit, tertium quod regitur et administratur. Imperat igitur anima, exequitur uigor eius in pectore constitutus, reguntur et dispensantur cetera pube tenus et infra.[89]

Surely the limbs of man follow the arrangement of the body of the world. For, if the world and the soul of the world consist of this arrangement, the result is that the summit is in fact measured by the heavens and is subject to them by means of the divine powers which [in the heavens] are called angels and demons, on earth, to be sure, earthly beings. Moreover, the celestial beings give orders, the angelic powers truly carry them out, and earthly beings are governed. At first they take hold of the highest place, then the middle, and finally those things which are subject on the bottom. Conse-

celum fastigio supereminet altiore; aer, terra, terra de infimo, aer de medio circumsistunt. De celo deitas imperat et disponit. Exequuntur jussionem que in aere vel in ethere mansitant potestates. Terrena que subterjacent gubernantur.[90]

In the lesser world, man, Physis understands that

[89] *Comm.*, cap. 232; p. 246.
[90] *Cos.* ii.13.95-102. Daniel of Morley sees the matter somewhat differently in the *Liber de Naturis*, ed. Sudhoff, p. 9.

quently, in the same manner there is in the nature of man something regal; there is something else in addition placed in the middle; [and] there is a third [area] on the bottom. The highest [is] what governs, the middle [is] what acts, the third [area is] what is governed and administered. Therefore the soul governs; its force, contained in the breast, executes; the rest are governed and managed as far down as the genitals and below.

there should be no error if she takes as a model for herself the likeness of the greater world. In this subtle apparatus of the "body of the world," heaven is located above in the higher summit; air and earth—earth below, air in the middle— are placed around [it]. From heaven divinity rules and manages. The powers, which dwell in air or in ether, execute the orders. The earthly beings which are thrown down below are governed.

There are certain differences in presentation between the two. For instance, Chalcidius incorporates the notion of *anima* into the description whereas Bernard has a more mechanical idea of how the body functions. Chalcidius also states the relationship between the earthly and bodily *daemones* more clearly. Yet in most respects the two explanations are fundamentally similar. A metaphor drawn from Chalcidius is thus imaginatively re-expressed by Bernard. Throughout the construction, moreover, it is Physis alone who is the "skilful artificer" of man's bodily parts and organs: except for brief notices, the other goddesses recede from the scene.

Particularly intriguing is Physis' fabrication of the head, the *futurum . . . intelligentie et rationis habitaculum.*[91] First she divides the head into three regions, the traditional formula. Then Bernard's imagination takes over:

[91] ii.13.81-82.

Secretis itaque rationibus, mollem cerebri liquidumque
quam crearat essentiam tegumentum intra testeum
occuluit ne ei facile noceretur. Molle et delicatum ad
creationem cerebri visa est delegisse, ut in liquido pos-
sent facilius rerum imagines insidere.[92]

Then, by a secret plan, [Physis] hid the soft liquid of
the brain, whose essence she creates, beneath a hard
covering, lest it be easily damaged. She seems to have
chosen something soft and delicate for the creation of
the brain, so that the images of things might easily
inhere in the liquid.

In the front part of the brain, a purely mechanical recorder
of impressions, *phantasia* anticipates the forms of all ob-
jects, further back, in the occiput, memory resides, "lest,
if at first the brain does not react to the initial appearance
of something seen, it will be aroused by the frequent coming and going of the images."[93] Reason resides in the middle area, so that a certain amount of judgment may be exerted over *phantasia* and *memoria*. In the "royal palace"
of the head, to continue the metaphor, messages go back
and forth between the different parts of the brain.

Bernard's mechanistic and sensorial account of the brain
owes a great deal to Constantinus Africanus. While the
philosophical and psychological aspects are drawn, in general, from Chalcidius' chapters on *De Capite* (213-35) and
De Sensibus (236-67), it is possible to derive the entire

[92] ii.13.117-21.

[93] ii.13.121-28: "Totam igitur capitis continentiam tres secernens
in thalamos, eos ternis anime efficientiis consecravit: in sincipite provi-
sum est fantasia, rerum formas anticipet et rationi renunciet que
viderit universa; in   occipitis reductiore thalamo memoria con-
quiescat ne, si primo visionum jacuisset in limine, figurarum fre-
quentissimis perturbaretur incursibus." The source is Constantinus,
Pantegni iv.9, cited by Gregory, 169-70 n. 2.

physiological outline from Constantinus' *Pantegni* and *Liber de Oculis*. From these sources Bernard took the general divisions of the brain, *phantasia* operating in the front, *ratio* in the middle, and *memoria* in the back. From them as well, he took the notion that "the brain is the origin and foundation of the senses and voluntary motion."[94] All the characteristics that Bernard imputes to the senses moreover are summarized in a single paragraph in the same book:

[Sunt] sensus quinque, quibus subtilior et acutior est visus. Ejusque sensus est igneus, igneam habens naturam, id est splendorem, ruborem, et lumen. . . . Post visum est auditus: cujus sensus est aereus, et quod aeri pertinet est vox. Vox enim non est aliud nisi aer ictus vel ictus aeris. Post auditum est odoratus, cujus sensus est fumosus: fumus enim est res inter aquam et aerem existens aeri commixta. Post odoratum est gustus: quidquid sentit est aquosum et aque pertinet; sapor enim qui sentitur nihil aliud est nisi aqua alicujus rei siccitati commixta calore in eo operante. . . . Ceteris autem sensibus tactus est grossior, quia quod sentitur est terreum vel terre pertinet, id est durum, molle, calidum, frigidum, siccum, et humidum et que ex eis procedunt.[95]

There are five senses, of which the most subtle and acute is sight. It is a fiery sense, that is, it has a fiery

---

[94] *Constantini Monachi Montecassini liber de oculis*, ed. P. Pansier (Paris [1933]), ii.1; p. 171: "Cerebrum autem intium est et fundamentum sensus et voluntarii motus, . . ." Bernard expresses a similar idea at ii.13.142-43: "Sensus igitur uno de fonte prodeunt, sed diversas expediunt actiones." He thus incorporates Constantinus' notion and that of identity and difference; *Liber de Oculis*, in *Opera omnia ysaac*, cap. 3, f. clxxii verso.

[95] *Loc. cit.* A somewhat different text is produced in the *Opera omnia ysaac*, *loc. cit.*

base [which produces] its splendor, glow, and light.
. . . After sight is hearing. It is an aereal sense, and
what pertains to the air is the voice; for the voice is
nothing but air struck or the striking of the air. After
hearing comes the sense of smell which is vaporous,
for vapor is something which exists between water
and air, mixed with air. After smell comes taste:
whatever it senses pertains to the aqueous and to water.
For the taste which is sensed is nothing but the liquid
of something mixed with dryness, with heat operating
in it. Of the other senses the least subtle is touch, since
what it senses pertains to the earthly or to earth, that
is, what is hard, soft, warm, cold, dry, or wet or what
is produced from these.

Among the senses, sight has a predominant importance
for Bernard because, like all medieval authors, he considered light to be the closest earthly manifestation of
divinity. His reasoning, again, is from the greater world
to the lesser. The eyes, located in the head, function like
the sun, the *oculus mundi*:

> Intima lux animeque dies concurrit ad ignis
>   solaris radios ethereumque jubar.
> De quo concursu vis et natura videndi
>   essendi causam materiamque trahit
> ad formas rerum; se porrigit hujus acumen
>   lucis, et examen judiciale facit.[96]

The inner light and daylight of the soul correspond to
the rays of solar fire [in the greater world] and to
their ethereal glory. From the [general] concourse
[of light], the power and capacity of seeing draws the
cause and matter of what exists towards the forms of
the things themselves. The piercing quality of this

[96] *Cos.* ii.14.15-20.

light stretches itself forth and makes a judicial examination.

Bernard perceives moreover that the eye does not possess an absolute but a normative capacity for discernment and that it works best with images similar to those it knows. Physis makes sure that this "domestic lighting system"[97] is housed in a suitable compartment and concludes her description with the anecdote of Empedocles, who, when asked why he was alive, replied, "so that I may see the stars. Take away the heavens, and I shall be nothing."[98] A similar treatment is given to hearing. Though less important than sight, it too is explained with a combination of poetic and mechanistic terms:

> Arteriis sonus egreditur vacuumque repellit
>   aera; percussus percutit ille alium,
> donec ad extremos elanguit ultima fines
>   motio per tractus extenuata suos.
> Aer materiam, formam, instrumenta resignant:
>   hinc illinc speciem vocis et esse trahit.
> Lingua sonos ferit in formam vocisque monetam
>   et suus huic operi malleus esse potest.
> Officiis formata suis substantia vocis
>   ad patulas aures articulata venit.
> Auriculis quasi vestibulo suscepta priore
>   vox sonat, et trahitur interiore domo.
> Sermonis numeros extraque sonantia verba
>   auris sed ratio significata capit.
> Quod foris auditus, interpres lingua quod intus est
>   monstrat et alterius postulat alter opem.[99]

Sound goes forth on its paths and strikes the empty air. One bit of air, being struck, strikes another, and

[97] ii.14.25: ". . . lucique domestica lux est."
[98] ii.14.45-48.   [99] ii.14.51-66.

the effect is extenuated through its waves until the final ending fades into nothing. Air redistributes the matter, the instruments [which strike?], the form: here and there [sound] draws the form of the voice and its being. The tongue forges sounds into the monetary form of the voice, and, [what is more], it is capable of being its own hammer for the job. The substance formed for the voice [to carry out] its own offices, once articulated, comes to the open ears. When the voice sounds it is taken into the first vestibule of the ears and then drawn into the interior compartments. The ear receives the numerical proportions of speech and the words sounding without, while reason grasps what is signified. What is outside, the hearing interprets; what is within, the tongue demonstrates, and each needs the other's help.

Like Bernard's conception of sight, then, hearing is primarily physical and physiological, revealing on every line a strongly empirical bias.

The most unusual feature of Bernard's outline of the senses, however, is his description of sexual reproduction, which is not only a fitting conclusion to the *Cosmographia*, which began with the symbolic portrait of the self-reproducing fertility of matter, but perhaps the most fascinating discussion of the theme in the twelfth century. Physis, again, is the *artifex*, but Bernard also brings into his physiology of sex the important relation between Natura and fate that operates in the greater world. Sexual reproduction is for Bernard a type of paradox, the ultimate mystery of life in death and death in life:

> Corporis extremum lascivum terminat inguen,
>   pressa sub occidua parte pudenda latent.
> Jocundusque tamen et eorum commodus usus,
>   si quando, qualis, quantus oportet erit.

Secula ne pereant decisaque cesset origo
et repetat primum massa soluta chaos,
ad genios fetura duos concessit et olim
commissum geminis fratribus illud opus.
Cum morte invicti pugnant genialibus armis,
naturam reparant perpetuantque genus.
Non mortale mori, non quod cadit esse caducum,
non a stirpe hominem deperiisse sinunt.
Militat adversus Lachesin sollersque renodat
mentula Parcarum fila resecta manu.
Defluit ad renes cerebri regione remissus
sanguis et albentis spermatis instar habet.
Format et effingit sollers Natura liquorem,
ut simili genesis ore reducat avos.
Influit ipsa sibi mundi Natura superstes,
permanet, et fluxu pascitur usque suo;
scilicet ad summam rerum jactura recurrit,
nec semel ut possit sepe perire perit.
Longe disparibus causis mutandus in horas
effluit occiduo corpore totus homo. . . .
Membra quibus mundus non indiget, illa necesse
Physis in humana conditione daret.[100]

The members for sex terminate the lascivious extreme of the body. The sexual organs lie hidden, pressed under a concealed part [of the body]. Yet their use is joyful and fitting if it takes place when, in what manner and to what extent it is necessary. Lest the centuries, cut off, perish, lest what has arisen cease to be and the dissolved mass repeat original chaos, the bringing forth of the newborn is conceded to two *genii* (for long ago this work had been entrusted to twin brothers). The unconquerable armies of procreation fight with death, renew nature, and perpetuate the

[100] ii.14.153-180.

species. They do not permit what is dying to die, what is falling to fall, nor do they allow mankind to perish from its stalk.

The sexual member fights against Lachesis and energetically reties the thread cut off by the hand of Fate. [During intercourse] blood, sent from the region of the brain, flows down to the loins. It has the appearance of white sperm. Skilful Natura shapes and fashions this liquid so that the process of reproduction brings back one's ancestors with a similar face. Natura herself, surviving the world, flows into herself and [yet] remains unchanged: to that extent she is nourished by her own flux. Clearly, what is discarded flows back to the highest and does not die once so that it may die often. The whole of man, who is to be changed continually by widely unequal forces, flows out from a body doomed to die. . . .

These are the members which [the greater] world does not need. It is necessary for Physis to present them in the human condition.

This verse physiology is developed out of a single well-known paradox, common to Christian and pagan writings. Bernard expressed it briefly in i.2, stating that the *fomes sensificus* of the world-soul "sic maneat ut perire non possit"[101] (may endure in such a way that it cannot perish). The notion is transformed in his closing verses into an enigmatic summary of his whole theory of creativity. The sexual member, he says, prevents humanity from reverting to the *massa soluta*, the chaos with which the *Cosmographia* began. The two *genii* are very probably the masculine and feminine aspects of creativity latent in matter. Repeated

[101] i.2.179.

at the level of the *microcosmus*, they may also be alluding to the twin *genii* of marriage mentioned by Censorinus,[102] for sexual reproduction should only take place at a suitable time—possibly a moment when the stars are right—in an accepted manner and presumably for the purpose of perpetuating the race. In a purely physiological context they may also represent the testicles.[103] In a brilliant series of parallels with the greater world, Bernard sees the *phallus* doing battle with fate, and Natura, vindicating both sides of the paradox, flows into man, the lesser world, thus surviving herself. What is not used in reproduction reascends immediately to the brain, just as the soul remigrates to the heavens after its sojourn on earth. Thus Bernard's description of sex, while primarily physiological, does not neglect to recapitulate three of the major themes in the *Cosmographia*: the self-regenerative qualities of primary substances; the One and the Many, which the reproductive process completes as a cycle in man; and the hierarchy, involving, in the lesser world, a certain descent and reassimilation. Physis, echoing the *Timaeus*, concludes the book by stating that the greater world, a perfect sphere, has no need of the limbs which, in the human condition, must be supplied.

---

[102] *De Die Natali*, cap. 3.3; ed. F. Hultsch, p. 5: "Nonnulli binos genios in his dumtaxat domibus quae essent maritae colendos putaverunt." Cf. T. Silverstein, *Modern Philology* 46 (1948-49), 109 n. 118. Firmicus mentions two similar *fratres* simply as *genii*, *Matheseos* i.5-6; vol. i, p. 16.

[103] Peter Dronke cites a relevant passage from Constantinus Africanus, *Liber Maior de Coitu*, in *SMed* 6 (1965), 415 n. 92. Cf. *De Testiculis*, in *Pantegni* iii.36; *Opera omnia ysaac*, f. 14va. The Cambridge commentary on Martianus Capella appears to base its discussion of sex on Constantinus; e.g. f. 2vb: "Semina dicunt quelibet rerum initia ut elementa et tempora mundi. . . ." There is a longer discussion of sex and reproduction at f. 4va.

Sources and Meaning

To summarize Bernard's use of his source material, attention may be drawn to certain general themes which run through the last act of *Microcosmus* (ii.9-14): the idea of fertility, presented in the opening scene in Granusion and reiterated in the closing lines on reproduction; the division of the sciences, which provide a division of labor in making man's frame and are then internalized as parts of human psychology; the union of Bernard's two favorite sciences, astrology and medicine, with classical theories of the human mind; a highly sensorial approach to the world and man, through which *homo*, like *terra* in the *Asclepius*, is himself a fount of creativity resonating with the higher levels; and finally, a further application of the oft-repeated idea of Identity and Difference, related now to the moral allegory through man, who completes the essentially beneficent process of descent and reascent.

Granusion is, as noted above, the stage upon which the climax of the drama is enacted. Man's creation there by Noys, Urania, Natura, and Physis is an entirely existential process; that is, it takes place on earth rather than in heaven (or even in the abstract) and involves principles which may be called natural laws. Even Urania, the most celestial of the three, has come down to earth for the event, and Bernard's preference for the empirically definable is evident throughout. Of the three *genii*, the chief role, besides that of Noys, is played by Physis. She is the *genius* of Granusion, master of the "vegetative soul" and the physical sciences. It is she who, as *faber*, makes man, and the terms she uses (*fabricata, machinamenta*) suggest a more mechanical process than in the *Timaeus*, as if Physis were literally hammering man together out of primitive materials. As in i.2 and 4, Bernard manages in his images to create the dual impression of matter as something divine and mysterious and at the same time mundane, earthly, and near at hand. The introduction of Physis may also be interpreted as a preference, as in *Megacosmus*, for the Stoic/Aristotelian as opposed to the neoplatonic in Chalcidius. Bernard seems, in fact, to have partially replaced the Platonic *demiurgos*, who, in the figure of Noys, hovers over the dark abyss of chaos in book one, with the more genial figure of Aristotle's conscious craftsman, who puts the body together from a pre-existent design. To this idea Bernard joins another: Physis as the preserver of the health of the body through the operations of the four humors. Man, like the world, is not only a *sensilis mundus;* he is a healthy *mundus.* And one of the most surprising features of *Microcosmus* as a whole is how profoundly Bernard's image of the world has been influenced by his image of man. The *sensilis mundus* is almost an "anthropological" idea in the *Cosmographia.*

The daughters of Physis, Theory and Practice, represent not only the normal division of the sciences in classical treatises like Boethius.[104] They incorporate the division of medical knowledge from the *Pantegni* of Constantinus Africanus. This work is not notable for its excursions into pure philosophy; Constantinus, unlike Abu Ma'shar, did not envisage medicine as the queen in a pyramid of sciences. He does however make it clear that medical knowledge is divided into theory and practice,[105] and it was this natural-scientific adaptation of the classical division which Bernard developed into a general categorization of all exact, predictive sciences. The twin aspects of Physis' pow-

[104] *Consol. Phil.* i, pr. 1, 16-22.

[105] *Pantegni* i.3; in *Opera omnia ysaac,* f. lvb: "Omnis ergo medicina aut theorica est aut practica. Theorica est perfecta noticia rerum solo intellectu capiendarum, subiecta memorie rerum operandarum. Practica est subjectam theoricam demonstrare in propatulo sensuum et operatione manuum secundum preeuntis theorice intellectum."

er also provide the key for relating her activities to those of Natura. In ii.9, Bernard refers to Natura as the *mater generationis*. The phrase, as noted above, is probably indebted to Abu Ma'shar. Its context, however, is largely Aristotelian. In the *Introductorium* i.2, the Arab astrologer treats in a general fashion the relation between the upper and the lower world and the relation of these to the two processes, *corruptio* and *generatio*. Nature is here conceived as one of the three fundamental forces bringing about change. She has an innate action, as when, for example, "fire, mediating heat, renders water hot."[106] In this sense Natura is said to be the "mother of generative change" since, as an innate force, she produces change "ex . . . actu et passione"[107] (out of activity and passivity). Throughout the *Cosmographia*, God, matter, and nature possess active and passive sides. In the case of the first two, this relationship is expressed as a difference of sex or as different aspects of the same thing (e.g. *silva/hyle*). In the case of Natura, it is translated into the theoretical and practical aspects of Physis, her helper; it is allegorized in her daughters. Thus Bernard, who emphasizes the practical over the purely theoretical in Natura's preference for Jupiter over Saturn, recreates the same idea by emphasizing Physis' mastery of the practical arts. In general, the growth of *praxis* would seem to be an integral part of Natura's initiation.

Granusion, then, is a type of earthly paradise which creates as well as represents perfect creation; it is the location in which Physis, that is, theoretical and practical knowledge at the earthly level, makes man. Is man then an

---

[106] *Introductorium* i.2; f.[a.5 recto]: ". . . ut cum ignis aquam mediante calore calidam reddit."

[107] *Ibid.* f.[a.5 verso]: "Quoniam et illius nature nec huiusmodi virtus inest et huius natura eiusmodi virtutis receptiva ex quo actu et passione mundi natura permixtio sit generationum omnium mater." Cf. Ch. II, n. 7.

"earthly" creature? Two aspects of his formation would point in the direction of such an interpretation: the mechanical way in which he works and his capacity to respond to sensorial stimuli. Although Bernard states on more than one occasion that man is both material and spiritual, his creation of man is almost entirely expressed in materialistic terms. It may be argued that the first act of *Microcosmus*, Urania's descent of the soul, is a spiritual activity, but even there Bernard's major preoccupation lies in presenting an astrological explanation of the heavens and of their influence on man. He has, so to speak, through astrology, dissipated some of the mystery of the soul, just as, through physics, medicine, and the mechanical arts, he proceeds to give a rational account of man. In Bernard's mind, moreover, matter, mechanics, and the senses are somehow linked to the amelioration of man: the *membra* of man, like the parts of the cosmos are, in Physis' term, *reformanda.*[108] Urania and Natura, in addition, are received on earth as guests; that is to say, *ratio*, after its ascent to the heavens, returns to earth with the knowledge of the heavens. What the two goddesses represent is then incorporated into man's psychology. And it is here that Bernard completes his union of classical theories of the mind with astrology and natural science.

Bernard has in fact incorporated a good deal of the eclecticism of *Megacosmus* into this part of *Microcosmus*. He does not, on the whole, present man's psychology in a systematic fashion. What results is the superimposition of parts of different theories, loosely united under the cover of allegory. As in his account of the greater world, he has absorbed certain fundamental features of human psychology from the *Timaeus*, for example, the view that the rational part of man is situated in the head, the emotive

---

[108] *Cos.* ii.13.64.

in the breast, and the appetite in the abdomen. Within the Platonic framework, however, other ideas make their appearance. From Stoicism and astrology Bernard draws the idea that sight is the most important sense, representing the *ignis divinus* and the sun's forces in man. From neoplatonism, and, very possibly, from the theological anthropology of Scottus Eriugena, he has taken the idea that Natura, representing the *causae primordiales* in the outside world, is internalized as *humana natura*.[109] Bernard's conception of Natura within man, however, is not primarily neoplatonic. Natura, like Urania, has a natural-scientific side. It is possible to see the incorporation of the attributes of the two goddesses into man as a recreation of Aristotle's interpretation of Plato's "divided and undivided" substance of the world-soul in terms of wisdom and prudence, theoretical and practical knowledge.[110]

But Bernard's idea is in fact even more subtle than this. For him, both Urania and Natura have an active and a passive, a practical and a theoretical side. Moreover, in the division of labor in making man, each has a specifically scientific function. Urania is assigned the stellar manifestation of Noys' providential design for man, while Natura, through fatalistic causality, is given its working out in time. Thus Plato's Intelligence and Necessity are recreated in a quite different ambience. Finally, in having man made in Granusion, Bernard is also subtly adapting astrological notions to Aristotle. For Macrobius and Abu Ma'shar, the lunar sphere governs vegetative activity inasmuch as man, as an earthly creature, shares certain characteristics in common with all things made in the *humecta substantia*. But Aristotle's interpretation of practical wisdom as prudence included the "polity" for which man is made. This

[109] See Stock, *SMed* 7 (1967) 1-57.

[110] M. McCrimmon, "The Classical Philosophical Sources," 146-47.

union is close to the suggestion of the following lines, cited
above:

> Cuditur artifici circumspectoque politu,
> fabrica Nature primipotentis, homo.[111]

Man, the contrivance of first-power Nature, is fashioned
for his craftsman [= Physis] and for one circumspect
to polish.

Thus man's cultivation, his improvement, his very creation
have two sides: he is both made in the image of his creator
for his greater glory and as a fitting culmination for
creation in the sense that he will rule over it.

Bernard, lastly, sees man as a *sensilis mundus,* a sensorial
cosmos. Man's senses are also related directly to the mechanical arts. In a period when the mechanical arts were
still, by and large, considered "adulterine,"[112] Bernard appears to have a more positive evaluation of their role. The
introduction of Physis, Natura's craftsman, at the climactic
moment in the drama cannot easily be interpreted in any
other way. It is worth recalling however that this positive
attitude towards the senses and the mechanical arts makes
its appearance very early in the *Cosmographia.* In i.3, when
the cosmos unfolds before the reader, Bernard indicates
that the *ornatus elementorum* is the result of necessity and
predictable from the stars. The world unfolds mechanically
in space and is primarily apprehensible through its material, sensible manifestation. It is no longer an image

---

[111] *Cos.* ii.14.1-2. See above, Ch. II, n. 27.

[112] E.g., Hugh of St. Victor, *Didascalicon* i.5, whose ideas may be
traced to the *Asclepius*; see J. Taylor, *The Didascalicon of Hugh of
St. Victor* (New York/London, 1961), 184 n. 32. The problem of
the mechanical arts in the twelfth century with special relation to
Hugh is treated by F. Alessio, *SMed* 6 (1965), 71-161. A useful
summary of medieval classifications of the sciences is provided by J.
Weisheipl, *MS* 27 (1965), 54-90.

but a reality. Certain of Bernard's classical sources present the visible world in a similarly positive light—notably the *Asclepius*—but none of them unites the senses with mechanical activity in quite this way. Nor are educational treatises written by his contemporaries as keenly aware of the problem as he was. A possible exception is provided by the Martianus *Commentary* in Cambridge University Library MS Mm.I.18. The division of the sciences in this work (ff. 5ra-vb) is in some respects similar to that of William of Conches, to whose pragmatic views on the role of the political and practical arts in civilization it may be compared.[113] Yet there are also important differences. The Martianus *Commentary* divides *scientia*, things which can be known, into four classes: *sapientia, eloquentia, poesis,* and *mecania*.[114] The virtue of each branch is to remedy its lack in the world at large. Thus, for example, wisdom relieves *ignorantia* and provides *agnitio*. The mechanical arts are said to relieve *defectus* and to establish *valetudo*. *Defectus* here may be interpreted simply as privation. The medical overtones of *valetudo* however suggest a context not dissimilar from Bernard's. In ii.7, Urania uses a variant of the same term (*defectius*) and Bernard throughout employs a number of synonyms to indicate that *ornatus*—in both a cosmological and a mechanical sense—relieves the defects *ab antiqua silve malitia*.[115] If this interpretation is correct, then Physis the craftsman is intimately involved not only in the creation of man but in his *reformatio*. This idea, however, compels an examination of Bernard's myth in the light of other conceptions of natural change in the twelfth century.

[113] E.g. [*Glosae super Boetium*], ed. C. Jourdain, *Excursions historiques et philosophiques à travers le moyen âge* (Paris, 1888), 34-35; *Glosae super Platonem*, ed. Jeauneau, cap. 2 (*accessus*); pp. 58-61.

[114] MS Mm.I.18, f. 5ra. Cf. Ch. I, n. 42. [115] *Cos.* ii.7.100-02.

CHAPTER V

Bernard and Twelfth-Century Naturalism

1. A Résumé

BEFORE turning to the problem of Bernard's relation to his contemporaries, it may be useful to summarize the myth of the *Cosmographia*. This will serve the purpose of bringing together the central points in the previous analysis as well as providing a framework for the discussion which follows.

In general, the *Cosmographia* may be viewed as a myth in two distinct senses. The first is that of a primitive myth, like the book of Genesis, the *Timaeus*, or the various poetic cosmogonies of the ancient world. As such it is an attempt to build a cosmic order before the reader's eyes, to allow him, through poetry, to participate actively in the unfolding of the cosmos from its primordial elements. In this sense the work recreates in a new context the formal features and doctrines of a number of earlier cosmogonies. It brings them up to date, so to speak, by the standards of its own day. The most important earlier model was Plato. Not only was the *Cosmographia* written towards the end of a half-century dominated by Platonism; it consciously adopts the mythical structure of the *Timaeus* as a foundation for constructing a new *narratio fabulosa*. Yet twelfth-century Platonism was not a unified phenomenon, and Bernard's work, which develops the naturalistic tendencies in it, differs in important ways from the original. The chief formal difference is the incorporation into the Platonic model of the structural encyclopedia. But there are others as well. Within the hierarchy of forces that remake the universe—God, Noys, Urania, Natura, Physis, and the astral divinities—Bernard's eclecticism rules out any faithful rapport with Plato. Instead of pure Platonism, one encounters a version of the middle-Platonist world view of the late classical period, typified by Chalcidius, Apuleius, the *Asclepius*, and Firmicus Maternus. To the natural-philosophic material already present in these authors Bernard adds new ideas derived in part from medical theory, through Constantinus Africanus, and Ptolemaic astrology, through Abu Ma'shar. Bernard has been called the medieval Lucretius. It is perhaps more tempting to think of him as an imaginative composite of two Hellenistic figures: Manilius and Posidonius.

The *Cosmographia* may also be considered a modern myth, provided that *modernus* is seen in a twelfth-century perspective.[1] To his contemporaries, Bernard was attempting to present a poetic solution to the problem of the creation of the world and of man, a subject which was treated, as William of Conches notes, by *fere omnes modernos*. Bernard's myth reveals how deeply the problem of cosmology had become impregnated with issues current in his own day. The allegorical figures who enact the drama of creation are not merely the recreations of classical arche-

---

[1] Chenu, 81, notes that Ralph de Diceto (1148-1202) understands *modernitas* to refer to his own period of history. This idea is corroborated by the philosophers. Gregory, 197 n. 1, cites *loci* in William of Conches as well as an anonymous commentary on the *Timaeus* derived from him and badly edited by T. Schmid, *Classica et Mediaevalia* 10 (1949), 220-66. Alan of Lille informs us that some among the *moderni* held the view that matter is eternal; *Quoniam Homines* 1.5d, ed. P. Glorieux, *AHDLMA* 20 (1954), 129: "Fuerunt etiam inter modernos quidam qui dixerunt primordialem materiam fuisse ab eterno et tamen ab ipso Deo procedere sicut splendor procedit ab igne." What better summary could one have of Bernard's view?

types. They all embody new and original, often scientific, elements. Noys, the Stoic *pronoia*, Chalcidius' *providentia*, and Macrobius' *mens divina*, is now as well an astrological figure, a Minerva who weaves together the cosmic fabric according to a predictable, if divine, model. Urania, Martianus' muse of the heavens, now looks after applied astronomy, that is, astrological calculation. Natura, the late classical intermediary between God and the world, is now the spirit of inquiry into the natural universe—perhaps the author himself—and the secrets she discloses on her Hermetic voyage of initiation turn out to be the new science making its appearance in Bernard's day. Physis, Aristotle's conscious craftsman, puts man together from the leftover elements and inquires in an experimental manner into all sublunary phenomena, thus preserving the medieval view of Aristotelianism as a science of the lower world. Yet she now emerges as Natura's indispensable helper and seems to be expert, not only in the topics of the *Categories*, but in a wide variety of disciplines including medicine and the mechanical arts. Even God hovers between Stoic, neoplatonic, and astrological configurations. What Bernard has effected, in short, is a metamorphosis of the late classical universe of allegory under the influence of twelfth-century natural philosophy. As noted elsewhere, the dusk of the ancient gods is for him the birth of rational science.

This second, consciously modern conception of myth, however, is absorbed into the first. Like Adelard, Thierry of Chartres, and William of Conches, Bernard remains faithful to the cultural ideals of the first half-century. He never allows his interest in the *quadrivium* to overpower the integrative capacities of the *trivium*. He remains, so to speak, between the two worlds of myth and science.

One means by which he bridges the two is by adopting a doctrine implict in the *Timaeus* and elaborated by later interpreters of it: namely, that ultimate philosophical or scientific realities cannot be adequately described in straight-forward language. Bernard's answer to this problem is to express them indirectly through metaphor, myth, and allegory. Throughout the *Cosmographia*, allegory is not only a literary device through which diverse ideas may be synthesized; it is a serious philosophical tool for which Bernard sees no alternative. There are, in fact, many overlapping uses of allegory in the work: to represent stellar divinities within the great living being of the cosmos, to symbolize disciplines, and, on occasion, to admit a certain degree of alienation from the dominant cultural dogmatics. The most important use however is not literary but philosophic; it is an attempt to revive Macrobius' vaguely expressed notion that mysteries like God and the soul cannot be reduced to hard cold facts. This idea, the catechism of neoplatonism, is refined and extended in Bernard's subtle imagination. In the *Cosmographia* not only God and the *anima mundi* but Noys, Matter, and, at times, the elemental forces and physical localities like Granusion are allegorized. They emerge suddenly onto the dramatic stage, make their epic appearances, and then recede when their parts are done. The most ingenious allegory is that of Matter. Here Bernard is surpassed by no one, not even by Lucretius. Some would dismiss him as a serious natural philosopher because he was a poet. But he would have seen the issue the other way round. For him, poetry was the only vehicle capable of overcoming the inherent weakness of the language of science.

On first reading, the *Cosmographia* presents the reader with a bewildering variety of forces, deities, and interrelationships, all cloaked quite intentionally in obscure and difficult language. Yet the major principles around which the work is organized are only three: order, creativity, and matter.

To the imagination in the twelfth century, Fr. Chenu has observed, order and hierarchy exerted the same seductive attraction as did the idea of evolution in the nineteenth.[2] Yet, he correctly adds, these notions were not interpreted by all writers in the same way.[3] Bernard's idea of hierarchical order, heavily indebted to the *Asclepius* and to Dionysian Platonism, is first of all natural-philosophic. Through the motion of the universal hierarchy, nourishment is provided by the stars and the celestial fire which surrounds them for all levels of life below, while from the earth, the process of natural regeneration reaches upwards towards the heavens. *Ordo*, however, is also related to *ornatus*, the structured unfolding of the contents of the universe in an ordered design. By conceiving order not as a static but as a dynamic process *in perpetuum*, Bernard unites the natural-philosophic hierarchy from Hermeticism with the *exornatio mundi* of Platonism. The synthesis is achieved through allegory. At every level of the creative process, an allegorical deity acts as a Hermetic *ousiarch*, presiding over the creative forces of its own sphere. As a poet, Bernard attempts to express this dynamic ordering of the elements in visual terms. In *Cosmographia* i.1 and 2, the rude elements of chaotic matter succeed to the ordered dance of creation; in i.3, the music is given words as the encyclopedic whole of creation springs to life. Even in the relation between the macro- and the microcosm order is given a high priority, for as man is created in both mind and body, he gradually begins to understand the music of the elements as an extension of his own sensorial world. Thus Bernard transforms in a highly individualistic way the notion of order so familiar to medieval thought between Augustine and Dante, which was given a classical treatment in Boethius, *Consolatio Philosophiae* iii, meter 9.

[2] Chenu, 33.　　　　　[3] *Ibid.* 129-30 n. 2.

Bernard's conception of order is much more readily understandable than his notions of creativity and matter. Again, the most formative influence on his doctrine of creativity was Hermeticism. Bernard was highly attracted by the *Asclepius*' combination of Stoic physical theory and eastern mystery religion, by its simultaneous acceptance of the real world and its refusal to reduce the hidden truths to banal exactitudes. Throughout the *Cosmographia* creativity is virtually synonymous with God himself. The *exsuperantissimus deus* in one of his aspects is the benevolent creator of Genesis and the *Timaeus*; in another, he displays himself as the operative principle of creativity in the world. For Bernard, the process of creation—which is for him the essence of the problem of creation—is continuous, having neither beginning nor end. From time to time the process submits to renewal, and at each stage, predictable from the stars, certain improvements are presumably made. Yet the creative changes themselves proceed eternally; they consist of a displacement of God's creative energies down through the cosmic order. At the elemental level they infiltrate the *primordia rerum* and their forms, which flow in an endless stream from the bosom of matter. At the celestial level they inform the world-soul and give it life. At all levels they complete the natural processes of *generatio* and *corruptio*. The same creativity is found in those two living creatures, *mundus* and *homo*, comprising an essential part of their divinity.

The originality of Bernard's idea of creativity is matched by his conception of matter. Matter is really the unsung heroine of the *Cosmographia*. Unlike Plato, Bernard did not see cosmogony as a story in which gods created by the god mould the body of the world out of the four elements, which are more or less passive, plastic instruments. He saw cosmogony as the working out of the *possibilitas* latent in matter: the imposition of form from without is matched by matter's internal longing for form. The creative element within matter is much larger than in either Plato or, on most occasions, in Chalcidius. It is closer to the modern view of matter as an active substance composed of charged atoms. Whether as a substance or as an allegorical deity, moreover, matter is never far from the dramatic action. In the opening verses, Silva is the subject of Natura's lament; *Megacosmus* consists, in large part, of the ordering of matter and what issues from it. In *Microcosmus*, matter is again the foundation for creative activity. Physis builds man from leftover matter and, in ii.13 and 14, man's physical frame is used to explain his sensorial reactions in an empirical manner. In sum, for a number of reasons matter may be described as a central force in the *Cosmographia*. First of all, it is coterminous with God; in one of his aspects God manifests himself in material form. Secondly, matter is self-reproducing; it thus perpetuates its own existence without interference from above. Thirdly, in the union of body and soul, matter is the more dynamic of the two. Thus Bernard, through his conception of matter, appears to be biased towards the empirical and tangible, not the spiritual, towards this rather than the other world. As noted above, the real world has acquired a value in his eyes that transcends the normal limits of Platonism. Through allegory he has evolved a philosophical position definable as a highly individualistic type of materialism.

One aspect of Bernard's materialism is an unusual interpretation of moral allegory. In twelfth-century Platonism, moral allegory is normally related to metaphysics; in Bernard it is limited to physics. He achieves this through a dual conception of matter, that is, before and after it has been ordered. Before *ornatus* takes place, matter is formless, chaotic, rude, and graceless; afterwards, it is patterned, obedient, polished, and beautiful. The attribution of value categories to unformed and formed matter is the essential element in Bernard's conception of moral allegory. His emphasis throughout is upon the experience of creativity within the creative act, not upon the created product; thus matter is never a static substance but a creational force that needs to have its primitive energy controlled and ordered. He speaks of the rigor, tension, and primordial force of matter. His cosmos is a network of interwoven forces and powers, maintained in a fragile state of stability as order (the good) just manages to overcome disorder (the evil). Tactile and, occasionally, Manichaean[4] images are employed to portray matter's release from the evil inherent in itself: in i.1, chaos is like the raging center of a molecule in which the atoms are continually opposing each other's forces; similar images occur in i.2, when Noys bridles the elements, and in ii.12, when Physis expresses her doubts about matter's capacity for order. Throughout the *Cosmographia*, therefore, the moral allegory is linked to the improvement of matter's external features. This is the reason why the *exornatio mundi* takes place.

What unites the two senses of myth, the "primitive" and the "modern," is the conception of reform that develops out of Bernard's replacement of moral with physical allegory. The idea of reform occurs at a number of important points in the *Cosmographia*, since it is of central interest to Bernard that the cosmos is in some mysterious way not only experiencing creation but recreation. In employing the concept, he is clearly building upon another foundation laid by his classical sources. As Gerhart Ladner has assiduously demonstrated,[5] the idea of reform is one of the central moral and physical doctrines of the patristic age. Throughout the period it acquires a largely moral significance which is embodied in Christian writings and adapted to institu-

---

[4] Cf. Gregory, 199 and 199 nn. 1-7.
[5] *The Idea of Reform*, 39-315.

tions like monasticism. The patristic tradition of reform reaches its apogee and turning point in John Scottus Eriugena, the ninth-century thinker whose notion of cosmic *reformatio* attempts, not altogether successfully, to unite the Augustinian and Greek patristic strands.[6] John's translation of the Pseudo-Denis helps to reintroduce the Greek idea of circular, physical reform into the West. In the twelfth century Hermetic and astrological notions are added to the Dionysian. No one is as radical in his interpretation of reform in the earlier twelfth century as Bernard. For him, it is entirely experienced in physical terms and only through them does moral reform derive any meaning. It is possible to regard Bernard as a reviver of the physical significance of the notion before the accretions of morality in the patristic age. Yet this view would neglect what is most fundamental in his idea of reform: its progressive character. In the *Cosmographia*, reform is not only brought about by the physical ordering of the elements in the world and in man. It also involves man's cultural achievements, especially the conquest of the secrets of the natural universe. It is progressive, inasmuch as the world is reformed, and therefore man, so that man may understand the world better. This view, a skilful blending of classical and twelfth-century ideals, may be described as a new stage of philosophical anthropology in the West, the re-emergence of naturalistic man.

The notion of reform occurs at various stages of the cosmic drama. It comprises, first of all, a good part of Natura's complaint. She is not only asking that chaos be resolved into order but that a new order, presumably to replace the old, be brought about. Thus, from the first, reform is predictable from the stars and progressive in nature. Again,

[6] For a brief summary, see Stock, *Harv. Theol. Rev.* 60 (1967), 213-20.

when Noys replies to Natura in i.2, she states that under her guidance "usie pepigi reformetur in melius"[7] (I have composed material being [so that] it be reformed into something better). In bringing the raging elements under control, Noys repeats the same formula;[8] and God, approving of the way in which his plan has been implemented, repeats it again.[9] God's approval is of course important in both the Platonic and astrological senses. For it is not only his *voluntas* that informs the world but his creative energy, through which all cosmic processes, including reform, take place. In *Microcosmus*, when man is being made, the idea occurs still again. Man, the *minor mundus*, is "able to be reformed" to the degree that his soul, entering his material frame, imitates the activity of the *anima mundi* in the world.[10] In this sense, the elaborate programming of the human soul in ii.5-9 is part of the ordering, or *reformatio*, of man. Lastly, the idea of reform is the ingenious device by which Bernard harmonizes the primitive and modern elements in his myth. The new man,

[7] *Cos.* i.2.36. [8] i.2.94: "species reformavit."

[9] i.2.127-34: "Bona vidit que fecisset omnia Deique visibus placitura. . . . Plenum enim et consummatum necesse erat compositum componentia reformarent, ubi plena et consummata perfectione, iota per essentiam, tota per potentiam, ignis, terra cetereque materie convenissent."

[10] ii.12.51-60:

Herentem rubuere due partesque laboris;
    has Urania subit:
expugnare malum silve fluidamque tenere
    limite materiam
humanumque genus, quamvis mortale trahatur
    conditione sua,
tale reformandum quod demigrare supernos
    possit adusque deos,
et dare sub leges quicquid torquente rotatu
    stellifer axis agit. . . .

the *fabrica Nature primipotentis*, is not just primeval man at the beginning of the world. He recapitulates human and cosmic history and restates them both in twelfth-century terms. There is not only a reform of the world and of man but of man's conception of reform which continually submits to renewal as new scientific information is discovered. Thus, for Bernard, reform is not an arbitrary act that concludes with the creation of the world and of man. It is a continuous aspect of creativity itself.

2. Thierry of Chartres, William of Conches, and Daniel of Morley

If the above interpretation is accepted, then Bernard's achievement as a mythmaker and as a natural philosopher ranks among the finest products of twelfth-century humanism. Yet the subject to which he gave poetic treatment— the origin of the world and of man—was dealt with by others in a wide variety of works: in hexaemera, in commentaries on Plato and later Platonists, and in original treatises on natural philosophy. Many of these works possess a similar problem orientation, and historians, viewing them in a broad perspective, have tended to assume that Bernard presents only slight variations on a generalized world picture. This assumption has never been genuinely put to the test, and it would be too large a task to do so in a comprehensive fashion here. Yet a specific comparison of texts between the *Cosmographia* and some other contemporary (or near contemporary) cosmologies may illustrate the degree to which it is supported by evidence.

Selecting the candidates for comparison is not easy, but three authors appear to stand out above the rest: Thierry of Chartres, William of Conches, and Daniel of Morley. Thierry was the master to whom Bernard dedicated the

Cosmographia, and his hexaemeron is found in a manuscript of Tours,[11] where Bernard taught. William is close to Bernard in his theory of myth, in his use of the structural encyclopedia, and in his close reading of the classics. Daniel, who belongs to the next generation, offers still another perspective. A student at Toledo until around 1175, he presents a fusion of the older Platonic cosmology, associated with Chartres, and the new science. He therefore offers a standard for evaluating Bernard's absorption of Arabic philosophy. To these three, two others should perhaps be added: Adelard of Bath and Hermann of Carinthia. Adelard's relation to Bernard, a possibly indirect one, has been discussed briefly in Chapters I and IV. Hermann, whose only original work was the *De Essentiis* of 1143, is similar to Bernard in dividing the question of cosmology into the superlunary and the sublunary, but quite unlike him on other central issues.[12] Points of comparison between the *Cosmographia* and the poetic myths of Alan of Lille and John de Hauteville could also be found. For the purposes defined above, however, a limited number of authors and texts provides the clearest set of distinctions.

Before turning to the texts, something should perhaps be said about the various careers of Thierry, William, and Daniel. While little is known of Daniel's life, Thierry and William were among the most famous teachers of their day. Thierry is first mentioned as *scholarum magister* at Chartres in 1121.[13] After teaching (it is presumed) at both

[11] Tours, Bibl. Mun., MS 85, ff. 181-83v; for this and other MSS, see N. Haring, *AHDLMA* 22 (1956), 181-82.

[12] Lemay, *Abu Ma'shar*, 204-05, notes: "[Hermann's] division of natural philosophy into a superior and lower science of nature resembles more the division between Metaphysics and Physics in Aristotle and in later scholasticism than it does the division of natural philosophy between celestial and terrestrial physics as in Bernard Silvester, Clarenbald of Arras, and Daniel of Morley."

[13] A. Clerval, *Les écoles de Chartres au moyen âge*, 169.

Chartres and Paris, he returned to Chartres to replace Gilbert Porreta[14] as chancellor in 1141. He was present at the Council of Reims in 1148[15] where Gilbert was on trial and where—however inappropriate to the occasion—Bernard is said to have read his *Cosmographia.* He is assumed to have died before 1155.[16] Of William much less is known for sure. He is thought to have been John of Salisbury's master at Chartres or Paris[17] during John's two sojourns on the continent, 1137-38 and 1140-41, and to have died sometime shortly after 1154.[18] Thierry wrote a grammatical commentary on Cicero's *De Inventione,*[19] a programme for the liberal arts called the *Heptateuchon,*[20] a theological commentary on Boethius' *De Trinitate,*[21] and a short treatise bearing the *incipit, De septem diebus et sex operum distinctionibus.*[22] Jeauneau,[23] William's latest biographer, divides his literary career into three periods: youth (1135-44), when he wrote his brilliant *Philosophia Mundi,* his commentary on Boethius, and the first redaction of his glosses on Priscian and Macrobius; maturity (1145-49), when he purged the *Philosophia* of its heresies and reissued it as the *Dragmaticon,* and, in addition, composed his

[14] *Ibid.* 171.

[15] *Loc. cit.,* where a misprint gives "1048" for 1148. Cf. N. Haring, *AHDLMA* 22 (1956), 138.

[16] Clerval, 172.

[17] Gregory, 1-3, favors Chartres; no genuine evidence has been brought forward to prove that it was not.

[18] M. Manitius, *Geschichte der lat. Literatur des Mittelalters,* vol. 3, 215; cf. E. Jeauneau, *Glosae super Platonem,* 10.

[19] See N. Haring, *MS* 26 (1964), 271-86.

[20] The preface of this work is edited by E. Jeauneau, *MS* 16 (1954), 171-75.

[21] Ed. N. Haring, *AHDLMA* 23 (1957), 257-325.

[22] Ed. N. Haring, *AHDLMA,* 22 (1956), 184-200. For an excellent, if brief, analysis, see E. Jeauneau, *Sophia* 23 (1955), 172-83.

[23] *Glosae super Platonem,* 14.

important commentary on the *Timaeus*; and old age (after 1149), when he completed the second redaction of his lectures on Priscian and perhaps as well on Macrobius. In sum, while Thierry and William were active during Bernard's lifetime and offer the possibility of contemporary influence, Daniel, writing a generation later, may himself have been influenced by all three.

Thierry of Chartres

To turn first to Thierry: whether it actually influenced Bernard or not, the short commentary on Genesis occupies an important place in the twelfth-century debate on myth and science since it is the only purely naturalistic exegesis of the text. It parallels the revival of naturalism in secular literary criticism and in the plastic arts. As a commentary it is a radical document. Instead of following the traditional method of fitting natural philosophy into the historical framework of the Bible, it fits the opening chapters of Genesis into the framework of natural philosophy. It opens with a brilliant statement which may be interpreted as a direct challenge to the Augustinian tradition:

> I propose to elucidate, according to the letter and to physics, the first part of Genesis, which treats the seven days and the distinct activities of the six kinds of works. First I shall say a few words about the intention of the author and the utility of the book. But then I shall proceed to expound the historical sense of the letter, with the result that I shall wholly pass over both the moral and the allegorical reading, which the holy commentators have clearly dealt with exhaustively. For the intention of Moses in this work was to show that the acts of the creation of the world and of the generation of man were carried out by one God only, to whom alone worship and reverence are due. By con-

trast, the utility of this book is a knowledge of God by means of the things he has made. To this God alone ought religious devotion to be displayed.[24]

Thierry thus sees naturalistic exegesis as the complement of moral allegory. Through it, he aims to demonstrate, not that God is omnipotent because he alone creates, but that his omnipotence and transcendence are most clearly revealed in his works. Later he will qualify this statement to avoid the pitfall of pantheism.[25] Yet his orientation towards the existing world rather than the ideal of which it is a copy is unmistakeable. His method, quite simply, is to employ the sciences of the *quadrivium* to demythologize the story of Genesis: "These instruments are to be employed succinctly in this theology, both in order that the artifice of the creator be made manifest in his works and, as I propose, that it be rationally demonstrated."[26]

How does he proceed? First by establishing the parallel between the causes of creation and their theological equivalents. God is the efficient cause; his wisdom, the formal

[24] The edition quoted is that of Haring (see n. 22 above), in which readings are occasionally taken from the notes. Ed. Haring, cap. 1; p. 184 [*accessus*]: "De septem diebus et sex operum distinctionibus primam Geneseos partem secundum physicam et ad litteram ego expositurus, imprimis de intentione auctoris et de libri utilitate pauca praemittam. Postea vero ad sensum litterae historialem exponendum veniam, ut et allegoricam et moralem lectionem, quas, sancti expositores aperte executi sunt, ex toto praetermittam. Intentio igitur Moysi in hoc opere fuit ostendere rerum creationes et hominum generationem factam esse ab uno solo Deo, cui soli cultus et reverentia debetur. Utilitas vero hujus libri est cognitio Dei ex facturis suis, cui soli cultus religionis exhibendus est."

[25] See J. M. Parent, *La doctrine de la création dans l'école de Chartres*, 83-87, and Gregory, 141-47.

[26] Cap. 30, p. 194: "Quibus instrumentis in hac theologia breviter utendum est, ut et artificium creatoris in rebus appareat et, quod proposuimus, rationabiliter ostendatur."

cause; his will, the final cause; and the four elements, the material cause. Since all earthly things are changeable and transitory, it is necessary that they have an author; since they are laid out rationally and by a certain order, that they exhibit wisdom; and since their creator is good, indeed perfect, that he should create the world out of his good will alone, so that he might both possess and participate in his own beatitude through the practice of love.[27] The world proceeds from disorder to order so that his wisdom may be made manifest to those knowledgeable to interpret it. All this, he maintains, will become apparent to one who observes carefully the skilful construction of the cosmos, the *fabrica mundi*.[28]

Each of the seven days of creation is called a *dies naturalis*, which is defined as "the space of time in which one whole revolution of the heavens is completed from beginning to beginning."[29] As the Bible is inconsistent on temporal relationships, Thierry adopts the traditional allegorical method of proposing different interpretations in order to harmonize them.[30] When the inconsistencies have been

[27] Cap. 2, p. 184: "Mundanae igitur substantiae (substantiae ACQR; subsistentiae, Haring) causae sunt quattuor: efficiens ut Deus, formalis ut Dei sapientia, finalis ut ejusdem benignitas, materialis, quattuor elementa. Necesse est enim, quia mutabilia et caduca sunt mundana, eadem habere auctorem. Quia vero rationabiliter et quodam ordine pulcherrimo disposita sunt, secundum sapientiam illa esse creata necesse est. Quoniam autem ipse creator juxta veram rationem nullo indiget sed in semetipso summum bonum et sufficientiam habet, oportet ut ea, quae creat, ex sola benignitate et caritate creet, ut scilicet habeat quibus beatitudinem suam more caritatis participet." On the analogy of the Trinity and the causes, see Parent, *La doctrine de la création,* 69-81.

[28] Cap. 2, p. 185.

[29] Cap. 4, p. 185: "Dies naturalis est spatium, in quo una caeli integra conversio ab ortu ad ortum perficitur."

[30] Thus Thierry collates the differing statements on time and

eliminated, the creation of the world may be viewed as a product of the *ordo naturalis*. To take the example of the first day, in the beginning God created matter; this is the meaning of *"In principio creavit deus caelum et terram."* Arguing from logic and physics, Thierry states that the heavens, once created, consisted of the "highest lightness." They could not remain still, nor could they move forward, since, by definition, they consisted of the space they occupied. Therefore from the first instant of time they began to move in a circle, which was the only option open to them.[31] When the first revolution was completed, the *prima dies* was ended.[32] From the creation of matter, and from the translation of matter's light-energy into motion, the creative process takes place along natural principles. In the next stage the four elements gravitate to their proper places and intermingle with each other.[33]

The growth of all living things also commences with heat and light. For instance, the natural force for producing grass and trees descends from the heat of the heavens.[34] The interrelation between the elements and their resultant qualities is determined by their inherent activity or passivity. Thierry summarizes the relationship as follows:

For fire is entirely active and earth entirely passive, while the two elements which are in the middle both

---

creation in Ecclesiasticus 18:1 and Exodus 20:11 in cap. 4, pp. 185-86.

[31] Cap. 5, p. 186: "Caelo vero creato, quia summae levitatis est et stare non potest et quia continet omnia, de loco ad locum in antea progredi non potuit." *In antea* here may mean *in anteriora*, as in cap. 21, p. 191, where the same idea is stated: "Cum enim necessario moveantur, aut in anteriora semper necesse erat ea moveri aut reverti."

[32] *Loc. cit.*

[33] Cf. P. Duhem, *Le système du monde*, iii (Paris, 1910), 187.

[34] Cap. 10, p. 187.

act and are acted upon like an instrument. Air is both
acted upon by fire and behaves like the conductor and
vehicle of fiery power towards the other elements.
Water is acted upon by air and by fire and behaves like
the conductor and vehicle of the power of the higher
to the remaining element [i.e. earth]. The result is
that fire is the craftsman, so to speak, the efficient
cause; the supporting earth, so to speak, the material
cause. The two elements which are in the middle [are]
like an instrument or something offering a union, by
which the action of the highest is administered to what
is lower down.[35]

Employing an Augustinian term to justify an essentially
Hermetic account of the physical processes, Thierry calls
these forces the *seminales causae.*[36]

The first part of the commentary, briefly summarized
above, treats *de causis et de ordine*; the second attempts
to incorporate the natural philosophy into a literal exegesis
of Genesis. An interesting feature of part two is how little
of the Bible is actually cited. The overall impression is not
of a commentary, but of an original theological cosmology
that uses Scripture as its point of departure.[37] The core of

[35] Cap. 17, p. 189: "Nam ignis tantum agit. Terra vero tantum
patitur. Duo vero elementa, quae sunt in medio (quasi instrumen-
tum, AC), et agunt et patiuntur. Et aër quidem ab igne patitur et
est quasi administrator et vehiculum igneae virtutis ad caetera elementa. Aqua vero ab aëre et igne patitur et est quasi administratrix
et vehiculum virtutis superiorum ad reliquum elementum. Ita igitur
ignis est quasi artifex et efficiens causa; terra vero subjecta quasi
materialis causa; duo vero elementa, quae sunt in medio, quasi in-
strumentum vel aliquid coadunativum quo actus supremi administratur ad infima."

[36] Gregory, 179-80, notes Thierry's use of Augustinian terminology, but Thierry himself, cap. 26, p. 193, cites "Mercurius" on
physical theory.

[37] In the chapters which Haring calls *Expositio Litterae* (18-29)

Thierry's thought is found in part three, which treats the topic of unity and diversity. Like many ancient (and modern) theorists, he attempts to defend numerology as the rationale behind all cosmic change.[38]

Part three begins with a typically neoplatonic statement of the relation between the One and the Many: "Unity precedes all otherness, since unity precedes duality which is the principle of all otherness. . . . Therefore unity precedes all change, for mutability draws its substance from duality."[39] If unity is the divine principle from which the

---

only phrases of Genesis are cited: e.g. cap. 18, p. 190: "In principio creauit Deus caelum et terram"; cap. 22, p. 191: "Terra autem erat inanis et vacua. . . . "; *ibid.*, p. 192: "Et tenebrae erant super faciem abyssi. . . . Et spiritus Domini ferebatur super aquas. . . ."; cap. 29, p. 194: "Et dixit Deus: Fiat lux." In terms of weight of citation, Thierry is more indebted in this literal exposition to Hermes, cap. 26, p. 193, of whom he cites a whole paragraph, supporting his quotation with references to Plato and Virgil (cap. 27). On the other hand, absence of citations from Genesis ought not to be interpreted as patent disregard for it. The text was, after all, hardly an obscure one. In addition, twelfth-century commentaries often develop out of relatively brief citations of the works they are supposed to be explaining. An example is the Martianus commentary in Cambridge, in which some twenty-seven folios are devoted to about a dozen lines of verse.

[38] While the number theory in the *De Septem Diebus* appears to be a combination of Platonic and Hermetic elements, Thierry derives similar ideas from Boethius in his commentary on the latter's *De Trinitate*. See, for example, his explanation of *alteritas* (cap. 1.30, ed. N. Haring, p. 274) and *intelligibilitas* (cap. 2.8, p. 280), as well as his description of *deus* as *unitas* (cap. 3.1-2, pp. 294-95). Twelfth-century thinkers, however, often attributed similar notions to other Platonists; e.g. William of Conches, *Glosae super Platonem*, cap. 12, ed. Jeauneau, p. 71 [on *Tim.* 17A]: "Plato igitur, ut Pitagoras. . . ." On the possibility that Thierry might have known the *Parmenides*, see Haring, *AHDLMA* 22 (1956), 163 and 163 n. 2.

[39] Cap. 30, pp. 194-95: "Omnem alteritatem unitas praecedit

diversity of the created universe derives, the procession from the One to the Many is also the solution to the dual problems of time and eternity and the individual and the universal:

> Indeed, every created thing is subject to mutability. For whatever exists is either eternal or the result of creation. Since Unity precedes every created thing, it is necessary that it is eternal; and eternity is nothing but divinity. Therefore this very divinity is Unity.
>
> Furthermore, the divine is the form of being for individual things. For just as something is illuminated by light or heated by heat, in the same way individual things draw their existence from divinity. Therefore, truly the whole of God is exhibited essentially everywhere.[40]

Maintaining a delicate balance between the conception of God as an abstraction and as a physical presence, Thierry neither allows him to be reduced to his worldly manifestation, nor the world to be reduced to an image of the divine. God exists outside the created universe, as the unifying principle in its diversity, and in the world, as the ordering and vivifying principle of its visible harmony. In the latter role, *divinitas* is the world's *forma essendi*. Thierry sum-

---

quoniam unitas praecedit binarium qui est principium omnis alteritatis. . . . Omnem igitur mutabilitatem praecedit unitas, siquidem omnis mutabilitas substantiam ex binario sortitur."

[40] Cap. 31, p. 195: "Sed mutabilitati omnis creatura subjecta est. Et quicquid est, vel aeternum est vel creatura. Cum igitur unitas omnem creaturam praecedat, aeternam esse necesse est. At aeternum nihil est aliud quam divinitas. Unitas igitur ipsa ⟨est⟩ divinitas. At divinitas singulis rebus forma essendi est. Nam sicut aliquid ex luce lucidum est vel ⟨ex⟩ calore calidum, ita singulae res esse suum ex divinitate sortiuntur. Unde Deus totus et essentialiter ubique esse vere perhibetur."

marizes these different aspects of deity in a later paragraph on number theory:

> For the unity which when multiplied puts together numbers (that is, the unities out of which numbers are produced) is nothing but the participations of unity in which consist the existences of created things. For as long as a thing participates in unity, it endures; but as quickly as it is divided, the same thing undergoes destruction. For unity is the preserver and form of being; but division is the cause of destruction. . . .[41]

Out of number, he continues, arise all the Aristotelian categories, which summarize and clarify the work of the *artifex aeternus*.[42] The whole process of creation amounts to this: "creatio numerorum, rerum est creatio"[43] (the creation of numbers is the creation of things).

Even so brief an exposition of Thierry's cosmology suffices to point out how different it is from Bernard's. Of course there are certain undeniable similarities. Both au-

[41] Cap. 34, p. 196: "Unitas vero, quae multiplicata componit numeros, vel unitates ex quibus numeri constant, nihil aliud sunt quam verae unitatis participationes quae creaturarum existentiae sunt. Quamdiu enim res unitate participat, ipsa permanet. Quam cito vero dividitur, eadem interitum incurrit. Unitas enim essendi conservatio et forma est; divisio vero causa interitus."

[42] Cap. 35, p. 196: cf. cap. 45, p. 199: "Si enim aequalitas unitatis est aequalitas existentiae et aequalitas existentiae rei facit ipsam rem existere et ipsum esse rei circumscribit ac terminat quasi quaedam lex et existendi aeterna regula, non est dubium quin ipsa unitatis aequalitas sit rebus omnibus forma essendi aeterna ac formalis causa secundum artifex aeternus modum existendi omnibus rebus constituit."

[43] Cap. 36, p. 196. Cf. *Comm.* on Boethius' *De Trinitate* 3.1-2, ed. N. Haring, *AHDLMA* 23 (1957), 294-95, and 3.18-19, p. 300, where Thierry asserts that, for a Christian, there can be no *diversitas* in God, an expression which recalls *Cos.* ii.13.1-5; cf. Ch. II, n. 75.

thors are interested in naturalistic allegory and each in his way treats cosmology as a story. In quite different ways both echo the language of classical poetry in describing chaos.[44] The closest rapport arises from their common use of the *Asclepius*. Yet even here the parallels may not be pushed too far. Thierry employs Hermeticism chiefly to provide a basis in physical theory for his notion of Unity and Diversity, while Bernard attempts a much more wholly naturalistic explanation of processes in the upper and lower worlds, distinguishing the two in a manner unknown to Thierry. Differences may also be noticed in their use of other common source material. For instance, Thierry defines wisdom, the formal cause, as follows: "Dei sapientia . . . nihil est aliud quam in coaeterna sibi sapientia futurae rei formam disponere"[45] (The wisdom of God . . . is nothing other than the arranging of the form of a future event in wisdom coeternal to himself). This captures the spirit of the Platonic side of Bernard's Noys, but omits the Stoicism and astrology. Similarly, speaking of the *aequalitas existentiae* between *deus* and *sapientia*, Thierry says: "Ancient philosophers have called this mode or equality of unity sometimes '*mentem divinitatis*,' sometimes '*providentiam*,' and sometimes '*creatoris sapientiam*.' "[46] Thierry and Ber-

---

[44] For example, cap. 22, p. 191: "*Terra autem erat inanis et vacua*, etc. Qualis terra tunc fuerit, plane ostendit dicendo eam tunc fuisse inanem, i.e. carentem forma quam postea suscepit ex aliorum elementorum ad ipsam concordia"; cap. 23, p. 192: "Inanitas vero eorum tunc in eo erat quod ita erant confusa, . . ."; cap. 24, p. 192: "Istam quattuor elementorum informitatem seu potius paene uniformitatem antiqui philosophi tunc hylen, tunc chaon appellaverunt . . . et illa elementa sic confusa una informis materia dicebantur." Thierry also refers to the clouds as *congeries*; cap. 7, p. 186.

[45] Cap. 3, p. 185.

[46] Cap. 42, p. 198: "Istum autem modum sive unitatis aequali-

nard may have the same *antiqui* in mind—possibly Macrobius, Chalcidius, and Augustine—but they do not use them in the same way. For his part Bernard never employs these sources to describe "four causes" of creation; unlike Thierry, he does not state that God created matter and time.[47] In addition, his interest in astrology in general and its influence on *homo microcosmus*[48] in particular is nowhere echoed in the Chartrain master. Aside from generalities, the points of similarity between the two are therefore very few.

William of Conches

Of William of Conches' numerous works perhaps the closest to Bernard in sources and content is the commentary on the *Timaeus*. For the purposes of comparison it has the added advantage of being a mature work which William wrote at the height of his career when he was "a master in full possession of his gifts."[49] In Chapter I, a broad similarity in format was pointed out between William's *Philoso-*

---

tatem antiqui philosophi tum 'mentem divinitatis' tum 'providentiam' tum 'creatoris sapientiam' appellaverunt."

[47] Cap. 5, p. 186. Cf. J. M. Parent, *La doctrine de la création*, 40-43; 95-106.

[48] It is interesting that Thierry, in following his own theology consistently, does not see man as a *minor mundus* in a purely naturalistic sense, as does Bernard, but as a miniature unity; cap. 43, p. 198: "Homo enim vel aliquid tale ideo est quia unum est. Si autem dividatur, interitum incurrit. Similiter ab ejusdem unitatis, qua homo subsistit, aequalitate forma hominis procedit. Si autem ipsi unitati, qua homo subsistit, aliquid apponatur vel inde diminuatur, non est 'humanitas' dicenda."

[49] E. Jeauneau, *Glosae super Platonem*, 15 (my trans.). Citations are made from this text alone, and cross-references to William's other works are not repeated from Jeauneau's notes, where they are listed fully, unless especially relevant.

phia Mundi and the *Cosmographia*. It was also suggested that the conception of myth which William employs in his commentary on Macrobius (and elsewhere) presents a useful language for interpreting Bernard's *narratio fabulosa*. In the commentary on Plato he turns to another central theme of the *Cosmographia*: the creation of the world, and, to a lesser degree, of man. William felt that Plato had adequately dealt with positive justice in the *Republic*; in the *Timaeus* he turned to natural justice,[50] which, as William defines it, is the equivalent of Thierry's *ordo naturalis*, since it treats the *creatio mundi*.[51] Like Thierry, William proposes that the secrets of myths like the *Timaeus* and Genesis may be unlocked by means of the *quadrivium*, and he divides the speculative wisdom which is to carry out the task into theology, mathematics, and physics.[52] Lastly, while William is chiefly indebted to Boethius, he also knows many of Bernard's Latin sources, including Chalcidius and Macrobius.[53]

---

[50] Cap. 3 ⟨*accessus*⟩, p. 59.

[51] *Ibid.* 59: "Unde possumus dicere quod materia huius libri est naturalis iusticia vel creatio mundi."

[52] Cap. 5 ⟨*accessus*⟩, p. 60. A rather better exposition of the relation between theory and practice is found in William's commentary on Boethius' *Consolatio Philosophiae*, ed. C. Jourdain, *Excursions historiques et philosophiques à travers le moyen âge* (Paris, 1888), 35: "A practica adscendendum est ad theoricam, non de theorica descendendum ad practicam, nisi causa communis utilitatis. Qui vero sint illi gradus philosophie, id est ordo ascendendi de practica ad theoricam, sic videndum est. Prius est homo instruendus in moribus per ethicam, deinde in dispensatione proprie familie per economicam, postea in gubernatione rerum per politicam. Deinde, cum in istis perfecte exercitatus fuerit, debet transire ad contemplationem eorum quae sunt circa corpora, per mathematicam et physicam, usque ad celestia; deinde ad contemplationem incorporeorum usque ad creatorem, per theologiam. Et hic est ordo philosophie."

[53] And like him, only gives lip service to Augustine; *Glosae super Platonem*, 26-27. Chenu, 115, argues that Augustine is the common

Thus from many viewpoints the lectures on Plato would appear to offer a solid basis for comparison. Yet, as in the case of Thierry, closer examination reveals many of the parallels to be superficial. William may be shown to differ from both Thierry and Bernard on central issues like the interpretation of Plato and Boethius, the idea of creation, the *anima mundi*, prime matter, and perception.

William's preferred classical authority is Boethius. Like his mentor he combines logic with neoplatonism, that is, a desire for clarity with a sensitivity towards the inner meaning of things. Citing Boethius at the beginning of his commentary, he states that reality may be understood *de divinis intellectualiter, de mathematicis doctrinaliter, de phisicis naturaliter.*[54] Throughout the commentary the three perspectives are kept in balance. For example, in explaining the four causes of the world, William states:

So that these may be better understood, [Plato] proposes a twofold division. In one part is contained the efficient, formal, and final causes of the world; in the other [is portrayed] the material [cause] and its effects. The division is as follows: whatever exists either lacks generation and always exists, or possesses generation and does not always exist. . . . *Generatio,* as Boethius states in his *Commentary on the Categories,* is the entrance into substantial being, that is,

---

denominator of all the syncretistic Platonisms of the twelfth century, a view that is echoed by Haring with reference to Thierry in his preface to the *De Septem Diebus.* This is an oversimplification. With regard to the *Glosae,* Jeauneau observes accurately (p. 26): "St. Augustine is named at least six times but one cannot say that his influence is exercised on the commentary itself" (my trans.).

[54] Cap. 12, p. 72. In cap. 5 of the *accessus,* p. 61, William states that "phisica vero est de naturis et complexionibus corporum: phisis enim est natura."

the principle of existence. Therefore, to have generation is to have a principle of existence. . . .[55]

The efficient, formal, and final causes, understood in their
theological equivalents as the Trinity, do not have a beginning; only "the elements and whatever arises from
them possess a principle of existence and undergo change
through the passage of time."[56]
From his understanding of Boethius, William then
develops his theory of the *anima mundi* and its relation to
physical forces. In a sense, he applies Boethius to Plato's
Timaeus ad litteram; in this arises his chief difference from
Thierry. Of course the two thinkers share certain Platonic
assumptions. For William, the *sensilis mundus* of the
Timaeus, made in the imitation of a divine archetype, has
as its principle of existence the *anima mundi*, which is similar in conception to Thierry's *forma essendi*.[57] Yet there is
an important difference. More than Thierry, William refers the principle of creativity back to the creator in a
purely theological sense.[58] Like Thierry, he will state that
"nothing is born without a cause, and not, by implication,

[55] Cap. 32, p. 98: "Que ut melius intelligantur, bimembrem pre-
ponit divisionem in cuius altero membro efficiens, formalis, finalis
causa mundi continetur, in altero vero materialis et effectus. Que
divisio talis est: quidquid est vel est carens generatione et semper est,
vel habet generationem nec semper est. . . . Generatio igitur, ut ait
Boetius in *Commento super Cathegorias*, est ingressus in substantiam
id est principium existentie. Habere igitur generationem est habere
principium existentie." Jeauneau, p. 98, n. b, notes the source from
Boethius, *In Categorias Aristotelis*, iv; *PL* 64, 290A.

[56] *Ibid.* 99: ". . . elementa et quidquid ex eis est principium habent
essentie et per successiones temporales variantur."

[57] E.g., Cap. 71, p. 144: "Et est anima mundi spiritus quidam
rebus insitus, motum et vitam illis conferens." For an exhaustive
discussion of the *anima mundi*, see Gregory, 123-74.

[58] Cap. 95, p. 177.

the world."[59] Yet he emphasizes that the cause of the world is not natural but divine. God is like a good craftsman, whose Wisdom acts as a model in providing a shape for the artistic product, "et sic mundus est imago divine sapientie"[60] (and thus the world is the image of divine wisdom). One of William's recurrent metaphors, in fact, is that the creator is a wise architect or sculptor, who, in a purely Platonic sense, fashions the cosmos as a beautiful work of art in the image and likeness of the divine.[61] On occasion he will even give the metaphor an Augustinian turn. Thus he states that man, with his limited capacities, can employ his reason in attempting to understand the musical and mathematical harmony of the universe; but its inner secrets remain beyond his grasp.[62]

As the world is the *opus creatoris*, it cannot be the *opus naturae*; William stresses the omnipotence of God whereas Bernard is oriented towards physical processes. William, of course, distinguishes the moral from the physical conception of nature. He does so on one occasion when he is discussing the problem of evil[63] and on another when he is referring to the possible types of motion.[64] Yet he is more disposed to divide up nature's duties than to treat them as physical forces. His tendency of mind is to subordinate physics to theology and to logic. The following passage summarizes his thoughts on nature and creation:

[59] Cap. 36, p. 103: "Nichil gignitur sine causa, ergo nec mundus."
[60] Cap. 38, p. 106.
[61] See, for example, William's commentary on *Tim.* 48E-49A, cap. 160, pp. 266-67.
[62] On this point William remains perhaps more Augustinian than Boethian; in cap. 45, p. 113, commenting on the fact that man cannot ever know fully the secrets of nature, he adds: ". . . Si loquamur de creatore, rationes divinas, invariabiles, incontradicibiles oportet nos invenire; quod est homini impossibile cuius sapientia est caduca, variabilis et fallax."
[63] Cap. 49, pp. 117-18.   [64] Cap. 107, pp. 195-96.

253

The world is that which is brought forth, but everything which is brought forth has a principle of existence. . . . In order that this might be understood better, according to what we have been teaching, six causes of things ought to be noted: four substantial . . . and two accidental, the latter being time and place. . . .

As it has been shown that nothing arises without a cause, it follows that what incurs effects does so from that which causes them. In this sense it should be understood that every work is either the work of the creator, the work of nature, or the work of a craftsman imitating nature. The work of the creator is first creation without pre-existing matter, such as the creation of the elements and the soul, or that which seems to us to be brought about against the accustomed course of nature, such as virgin birth, etc. A natural work is that which gives birth to like from like, from a seed or a sprout. For nature is a power latent in things, producing like from like. An artificial work is the work of a man and is produced according to his need, like clothes against the cold, a house against intemperate weather. But in everything he does [man] imitates nature. . . .

Moreover, a work derives its characteristics from its craftsman. The work of the creator is perpetual, free from dissolution; for neither the cosmos nor the soul are destroyed. A work of nature, though it lacks being in itself, nonetheless reproduces something from itself as a seed. But the work of a craftsman imitating nature neither remains in itself nor produces anything from itself.[65]

[65] Capp. 36-37, pp. 103-05: "Mundus est id quod gignitur, sed omne quod gignitur habet principium existentie. . . . Quod ut melius

254

It is revealing to compare this summary to Bernard's and Thierry's views of creation. All three posit an ultimate creator, but William does not involve him in anything but the original creation of the world and man. Between William and Bernard there is a fundamentally different conception of deity. For William, God creates matter as he creates the soul; for Bernard, matter and soul are different aspects of God. In William nature is a far more limited principle than in Bernard. As a force latent in things, *natura* governs their reproduction of like from like. Bernard's idea of nature (which is not synonymous with the goddess Natura) is that of a mediator between the heavens and earth. Thus for him nature is both a biological principle, governing growth, and a deterministic principle, whose laws are translated into fate at the earthly level. In other words, in the *Cosmographia* there are not different types of creativity; there is a similar type, adapted to different levels of descent from heaven to earth. Moreover, unlike

---

intelligatur, attendendum est sex esse causas rerum: quatuor substantiales . . . et duas accidentales scilicet tempus et locum. . . .

"Ostenso quod nichil est sine causa, subiungit quid contrahat effectus ex efficiente. Et sciendum quod omne opus vel est opus creatoris, vel opus nature, vel artificis imitantis naturam (cf. Chalcidius, *Comm.*, cap. 23, p. 73). Et est opus creatoris prima creatio sine preiacente materia ut est creatio elementorum et spirituum vel ea que videmus fieri contra consuetum cursum nature ut partus virginis, etc. Opus nature est quod similia nascuntur ex similibus, ex semine vel ex germine. Et est natura vis rebus insita similia de similibus operans. Opus artificis est opus hominis quod propter indigentiam operatur ut vestimenta contra frigus, domum contra intemperiem aeris. Sed in omnibus que agit naturam imitatur. . . .

"Sed ex artifice opus contrahit qualitatem. Opus enim creatoris perpetuum est, carens dissolutione; neque enim mundus neque spiritus dissolvuntur. Opus nature, etsi in se esse desinat, tamen in semine remanet. Opus vero artificis naturam imitantis nec in se remanet nec aliquid in se gignit."

William, Bernard does not merely consider man, the crown of creation, as a *creatura*. Like *mundus*, he is a creating element within the cosmic system. William adheres faithfully to the Platonic notion of man as a model of the divine. Through astrology and biology, Bernard adds the notion of *homo viator*. William's theory of creation, in fact, has even less rapport with Bernard's than does Thierry's. Through the *Asclepius*, Thierry develops the naturalistic tendencies in Platonism, while William stresses the logical and theological.

This difference between William and Thierry may be illustrated in another way. Both authors agree that the world has a cause, its creator, who created both matter and time.[66] But while Thierry accounts for the physical properties of the elements through natural laws, as does Bernard, William emphasizes the purely logical. A good example of William's approach is provided by his answer to a specific problem in twelfth-century philosophy: whether, before God ordered the elements according to the divine plan, they occupied the positions relative to each other that they do at present. Disagreeing with *fere omnes*,[67] including presumably Bernard, William states that the elements always occupied the same positions. For as bodies, he reasons, they had to occupy a position somewhere, and as there was nowhere else for them to go, "they were where they are now, although they were not arranged as they are now."[68] Those who assert that fire was not always on top,

[66] Cap. 97, pp. 180-81. See Parent, *La doctrine de la création*, 95-106.

[67] Cap. 50, p. 118: "Dicunt igitur fere omnes elementa in prima creatione certa loca non obtinuisse sed modo simul ascendere, modo simul descendere." This is an accurate paraphrase of Bernard's conception of elemental chaos in *Cos.* i.i.

[68] Cap. 50, p. 118: "Erant ergo ubi nunc sunt etsi non essent sic disposita ut nunc sunt."

earth on the bottom, and air and water in the middle are merely attempting to ascribe to God powers that he does not possess, which amounts to "an incorrect position unsuitable to reason."[69]

> For they [who urge this position] present an inadequate reason, namely that God had done this so that he might demonstrate how great a confusion might exist in the world if he had not ordered the elements. To whom might he offer this demonstration? To an angel? But the angel knows the nature of the universe through his own nature and divine grace. To a man? But man did not yet exist.[70]

He concludes that "the elements existed from the beginning of creation where they are now, possessing the same qualities which they have now but not the accidents."[71]

Another example of William's distinctive approach is provided by his solution to a problem related to the above: prime matter. In his lengthy discussion of matter at the end of volume two, he states:

> Some say that the elements in chaos consisted of such [a prime] matter. But I maintain that the elements could not be prime matter, neither in chaos nor outside, since some of it belongs to each. This may be proven as follows: of whatever there is a form there

[69] *Loc. cit.*: ". . . falsam sententiam et rationem non convenientem."

[70] Cap. 50, p. 119: "Inconveniens vero est ratio quam inducunt scilicet Deum ad hoc fecisse ut ostenderet quanta rerum confusio foret nisi eas ordinaret. Cui ostenderet? Angelo? Sed angelus naturas rerum scit natura propria et gratia divina. Homini? Sed nondum erat homo."

[71] Cap. 51, p. 119: "Nostra vero sententia est elementa in prima creatione fuisse ubi nunc sunt et easdem quas nunc habent substantiales qualitates obtinentia, sed not accidentales."

must also be matter, for form cannot exist without matter. But there exists a certain form of the elements, for fire is sharp, earth dull. . . . Therefore the elements are not primordial matter, neither in chaos nor outside. For in chaos they possess the same substantial qualities that they have now (and nothing can exist in any way without substantial qualities). Therefore it is my position that the matter of the elements is prime matter.[72]

In suggesting that the elements are definable in terms of their substantial qualities rather than as an indefinable substratum, William is not far from the *phisici*; but in accounting for the origin of the elements themselves, he returns to a position of idealism. In the same discussion, he asks whether matter is a *creator* or a *creatura*. The latter, "for God was of such great potency that he was able to create at once the elements and their matter."[73]

This brief comparison suggests that, while they are both indebted to the *medici*, Bernard and William differ sharply

---

[72] Cap. 154, pp. 258-59: "Dicunt enim quidam quod elementa in chao fuerunt talis materia (i.e. prima materia). Nos vero dicimus elementa nec in chao nec extra posse esse primam materiam, quia est aliqua eorum materia. Quod sic probatur. Cuiuscumque est forma, eiusdem est materia: forma enim sine materia esse non potest. Sed elementorum est aliqua forma: est enim ignis acutus, terra obtusa. . . . Non sunt ergo elementa primordialis materia nec in chao nec extra. In chao enim habebant easdem substantiales qualitates quas modo habent: nichil enim sine suis substantialibus qualitatibus aliquo modo potest esse. Est ergo nostra sententia quod materia elementorum est prima materia."

[73] Cap. 155, p. 260: "Si iterum queratur utrum sit ile (= hyle) creator an creatura, dicimus quod est creatura. Fuit enim Deus tante potentie quod simul elementa et eorum materia creare potuit." This view, of course, is the opposite of Bernard's, as he considered matter to be an aspect of God, and therefore a creating as well as created force.

in their conceptions of creation, nature, and matter. They disagree even more profoundly on the problem of the senses and perception. Bernard's view may be described as sensorial and empirical perception, since the data from the external world, reflected directly by the senses, are analysed by the brain, which in turn sends messages to the various parts of the body. This is essentially a physical approach and Bernard's debt to Galen is clear. For William, in contrast, the problem of perception is inseparable from the classical theory of the mind.[74] Any attempt to separate the empirical and philosophical elements in his approach would do a serious injustice to his thought as a whole. Stated in its simplest terms, his theory derives from the notion of the *anima mundi*, which he sees providing the life-forces, both spiritual and physical, for the world and man:

> The whole soul of the world is one and the same. It brings about respectively motion in the planets, quickening of life in the grass and trees, sense in brute animals, and reason in man. Thus it works in individual things according to the nature of individual things, existing as a totality in them but not exercising all of its powers [at any given time and place].[75]

[74] See Parent, *La doctrine de la création*, 29-34 and Gregory, 145-54, 167-72.

[75] Cap. 71, p. 146: "Una enim et eadem anima mundi tota est, in planetis sed motum ibi operans, in herbis et arboribus vegetationem, in brutis animalibus sensum, in homine rationem. Ita iuxta naturam singulorum in singulis operatur, tota in eis existens, sed non omnes potentias exercens." A fuller account is found in the commentary on Boethius, ed. Jourdain, pp. 36-37: "Anima mundi est naturalis vigor quo habent quedam res tantum moveri, quedam crescere, quedam sentire, quedam discernere. . . . Sed, ut mihi videtur, ille vigor naturalis est spiritus sanctus, id est, divina et benigna concordia. . . . Qui bene dicitur naturalis vigor, quia divino amore omnia crescunt et vigent. Qui bene dicitur anima mundi, quia solo

Just as the *anima mundi*, in essence, is the same no matter where it operates, so the virtues of the human soul are united in the mind, but operate according to the different demands made on them:

> For the creator conferred on the soul of man an indissoluble essence, a complete range of knowledge, and freedom of will. But since diverse kinds of things are related to knowledge, and the same thing is often perceived in different ways—in order that diverse things may be perceived or the same thing in diverse ways—[God] conferred on it diverse powers: namely sense, imagination, reason, [and] intellect.[76]

These powers, which increase as a man matures with age, are aided by three others: inventiveness, memory, and opinion.[77] Even the passions, which Bernard sees in relation to the astrological control of the four humors, are related to the faculties of the soul. Thus William will state that once

---

divino amore et caritate, omnia quae in mundo sunt, vivunt et habent vivere. Viso quid sit anima mundi, videndae sunt proprietates ejus juxta corpora, quae tales sunt, scilicet sensualitas, vegetatio, ratio. Quedam enim corpora vegetat et facit crescere, ut herbas et arbores; quedam facit sentire, ut bruta animalia; quedam facit discernere, ut homines, una et eadem manens anima; sed non in omnibus exercet eamdem potentiam. . . ."

[76] Cap. 34, p. 100: "Creator igitur anime hominis essentiam indissolubilem, scientie perfectionem, arbitrii libertatem contulit. Sed quoniam diversa genera rerum scientie subiacent idemque sepe diversis modis percipitur, ad diversa percipienda vel idem diverso modo, diversas illi contulit virtutes scilicet sensum, imaginationem, rationem, intellectum."

[77] *Ibid.* p. 102: "Preter has virtutes sunt alie rationi et intellectui servientes ut ingenium, memoria, opinio. Et est ingenium naturalis vis animi ad aliquid cito percipiendum, dictum ingenium quasi intus genitum. Memoria vero est vis firme retinendi cognita. Opinio vero est perceptio rei cum dubitatione: que si de corporibus sit confirmata fit ratio, si de incorporeis intellectus."

Plato has shown "where the passions of the soul arise, he shows how and why they are called senses: because they make the soul sense."[78] At the same time, he incorporates the views of the *medici*, stating that "after one removes from the body the power of sensing, he will remove from it as well the power of discerning and understanding."[79] In other words, while sensorial psychology is related to the powers of the soul, the external world is not reduced to the reflection of sense data.

The sense to which William devotes the most attention is *visus*, under which rubric he includes *contuicio*, *intuicio*, and *detuicio*.[80] The spirit of his approach is perhaps best conveyed in a brief anecdote in which he relates to his students the origin of reflective philosophy:

> Here [= *Tim.* 47A] [Plato] demonstrates the special utility of seeing, the particular application of which is philosophy. For nothing is more important than wisdom, the source of which is seeing, for the following reason. When man distinguishes by sight the creations of the world and the arrangements of created things, he is charged with the duty of inquiring into the natures and properties of things. On encountering them, he sees that they are both created and arranged wisely; and he asks whose wisdom might create and arrange things in this fashion. But finding the wisdom of no created thing capable of bringing this about, he establishes that the same substance whose wisdom brought this about is unborn, eternal. And what he has found out, he teaches to others by writing and by

[78] Cap. 129, p. 227: "Ostenso unde nascantur passiones in anima, ostendit qualiter et quare scilicet sensus dicuntur: quia faciunt animam sentire."

[79] Cap. 147, p. 250: "Postquam removit a corpore vim sentiendi, removet etiam ab eodem vim discernendi et intelligendi."

[80] Cap. 142, pp. 243-44.

word; and in this way was philosophy discovered. Seeing, therefore, is the source of philosophy.[81]

This little story is a reminder that William's commentary on Plato is a series of lecture notes, not a polished example of rhetoric like his encyclopedic dialogues, and that it is not only in content but in literary form that it differs from the *Cosmographia*.

Daniel of Morley

The cosmological theories of Thierry and William, as well, perhaps, as Bernard himself, provide a necessary preface for understanding those of Daniel of Morley. Daniel returned, he tells us, from the continent sometime after 1175 and composed for his patron, bishop John of Norwich, his *Liber de Naturis Inferiorum et Superiorum*.[82] A product of the next generation, he would have been

[81] Cap. 149, p. 252: "Hic ostendit precipuam utilitatem visus, cuius precipua utilitas est philosophia. Nichil enim maius est sapientia. Huius causa est visus sic. Cum homo visu notaret creationes rerum creaturarum dispositiones, iniuncta est ei cura inquirendi naturas rerum et proprietates. Quas inveniens, vidensque eas et sapienter creari et sapienter disponi, quesivit cuius sapientia sic res crearet et disponeret; reperiensque nullius creature sapientiam hoc agere posse, confirmavit quamdam substantiam esse ingenitam, eternam, cuius sapientia hoc ageret. Et ea que invenit, scripto et voce alios docuit: et sic philosophia inventa est. Visus igitur est causa philosophie." (I have changed some past to present tenses in my translation.)

[82] Ed. K. Sudhoff, *Archiv für die Geschichte der Naturwissenschaften* 8 (1917), 1-40, with corrections by A. Birkenmajer, *ibid.* 9 (1918), 45-51. This text is cited below with Birkenmajer's corrections added where necessary. Other mss of the *Liber de Naturis*, of which a critical edition would be useful, are listed by M. Müller, *Philosophisches Jahrbuch . . . der Görres-Gesellschaft* 41 (1928), 301-04, whose views are criticized by Silverstein, *MS* 10 (1948), 195-96. To the summary of scholarship pertaining to Daniel in Silverstein's article, 179 n. 1, should now be added Lemay, *Abu Ma'shar*, 313-42.

more at home at the Chartres, Tours, or Paris of the 1140s. Finding Paris by the sixties dominated by the study of law and theology, he fled to Toledo to work with the Arabs on scientific questions.[83] His *Liber de Naturis*, Silverstein notes, turns out to be "not so much a summary of the new astronomical lore as a neatly organized cosmogony which uses it."[84] This observation is substantiated by Daniel's source material, which is evenly divided between the Latins and the Arabs. Among the former he is particularly indebted to Adelard and to William of Conches; among the latter, to Alfergani's *Rudimenta Astronomica*, Alfarabi's *De Ortu Scientie*, Abu Ma'shar's *Maius Introductorium* (in Hermann of Carinthia's version), and an obscure Hermetic book called the *Liber Triplicis Mundi*.[85] In addition to the Arabic books, which Daniel claims, somewhat contrary to the evidence,[86] to have used extensively, he learned from Gerard of Cremona, his *magister*, the *Libri Naturales* of Aristotle, as well as a number of other scientific books that are not easily traceable from the titles he reports.[87] Daniel thus represents an interesting blend of the old and the new science. He offers a standard for measuring Bernard Silvester's intellectual distance from Chartres and from Toledo.

In reviewing Daniel's work, historians have stressed the debts he owes to his sources, neglecting the originality of his cosmology as a whole. Daniel represents the last stage of development of the Platonism of the first half-century

---

[83] *Liber de Naturis*, p. 6.   [84] *Art. cit.*, 179.

[85] Daniel's Latin sources are dealt by Müller, while Silverstein concentrates on the Arabic *fontes*. Silverstein and Lemay agree that Abu Ma'shar is the most important single Arab author cited by Daniel and that he is cited in Hermann of Carinthia's version. Lemay argues that Daniel also knew Hermann's *De Essentiis* (p. 319), but does not prove it adequately; see his own remarks, 321-22.

[86] See Silverstein's remarks, 181.

[87] See Silverstein, 180 n. 5 and Lemay, 333-40.

before it is overwhelmed by Aristotelianism. He also develops to their logical conclusion the tendencies towards naturalism originated by Thierry and William. Although, like both, he is a Christian[88] who, at the beginning of his discussion of sublunary generation in book two,[89] cites Genesis and Augustine, he abandons, to an even greater degree than either, the hexaemeral pattern as a rational mode of explanation. As in the case of Bernard, one feels that in Daniel the era of the hexaemera has come to an end, to be superseded by the new physical and astronomical theory.[90]

If the *Liber de Naturis* is a faithful witness to trends in thinking in the third quarter of the century, it also illustrates the degree to which, in both language and ideas, the Latin and Arab traditions had become intermingled. There is even the suggestion that Chartres may have influenced Toledo. A good example of the interpenetration of different sources is furnished by Daniel's account of the manner in which God generates the image of the world from his own wisdom, near the beginning of book one. Here his language and metaphors are close to Bernard's, while his meaning is close to William of Conches.[91] Elsewhere in book one Daniel presents a number of borrowings from William. For both authors, the world is an archetype, an effigy or work of art constructed in the likeness of an eternal

---

[88] *Liber de Naturis*, p. 7.   [89] *Ibid.* 23.

[90] Cf. Lemay, 340.

[91] *Liber de Naturis*, p. 7: "Sed quia sapiens artifex nichil inconsulte facere suam sapientiam consuluit, sed quoniam, quicquid fit, uel ad similitudinem existentis, ut imago, que in se alicuius rei formam gerit, ideo summus fabricator, que fieri disposuit in noy, id est in mente diuina, tanquam in spera aurea scelata, sigillo perpetue memorie signauit." Cf. *Cos.* i.2.8-15. Bernard, unlike William of Conches, does not speak in this passage of a *summus fabricator* acting directly on the world, as does Daniel. Here Daniel betrays his affinity for Chartres rather than Tours or Toledo.

model; to support this idea, Daniel even cites the same passage of Augustine as does William.[92] Again, like the Chartres group, Daniel holds that God created matter. Chaos is not a pre-existing state but merely the *forma confusionis* of matter.[93] The violence of Daniel's attack on Chalcidius suggests that his astronomical theories, like those of Macrobius and Martianus, were being soundly criticized by the Toledan masters;[94] yet on other fundamental issues affecting cosmology he appears to be satisfied with the solutions proposed at Chartres. Echoing William's formula, he states that "omne . . . opus aut est opus dei aut opus nature aut opus artificis imitantis naturam"[95] (all work is either the work of God, the work of nature, or the work of a craftsman imitating nature). Soon after he adds that there are four principle causes of things, which turn out to be those of Chartres, purged of their controversial parallels with the Trinity.[96] If Daniel remains discreetly silent on this issue, he assures the reader at the beginning of book two

[92] *Ibid.* 9-10: "Igitur uulgari philosophie haut dubium est, quin mundus iste uisibilis ad exemplar et similitudinem eterni mundi sit fabricatus. Eternum mundum uoco mundum illum archetypum, qui semper uelut ars quedam cum suo artifice incommutabilis manet. Nec tamen ideo necesse est, istum uisibilem ad illius effigiem compositum ab illo etiam eternitatem mutuari, verbi gratia si forte aliquis faber arcam uelit fabricare, prius in animo suo latitudinem, longitudinem et profundum disponit." Cf. Augustinus, *Tractatus in Iohannen* i.17; *PL* 35, 1387: "Faber facit arcam. Primo in arte habet arcam: si enim in arte arcam non haberet, unde illam fabricando proferret?" William's metaphor, along with the above citation of Augustine, are found in the *Glosae super Platonem*, cap. 32, p. 99 and p. 99 n. c. It is worth noting that Daniel's metaphor is not exactly the same as William's, perhaps indicating that they are both reacting independently to Augustine and Chalcidius.

[93] The relevant texts are compared in Silverstein, *art. cit.*, 193-94.

[94] Cf. Silverstein, *loc. cit.*   [95] *Liber de Naturis*, p. 12.

[96] *Ibid.* 13-14; cf. Silverstein, 191-92.

that his division of creation into lower and upper regions is, in one sense, a gloss on the text, "*In principio. . . .*"[97] Yet in another sense it is not. In many respects he parallels, at a later stage of development the attempt Bernard makes to adapt the Platonic cosmology to Arabic science. In book two, for instance, immediately after the abovementioned reference to Genesis, he states that in the order of nature change begins with the motions of the heavens.[98] The conception of *caelum* itself, to which he devotes considerable attention, is an ambitious attempt to reconcile Plato, Aristotle, and the astrologers.[99] It may be considered a continuation of the last of Adelard's *Questiones Naturales.* Daniel, as well, is heavily indebted to the astrologers. Like Bernard, he conceives the stars as divinities[100] and discourses upon the astrological virtues of the sun.[101] A still more important parallel between the two arises from Daniel's sensuous approach to the real world.[102] Like Bernard, he maintains that the world is knowable, in part, through the empirical manifestation of a divine model. Yet he goes considerably beyond Bernard in incorporating the vocabulary of stellar and material mixing from Abu Ma'shar. Where Bernard, inspired by Hermes, speaks of "cosmic physiology," he refers to *compositio*.[103] In addition, quite aside from his absorption of the quasi-Aristotelian language of mixtures, Daniel disagrees with Bernard on a number of major and minor issues. For instance, while both authors agree that the world and time arose from a single principle, they disagree on the solution to the problem of identity and difference.[104] Again, Daniel will cite

---

[97] *Liber de Naturis,* p. 23. [98] *Loc. cit.*
[99] *Ibid.* 24-28.
[100] *Ibid.* 28, citing, of course, Abu Ma'shar and Ptolemy.
[101] *Ibid.* 33. [102] Cf. Silverstein, 190.
[103] *Liber de Naturis,* p. 17. See the comparison of Lemay, 329-30.
[104] The major difference is that Daniel attempts to introduce into

a passage of the *Asclepius* that Bernard knows, but point out that Mercury is really two figures, possibly alluding to the distinction between theological and scientific Hermeticism.[105]

The similarities and differences in the two thinkers are aptly summarized in the following analysis by Daniel of the interrelationship between God, nature, and creation. After implying that Chartrain cosmology is a prelude to his own advanced views, he proposes that there are four kinds of lower things without the activity of which no creation may take place. These are *materia, forma, compositio,* and *compositum.*[106] After a brief discussion of the first two, he turns in the more original part of his analysis to the manner in which the thing being composed (*compositio*) becomes the thing composed (*compositum*):

Indeed, so fine a compositor cannot be anyone but God, the begetter of all things, who, to the extent of their differences, created from nothing by his own wisdom at once and once and for all, the two primordial materials, that is, of the lower and upper [worlds]. And in order that they might serve the law of their unalterable creation that was given inviolate, he animated them in this creation by an eternal breath of that same divine source of breath. Furthermore, I call the natural law that which arranges, according to the prop-

---

the Platonic and Hermetic conceptions the Aristotelian inspired dichotomy between *compositio* and *compositum*; see, for example, his commentary on Hermes, *Liber de Naturis*, p. 14.

[105] *Ibid.* 16.

[106] *Ibid.* 17: "Supradictis igitur in hunc modum determinatis (i.e. having dealt with the cosmological theories of the School of Chartres), qua uia preparata ad creationem mundi pedetentim accedendum est, quod ut melius fiat, inprimis ponenda sunt quatuor rerum genera, extra que nulla inferioris mundi species inueniri potest. Sunt autem hec: materia, forma, compositio et compositum."

erty of the subject, motion or rest for every corporeal thing. But this [law of nature], since it does nothing without a plan, takes counsel from the soul, so that, so to speak, neither may accomplish anything without the other.

These are the two instruments of the great craftsman, which, since they have learned from the master, put together all composed things by a certain harmony in the lower world and dissolve them again by a certain dissonance. And yet all this is ascribed to the craftsman, since they have been made aware of this instruction from the beginning by his artifice. For, although any workman may work with his tools, the work is nonetheless not said [to be] by the tools but by the workman. Thus, even though God has produced a form for the world from pre-existing matter by means of these two instruments, the world is, for the sake of the term, correctly to be called not the work of nature but the work of God. Although Nature, whose duty it is to make an impression of the human figure for man, may, in the material uterus, form, hollow out and arrange the limbs, nonetheless man, on account of his more worthy part, is the work of God. . . .[107]

[107] *Ibid.* 17-18: "Compositor uero talis non nisi genitor uniuersitatis deus esse potest, qui, sua sapientia semel et simul, unde singula prouenirent, duas quantum ad distinctionem primordiales inferiorum uidelicet et superiorum materias ex nichilo creauit, easque, ut datam legem rate conditionis inuiolatam seruarent, in ipsa creatione eterno cuiusdam, diuini spiraculi flatu animauit. Hanc enim legem naturam appello, que unicuique rei corporee secundum subiecti proprietatem, motum uel quietum disponit.

"Ista uero, quia sine ratione nichil facit, ab anima consilium capit, ita tamen, quod neutra sine altera aliquid operetur. Hec sunt duo instrumenta magni artificis, que sicut a magistro didicerunt, in his inferioribus omne compositum quadam armonia componuntur et

The most remarkable feature of this description is its capacity to absorb the language of the new science without necessarily committing itself to any of its positions. In spite of his Hermetic vocabulary and his interest in astrology, Daniel has not moved very far from Chartres. His metaphor of the craftsman appears to be an adaptation of William's. In spite of his more elaborate description of the creative process, he also refers creation back to the creator. In these two respects he would seem to have adapted a new vocabulary to a relatively conservative philosophical position. Only in his conception of nature does he display audacity. In analysing her powers, he states:

> Moreover, the aforesaid Nature, like a craftsmanlike assistant, when it had purified the elements and separated them from each other, commanded each one to keep the place congruent to it, according to what the plan demanded, in order that it might illuminate the future world.[108]

This *prouida natura*[109] appears to perform for Daniel what Noys does for Bernard with the aid of Natura: to render

---

iterum quadam dissonantia dissoluunt, et tamen hoc totum artifici ascribitur, quia (qui, Sudhoff) ab artifice hunc originis ducatum senserunt. Licet enim aliquis faber suis instrumentis operetur, non tamen instrumentorum sed artificis opus dicitur. Sic, quamuis deus hiis duobus intrumentis ex iam preiacente materia formam mundo prestauerit, non tamen mundus opus nature, sed opus dei recte nominatur, verbi gratia, licet natura, cuius est officium humanam homini imprimere figuram, in utero materno membra informet, concauet et disponat, tamen homo propter partem digniorem opus dei . . . est. . . ."

[108] *Ibid.* 18: "Predicta siquidem tandem natura, uelut artificiosa ministra, depuratis elementis et ab inuicem separatis, ut mundum profuturum serenaret, iussit unicuique, secundum quod ratio exigebat, congruum sibi locum tenere."

[109] *Loc. cit.*

the cosmos an orderly imitation of the divine. Yet Daniel has not committed himself as completely as Bernard to naturalism. Daniel's nature arranges the elements into the desirable proportions that the *phisici* call obedience, harmony, and necessity.[110] The resultant *ornatus* is similar to Bernard's, but is presented in noticeably more static terms. The basic difference is that, in describing the change from *compositio* to *compositum*, Daniel employs the two terms *elementum* and *elementatum*. According to this process, as the *uisibiles elementorum ornatus* takes place, the elements become the *elementata*, the composed products of the creative action.[111] Bernard mentions *elementatum* once when he

[110] *Loc. cit.*: "Primum uocant phisici obedientiam, secundum armoniam, tercium necessitatem."

[111] On *elementatum* in the twelfth century, see T. Silverstein, *MS* 16 (1954), 156-62, and, with special reference to William of Conches, Lemay, *Abu Ma'shar*, 176-79. In assimilating Daniel's notion, in part, into Dominicus Gundissalinus, Silverstein perhaps gives the impression that it is more carefully thought out than it is. In the *Liber de Naturis*, p. 19, Daniel summarizes his position on the ordering of the elements in the lower world as follows: "Hec uero, que dicta sunt de yle et elementis, doctrinalia sunt, quia yle non fuit, nisi dum pura elementa fuerunt, que quam cito corrumpebantur, ut generacio rerum fieret yle, que grece initium mundi interpretatur, desunt esse. Similiter et elementa, per supradictam generationem a suis principiis alienata, qualitatibus tantum conseruatis in essentiam elementatorum transierunt, in quibus nichil remanet nisi elementorum proprietates. Dicimus tamen elementata ex elementis constare, sicuti panem ex farina et aqua, quia non debemus destruere principia facultatem." Birkenmajer (p. 51) suggests that these lines are not Daniel's, but if they may be accepted as a reasonable summary of his doctrine they shed light on the more abstruse description of the same process in the *Liber*, pp. 10-12, which culminates with the passage cited by Silverstein in his article (161), and concludes with the definition of *elementorum ornatus* as the *elementata* (*Liber*, p. 12). In this analysis, Daniel begins with the position on the elements in Chartres and attempts to incorporate notions which, he claims, come from Aristotle and Hippocrates (p.

is summarizing his theory of identity and difference,[112] but it is not so centrally important in his cosmology. On the whole he assigns a larger role than Daniel to natural and physical processes in the creative act. In sum, while Daniel knows more advanced sources than Bernard, his cosmology, on the whole, is more conservative, less dynamic, and less committed to a naturalistic mode of explanation.

As stated above, this brief outline makes no pretence at offering a comprehensive exposition of the cosmologies of Thierry, William, and Daniel. It does however point out how much each differs from the other and from Bernard.

Thierry's originality lies in his brilliant reworking of the hexaemeral tradition. He purges it of its imprecision, mysticism, and irrationality; he readapts it to a new, more logical physical theory. Yet its originality operates within limits, the *distinctiones* or distinct acts of the six days themselves. Haskins characterizes the *De Septem Diebus* as "a daring piece of Platonism," in which "the traces of Aristotelian physics carry us no farther than Macrobius."[113] The choice of Macrobius rather than Hermes is unhappy, but Haskins is essentially correct. Thierry reflects neither the new Aristotelianism nor the new astronomy. His significance for twelfth-century scientific thought arises from his introducing the *ordo naturalis* into hexaemeral literature. He thereby legitimizes the activity of logical scientific investigation, distinguishing clearly between what is leg-

---

11). Yet these notions may not really consist, as Silverstein and Lemay argue, of a profound assimilation of Arabic doctrines, but merely of a logical and linguistic justification for a sensuous appreciation of the existing world.

[112] *Cos.* i.4.51. And did Bernard see *elementatum* in relation to *elementans*, which he associates with Natura, *Cos.* i.4.50, 57?

[113] Haskins, 90.

endary or mythical and what is capable of rationalistic explanation.

William, by contrast, is more difficult to assess. He is aware of the translations and some of their doctrines, but he incorporates no more than a *soupçon* into his lectures on Plato. His physics is heavily indebted, as he acknowledges, to the *medici*, whose works had been available for some time even if they had not previously been put to such use. His response to Plato is first of all a personal one. Yet he is heavily indebted to Boethius, and his interest in science cannot be separated from his desire to solve certain classical philosophical problems. What Bernard perhaps owes to him—although it is nowhere stated directly—is a theory of myth which builds on Macrobius and offers a theoretical background for the *Cosmographia*. Bernard's work cannot be reduced to William's critical vocabulary for discussing myth, but once the reader has mastered that language many of its secrets are unlocked.

Daniel, on the other hand, at least knows the new physics and astronomy at first hand. He has the advantage of belonging to the next generation, although it is questionable whether he pursues that advantage fully. He has the added qualification of having studied with the Arabs himself, whereas Bernard, if he knew Arabic at all, probably learned it from Hermann of Carinthia. He has heard of Aristotle's *Libri Naturales* and can cite (if somewhat inaccurately) individual works from within the corpus; he also knows Alfarabi, Alfergani, and at least one Hermetic book in addition to the *Asclepius*. Yet his acquaintance with these works is often superficial and the underlying conservatism of his philosophy belies any real commitment to their positions. His relation to Bernard, who may perhaps also be numbered among his sources, is twofold. First, he abandons the hexaemeral pattern virtually altogether and substitutes for it a combination of Plato and Ptolemy. Secondly, he leans very heavily on a single Arab source, Abu Ma'shar. Bernard and Daniel, in fact, argue strongly for the early penetration of Aristotelian naturalism and Ptolemaic astrology through this author.[114] While other astronomers are mentioned by name only, Abu Ma'shar seems to have inspired at least two thinkers to reformulate the fundamental problem of Identity and Difference.

In a larger perspective this brief comparison between Bernard and his near contemporaries also illustrates the futility of attempting to interpret all their works as variations on a single world view without drawing attention at the same time to the individualizing features of each. To date, the treatment of the twelfth century, in this respect at least, has been somewhat paradoxical. While praising the period's achievements as "the foundations of European civilization," historians have fallen back on hundred-year-old platitudes like "Chartrain cosmology" in attempting to evaluate its philosophical and scientific originality. The present study, by implication, argues for a more subtle and refined assessment of figures like Adelard, Thierry, William, Hermann, and Daniel—to say nothing of the numerous *anonymi*—in terms of their own responses to tradition and innovation. When the large number of texts which still remain in manuscript have been edited, and monographic studies provided where necessary, it will be clear that the twelfth century was not only a great period for the reassimilation of the ancients but also for reorienting the fundamental problems of European philosophy. Within that reorientation the modern scientific consciousness was born.

3. Conclusion: Literature or Science?

The above observations have emphasized Bernard's doctrinal differences from his near contemporaries, but a more

[114] Cf. Lemay, *Abu Ma'shar*, 345-52.

profound disparity arises from the simple fact that, in contrast to the dialogues and commentaries, the *Cosmographia* is primarily a work of literature. There is really no parallel in Thierry, William, or Daniel for Bernard's poetry. While all adhered to the twelfth-century ideal of uniting rhetoric and philosophy, and while all, in theory, may have possessed a poetic vision of the cosmos, none translated it into poetic practice. It is arguable, in fact, that the commentaries and philosophical dialogues are essentially demythologizations. They all bear, to a greater or lesser degree, the stamp of the scholastic form in which they are conceived. The arguments emerge from their own inner, logical consistency, not from the imposition onto the older models of a new symbolic view of the cosmos. An argument may be advanced that Adelard and Daniel present relatively new cosmologies. Yet they do not do so as new myths, and the lack of a literary as opposed to purely philosophic unity separates them from Bernard. Again, William's mind is much more rational than Bernard's. He possesses the capacity to distinguish clearly between rival arguments and to forge from them a new unity. Moreover, his *model* of the universe presents a number of new and original features. But it is not a new *myth* of creation. Bernard lacks William's didactic gifts, but he has just the right combination of interest in myth and science to create a new and original cosmogony. That is why the *Cosmographia* is so unusual an event in medieval Latin literature.

Yet, because of its very uniqueness, it is difficult to state with precision just what Bernard's place is in medieval letters. Some historians have neglected his role, while others, like C. S. Lewis, have attempted to show that he played a large part in framing the theoretical background for the vernacular literature of courtly love. An accurate assessment perhaps lies between the two extremes. On the one hand, it is easy, through selective quotation, to overstress

Bernard's influence on thirteenth- and fourteenth-century literature. It should be recalled that medieval authors were much less exact in specifying their sources than modern editors. From the perspective of the fourteenth century in particular it would have appeared that many authors were spreading ideas in philosophical verse not so very different from Bernard's. In numerous codices the *Cosmographia* is bound with treatises on composition, like Geoffroi de Vinsauf, or other twelfth-century poets, like Alan of Lille. Therefore the question of direct influence, even where the manuscript evidence supports it, is difficult to assess. On the other hand, the general neglect of Bernard has left a considerable lacuna in medieval literary scholarship. In his stylistic superiority, in his ability to capture in verse the most advanced ideas of his contemporaries, Bernard is one of the most important literary innovators of his time. Moreover, in uniting poetry and philosophy so harmoniously, he becomes the successor to the author of the *Consolatio Philosophiae*, foreshadowing the philosophical epics of Alan of Lille, Jean de Meung, and Dante.

The central idea of the *Cosmographia* is that man is a microcosm of the elements, principles, and forces in the world. His creation recapitulates the mythical cosmogony that brought the world into being. Once created, he is the crowning glory, the *raison d'être*, of creation. Made in the image of his maker through the cooperation of the natural forces, he alone is able to understand the processes by which he is formed and by which the world perpetuates its existence. With this splendid design of man, the *fabrica Nature primipotentis*, Bernard bridges one of the great ideas linking classical and renaissance thought.

Yet Bernard is not the only twelfth-century author to think that man is a little cosmos.[115] As mentioned briefly in Chapter IV, the notion undergoes a rapid development

[115] Cf. Chenu, 38.

275

in the first half-century that is virtually unforeseen in the previous literature. It is not simply a reworking of Plato but a new movement uniting various currents of ancient and modern thought. It makes its appearance in the exegetical writings of William of Conches, Gilbert Porreta, William of St. Thierry, and Peter Lombard. It provides a foundation for major works of theological literature in Hildegard of Bingen, Godefrey of St. Victor, and Alan of Lille. In all these authors the idea has certain common features that are admirably summarized in the illustration of Hildegard's *Liber Divinorum Operum* in the famous Lucca codex [Plate VI]. The (presumably) thirteenth-century artist has caught the essential spirit of the twelfth-century idea. Here man is the center of the cosmos; he is its most important creation and the summary of all its parts. The four elements out of which he is made are arranged according to their natural properties in concentric circles: earth in the middle, water and air in various layers around it, and, in the celestial heights, divine fire in a red ring. The twelve signs of the zodiac inhere in the firmament, while the four winds moderate the climate of the globe. Hildegard has no figure called Noys, but God's wisdom, who hovers over the animating fire, fulfils the same function. Nor is there a Natura, unless one sees her in the figure of the saintly abbess herself, who records her own vision in the lower left-hand corner. Various twelfth-century authors would emphasize different aspects of the cosmology. Bernard assigns a large role to astrology and distinguishes more sharply than the picture suggests between macro- and microcosmic influences. Yet there can be no doubt about the common features.

The use of the topos, *homo microcosmus*, by a number of writers in different disciplines, however, again raises a question about the literary form of the *Cosmographia*. Immediately above, it was suggested that the work is a myth rather than a demythologization. It should also be stressed that it is not a work of natural philosophy or theology, nor should it be assessed by the criteria of either discipline. This means, on the one hand, that it should not be assessed as a work of pure science. In the history of astronomy, its major scientific discipline, its influence was only momentary. It summarized and expressed for the Latin world trends of thought that were being worked out with greater precision elsewhere. The subordination of natural philosophy to literature in the work is implicit in treating cosmology as a story and in making the *quadrivium* serve the interests of the *trivium*. On the other hand, the *Cosmographia* should not be viewed through the perspective of its sister discipline, theology. In his outline of the types of subject-matter suitable for treatment in a mythical format, Macrobius specifically excludes the ultimate mysteries of theology, and Bernard seems to have followed him to the letter. The subject of the *Cosmographia* is not the initial origin of matter and of God but the periodic and predictable renewal of matter under God's design: not *initium mundi* but *exornatio mundi*. At a suitable time the cosmos dissolves into its primitive elements only to be remade again according to a divine model. While Bernard holds radical views on individual scientific issues, the *Cosmographia* should not be interpreted primarily as an attack on the theological view of reality but simply as a work of literature inspired by the "new science." Like any work of literature, it is a representation of reality, a dramatic enactment. In twelfth-century terms, it is an "organization" of that reality within the scope of the poet's role as divine philosopher. As Virgil, Ovid, and the late Latin allegorists had told the story of the world's creation in their terms, so Bernard does in his. The failure to recognize that the *Cosmographia* is a work of literature written at a time when this discipline is again re-entering the school curriculum on a large scale has been at the source of many mis-interpretations of it.[116]

Within the literary mode, then, natural philosophy makes its appearance, and it does so in two ways, both as a set of doctrines on specific issues like *homo microcosmus* and as a more general attitude towards the empirically definable world. The latter aspect of Bernard's mind is difficult to describe in a few words. Some have attempted to define his approach as "pantheistic" or "realist," but these theological and philosophical categories that at once say too much and too little.[117] Bernard is not a pantheist; he

[116] In almost all previous accounts of the work, in fact, historians have shown a compulsive desire to prove that Bernard was either a Christian or pagan author. In the first "modern" study of Bernard, Gilson argued unconvincingly that he was a Christian writer; *AHDLMA* 3 (1928), 5-24. He was answered by two hardly more convincing accounts by E. R. Curtius; *Zeitschrift für romanische Philologie* 58 (1938), 180-97 and *Europäische Literatur und lateinisches Mittelalter*, 118-23. An expectedly pagan reading was also given by Thorndike, *A History of Magic and Experimental Science*, vol. 2, 102-06, while Silverstein attempted to strike a compromise; *Modern Philology* 46 (1948-49), 92-116. Even Lemay, *Abu Ma'shar*, 259-84 assimilates Gilson's view into an account that, on all specific points, refutes it and, in a unusual moment of bad judgment, Chenu, 115 n. 2, affirms the approach of Gilson "qui souligne fortement le christianisme du fond sous le paganisme de la forme." This problem has happily not been made the center of focus of my study. Yet it is worth noting that two excellent refutations of the thesis that Bernard was, in a theological sense, a Christian writer, have been available for some time. The first is Vernet, whose introduction and notes settle the matter decisively in favor of pagan sources. The second is the thesis of M. McCrimmon, which supports Vernet's statement that, while there are perhaps *parallels* to the book of Genesis in the *Cosmographia*, there are no *sources*. As this study has suggested in numerous places, however, it is no more discerning to interpret the *Cosmographia* as a work of theology than it would be to use such an approach in reading *Paradise Lost*.

[117] Clerval, *Les écoles de Chartres*, 260-61 claims that Bernard was a pantheist, a notion that is taken up by M. de Wulf, *Histoire*

does not absorb God into his works. Like Thierry, he maintains a respectful balance between a this- and otherworldly conception of deity. Nor does realism describe with accuracy his approach to what exists, since he does not speak in terms of individuals or universals. The much abused term "Platonist," which is normally applied to the whole period 1100-1150, also fails to account for what dominates his experience of nature: its sensuous presence. It has the added disadvantage of reducing new and original problem-orientations to the categories of thought of a previous age. Tullio Gregory has suggested that the Platonism of the first half-century has strong doctrinal links with the Aristotelianism of the last half.[118] No better example of a

de la philosophie médiévale, 5th edn., vol. 1 (Louvain, 1924), 180-81. De Wulf adds "le monisme" to the characterization, *ibid*. 203, and suggests, 141-47, that the entire School of Chartres, including Bernard, were realists. Gilson, *AHDLMA* 3 (1928), 5, states that the question cannot be answered without a study of the sources of the *Cosmographia*. Despite the partial and inaccurate manner in which Gilson does this, de Wulf, citing no other authority, retracts his essentially well-argued views in the 6th edition of his *Histoire*, vol. 1 (Louvain, 1934), 191: "Cette oeuvre, dans laquelle Gilson voit une interprétation des données de la Genèse, ne contient rien, au point de vue philosophique, que Bernard n'ait appris chez ses maîtres. Elle n'est ni moniste, ni panthéiste." Cf. p. 194. Somewhat qualified, de Wulf's views from the 5th edition (1924) are substantiated by this study, but they have been placed in the wider context of Bernard's sources. In this sense, they complete the picture of Bernard offered by Liebeschütz, *Vorträge der Bibliothek Warburg 1923-24*, 133-43.

[118] Gregory, 263: "From the Platonism of the twelfth century to the Aristotelianism of the next there is no antithesis or brusque transition" (my trans.). Cf. E. Gilson, *History of Christian Philosophy in the Middle Ages* (London, 1955), 144, speaking of the twelfth century: "The more one studies the Middle Ages, the more one notices the polymorphism of the Platonic influence. Plato himself does not appear, but Platonism is everywhere: let us say rather that there are Platonisms everywhere."

union of the two through naturalism could be found than Bernard. Essentially, Bernard's philosophic achievement consists in maintaining the idea of order inherent in twelfth-century Platonism while asserting at the same time that this order is an abstraction of the existing world. Thus, in his work there is a meeting between the divine order in the mind of God and the empirical order of the created universe. Thierry and William call the divine element the *forma* or *principium essendi*; the earthly, *exornatio mundi*. The position of all three in this regard is both a philosophical and scientific naturalism. From time to time in this study it has been called an *existential naturalism*: existential inasmuch as it involves the empirically definable world and natural inasmuch as it involves the abstract patterns by which twelfth-century philosophy understood natural laws.

Important in developing this two-sided approach to nature is the structural encyclopedia. Bernard commences the cosmic process of *ornatus mundi* with a divine model in mind, but when the world is finally created it is divided into the realms of the living universe as his contemporaries knew them. The unfolding of the world results in the world as it is. The model is not an ideal held out to be imitated but actually informs the cosmos. In his description of the contents of the universe in i.3, he makes this abundantly clear. The reader encounters a catalogue made up of items drawn from mythological handbooks as well as from treatises on natural philosophy. The juxtaposition of the mythical and the scientific is hardly accidental in so calculating a literary artist as Bernard. It is possible to see his attitude as an essentially empirical outlook from which the mythical has not been eliminated, or, as is more probably the case, as a mythical outlook to which a nascent interest in the real world has been added. Through this unusual approach to the natural universe, Bernard conveys an impression that is rare before the 1140s: a sense of the tangible, the individual, and the material which is at once intangible, universal, and mysterious. A century earlier this stylistic combination is unheard of; a half-century later it is more familiar in literature and in the plastic arts, but must be viewed through the perspective of *Aristoteles latinus*. At this particular moment in the revival of classical learning it possesses a highly attractive union of erudition and joyful naïveté.

In its broadest context the naturalism of the first half-century has a very profound and far-reaching effect on the cultural history of Europe. One may trace it, indirectly, in the continuing debate over individuals and universals, and, more directly, in cathedrals like Chartres, in which the Romanesque is incorporated into the Gothic in a perfect union of Platonic order and existential naturalism. Perhaps the most lasting influence arises from legal and political theory and practice. The idea of *homo naturalis*, who is formed and maintained according to natural laws, holds important implications for the practical arts of civilization, for if man is now an autonomous being in physical terms, his laws and institutions are the result of his own collective experience. In this way the normative begins to make its appearance alongside the inherited authority of ideal moral law; the existing world and its legal framework find their own legitimation. This development is more than a revival of Roman legal practice; it is a new beginning. In this area much research of a cross-disciplinary nature remains to be done, so that twelfth-century naturalism may be shown to reveal changes not only within individual disciplines but in more general attitudes affecting the state and its institutions.

Not all of these developments, of course, may be traced to Bernard Silvester. In terms of his immediate influence a special place is reserved for Alan of Lille. Alan's *Anti-*

claudianus de Antirufino, which was finished around 1184, holds somewhat the same position in poetry as does Daniel's *Liber de Naturis* in cosmology: it summarizes the trends of the previous half-century, providing the link between Chartres and Toledo on the one hand and the thirteenth century on the other. In Alan's theological and poetic writings the goddess Natura is quite different from what she is in the *Cosmographia*. From physical allegory the reader has returned to moral allegory, and morality now has the upper hand. Yet this new moral allegory is quite different from any that has appeared before, since it has absorbed into its eclectic fabric the essential elements of the earlier naturalism. It is a fusion of natural philosophy and theology. The *Anticlaudianus* may be described as a twelfth-century *Psychomachia* in which various allegorized virtues and vices fight for man's soul. Amid the vast gallery of personifications in the work, Alan remains faithful to Bernard, whose work he knew,[119] in one important respect: the conception of naturalistic man. Whether as a "universal" figure who unites all the physical and moral virtues in one, or as an "individual" who fights alone against the vices that encroach upon him from all sides, Alan's *nouus homo* is a direct continuation of Bernard's *homo, fabrica Nature primipotentis*. By building on Bernard's achievement, Alan effectively translates the whole machinery of man's moral drama to the existing world. In book nine, when man, exhausted at having conquered the vices, looks out over the "epic" battlefield and foresees a new golden age, Alan has in mind a utopia not of the future but of the present. The existential naturalism

---

[119] Vernet (1938), 120 notes wryly: "Alain de Lille n'a pas prononcé le nom de Bernard, peut-être parce qu'il le pille à chaque page: l'*Anticlaudianus* est farci de vers empruntés à la *Cosmographia* et de développements qui reprennent—en les délayant—des passages analogues de Bernard."

of the *Cosmographia* has become the moral golden age of perpetual harmony in the real world, in which natural laws, guided by love, govern man in society. Yet in Alan the reader has lost something essential to Bernard: his optimism. Alan knows that man is a fallen creature who can never quite repair his sinful nature, while Bernard finds man, as on that primeval first day, waiting to see the world unfold before him. Of the two views Bernard's is by far the more unusual for its time and place. It is also, perhaps, a more faithful reflection of the social and cultural milieux. Bernard's preoccupation with origins, with man's place in the natural order, with change in general, corresponds loosely to a contemporary picture of man in a society of change. Allusions to everyday life are anything but abundant in the *Cosmographia*; yet, indirectly, the work reflects the prosperity of the towns and the active intellectual life of the cathedral schools, and, as a result, an unmistakably secularized sensibility. Bernard's images often illustrate the utilitarian, the mechanical, and the notion of man as the measure of all things. He is virtually alone in his day in stating that the present, not the past, is the *receptaculum* of the future, a sentiment that transmits in an acceptably classical format the contemporary ideals of progress and change. His *homo naturalis* was in fact so popular in its own day and so widely utilized by subsequent writers that it must have touched the sensibilities of its period very closely. It was indeed a suitable image for such an optimistic age to frame of itself and of the men who were making it.

Selected Bibliography

[Abelard, P.]. *Petri Abaelardi Introductio ad Theologiam, in libros tres divisa. PL* 178, 979-1114.

[Abu Maʿshar]. *Introductorium in astronomiam Albumasaris abalchi octo continens libros partiales.* [Venezia, 1506].

[Adelard of Bath]. *Des Adelard von Bath Traktat De Eodem et Diverso. Zum ersten Male herausgegeben und historisch-kritisch untersucht.* Edited by H. Willner. *Beiträge* 4.1, Münster, 1903.

————. *Die Questiones Naturales des Adelardus von Bath.* Edited by M. Müller. *Beiträge* 31.2, Münster, 1934.

[Alan of Lille]. *Alain de Lille Anticlaudianus. Texte critique avec une introduction et des tables.* Edited by R. Bossuat. Textes philosophiques du moyen âge, 1. Paris, 1955.

————. "La somme 'Quoniam homines' d'Alain de Lille." Edited by P. Glorieux. *AHDLMA* 20 (1953), 113-364.

Alessio, F., "La filosofia e le 'artes mechanicae' nel secolo XII." *SMed*, 3rd ser., 6 (1965), 71-155.

[Alkindi]. *Die philosophischen Abhandlungen des Jaʿqūb ben Isḥāq al-Kindi.* Edited by A. Nagy. *Beiträge* 2.5, Münster, 1897.

Allers, R. "Microcosmus from Anaximander to Paracelsus." *Traditio* 2 (1944), 319-407.

Arbusow, L. *Colores Rhetorici. Eine Auswahl rhetorischer Figuren und Gemeinplätze als Hilfsmittel für akademische Übungen an mittelalterlichen Texten.* 2nd edn., revised by H. Peter. Göttingen, 1963.

Auerbach, E. "Figura." *Scenes from the Drama of European Literature. Six Essays,* pp. 11-76. New York, 1959. (=*Gesammelte Aufsätze zur romanischen Philologie,* pp. 55-92. Berne/München, 1967.)

————. *Typologische Motive in der mittelalterlichen Literatur.* Schriften und Vorträge des Petrarca-Institutes Köln. Krefeld, 1953.

[Bernard of Clairvaux]. *Sancti Bernardi Abbatis Clarae-Vallensis De Consideratione Libri quinque ad Eugenium Tertium. PL* 182, 727-807.

285

[Bernardus Silvestris]. *Commentum Bernardi Silvestris super sex libros Eneidos Virgilii.* Edited by W. Riedel. Greifswald, 1924.

―――. "Il 'Dictamen' de Bernardo Silvestre." Edited by M. Brini Savorelli. *Rivista critica della storia della filosofia* 20 (1965), 182-230.

―――. "Un manuale de geomanzia presentato da Bernardo Silvestre da Tours (XII secolo): l'*Experimentarius.*" Edited by M. Brini Savorelli. *Rivista critica della storia della filosofia* 14 (1959), 283-342.

Bezold, F. von. "Astrologische Geschichtskonstruction im Mittelalter." *Aus Mittelalter und Renaissance,* pp. 165-95. München/Berlin, 1918.

―――. *Das Fortleben der antiken Götter im mittelalterlichen Humanismus.* Bonn/Leipzig, 1922.

Birkenmajer, A. "Eine neue Handschrift des Liber de naturis inferiorum et superiorum des Daniel von Merlai." *Archiv für die Geschichte der Naturwissenschaften und die Technik* 9 (1918), 45-51.

―――. *Le rôle joué par les médecins et les naturalistes dans la réception d'Aristote au XIIe et XIIIe siècles.* Extrait de la Pologne au VIe Congrès International des Sciences Historiques, Oslo, 1928. Warzsawa, 1930.

Bliemetzrieder, F. *Adelhard von Bath. Blätter aus dem Leben eines englischen Naturphilosophen des 12. Jahrhunderts und Bahnbrechers einer Wiedererweckung der griechischen Antike. Eine kulturgeschichtliche Studie.* München, 1935.

Bober, H. "An Illustrated Medieval School-Book of Bede's 'De Natura Rerum.'" *The Journal of the Walters Art Gallery* 19-20 (1956-57), 65-97.

Borkenau, F. *Der Übergang vom feudalen zum bürgerlichen Weltbild.* Paris, 1934.

Brinkmann, H. "Verhüllung ("Integumentum") als literarische Darstellungsform im Mittelalter." In A. Zimmermann, ed., *Miscellanea Mediaevalia 8, Der Begriff der Repraesentatio im Mittelalter. Stellvertretung, Symbol, Zeichen, Bild,* pp. 314-39. Berlin/New York, 1971.

Callus, D. A. "Introduction of Aristotelian Learning to Oxford." *Proceedings of the British Academy* 19 (1943), 229-81.

Carmody, F. J. *Arabic Astronomical and Astrological Sciences in Latin Translation. A Critical Bibliography.* Berkeley/Los Angeles, 1956.

[Censorinus]. *Censorini de die natali.* Edited by F. Hultsch. Leipzig, 1867.

Chenu, M.-D. "Involucrum. Le mythe selon les théologiens médiévaux." *AHDLMA* 22 (1956), 75-79.

———. *Nature, Man and Society in the Twelfth Century. Essays on New Theological Perspectives in the Latin West.* Selected, edited, and translated by J. Taylor and L. K. Little. Chicago, 1968. (= *La théologie au douzième siècle,* Paris, 1957.)

Cicero. *De Natura Deorum. Academica.* Translated by H. Rackam. London/New York, 1933.

———. *M. Tulli Ciceronis scripta quae manserunt omnia,* fasc. 45, *De Natura Deorum.* Edited by O. Plasberg. Leipzig, 1933.

[Claudian]. *Claudii Claudiani Carmina.* Edited by J. Koch. Leipzig, 1893.

Clerval, A. *Les écoles de Chartres au moyen âge du Ve au XVIe siècle.* Mémoires de la Société archéologique d'Eure-et-Loire, XI. Chartres, 1895.

[Constantinus Africanus]. *Constantini Monachi Montecassini liber de oculis. Galieni littere ad corisium de morbis oculorum et eorum curis.* Collectio Ophtalmologica Veterum Auctorum, II, fasc. VII. Paris [1933].

———. *Liber Pantegni ysaac israelite filij adoptiui Salomonis regis arabie, quem Constantinus aphricanus monachus montis cassinensis sibi uendicauit.* In *Opera omnia ysaac.* . . . Lugduni, 1515.

Cornford, F. M. *Plato's Cosmology. The Timaeus of Plato translated with a Running Commentary.* London, 1937.

Courcelle, P. "Etude critique sur les commentaires de la *Consolation* de Boèce (IXe-XVe siècles)." *AHDLMA* 14 (1939), 5-140.

Cousin, V. *Ouvrages inédits d'Abélard pour servir à l'histoire de la philosophie scholastique en France.* Paris, 1836.

Cumont, F. "Jupiter summus exsuperantissimus." *Archiv für Religionswissenschaft* 9 (1906), 323-36.

Curtius, E. R. *Europäische Literatur und lateinisches Mittelalter,* 2nd edn. Berne, 1954.

———. "Rhetorische Naturschilderung im Mittelalter." *Romanische Forschungen* 56 (1942), 219-56.

———. "Zur Literarästhetik des Mittelalters II." *Zeitschrift für romanische Philologie* 58 (1938), 129-232.

Dales, R. C. "Anonymi *De Elementis*: From a Twelfth-Century Collection of Scientific Works in British Museum MS Cotton Galba E.IV." *Isis* 56 (1965), 174-89.

d'Alverny, M.-T. "Alain de Lille et la *theologia.*" In *L'homme devant Dieu. Mélanges offerts au Père Henri de Lubac,* vol. 2, *Du moyen âge au siècle des lumières.* Théologie . . . 57 [Paris], 1964, 111-28.

———. "Le cosmos symbolique du XIIe siècle." *AHDLMA* 20 (1954), 31-81.

[Damian, Peter]. *L'opera poetica di S. Pier Damiani.* Edited by M. Lokrantz. Acta Universitatis Stockholmiensis, Studia Latina Stockholmiensia, XII. Uppsala, 1964.

[Daniel of Morley]. "Daniels von Morley Liber de naturis inferiorum et superiorum nach der Handschrift Cod. Arundel 377 des British Museums zum Abdruck gebracht." Edited by K. Sudhoff, *Archiv für die Geschichte der Naturwissenschaften und die Technik* 8 (1917), 1-41.

Destombes, M., ed., *Mappemondes A.D. 1200-1500. Catalogue préparé par la Commission des Cartes Anciennes de l'Union Géographique Internationale.* Monumenta Cartographica Vestustioris Aevi A.D. 1200-1500, I. Amsterdam, 1964.

Dodd, C. H. *The Bible and the Greeks.* London, 1935.

Dronke, P. "L'amor che move il sole e l'altre stelle." *SMed,* 3rd ser., 6 (1965), 389-422.

———. "New Approaches to the School of Chartres." *Anuario de estudios medievales* 6 (1971), 117-40.

———. *Poetic Individuality in the Middle Ages. New Departures in Poetry, 1000-1150.* Oxford, 1970.

Duhem, P. *Le système du monde. Histoire des doctrines cosmologiques de Platon à Copernic,* vol. 3. Paris, 1915.

Ebel, U. "Die literarischen Formen der Jenseits- und Endzeitvisionen." In H. R. Jauss and E. Köhler, eds., *Grundriss der romanischen Literaturen des Mittelalters* 6.1, *La littérature didactique, allégorique, et satirique,* pp. 181-224. Heidelberg, 1968.

Edsman, C.-M. *Ignis Divinus. Le feu comme moyen de rajeunissement et d'immortalité: contes, légendes, mythes, et rites.* Publications of the New Society of Letters at Lund, 34. Lund, 1949.

Faral, E. "Le manuscrit 511 du 'Hunterian Museum' de Glasgow." *SMed,* nuova serie, 9 (1936), 18-119.

———. *Les arts poétiques du XIIe et du XIIIe siècle. Recherches et documents sur la technique littéraire du moyen âge.* Paris, 1924.

[Firmicus Maternus]. *Iulii Firmicii Materni Matheseos libri VIII.* Edited by W. Kroll and F. Skutsch. 2 vols. Leipzig, 1913.

[Fulgentius]. *Fabii Planciades Fulgentii V.C. Opera accedunt Fabii Claudii Gordiani Fulgentii V.C. De Aetatibus Mundi et Hominis et S. Fulgentii Episcopi Super Thebaiden.* Edited by R. Helm. Leipzig, 1898.

Gain, D. B. "Gerbert and Manilius." *Latomus* 29 (1970), 128-32.

Gilson, E. "La cosmogonie de Bernardus Silvestris." *AHDLMA* 3 (1928), 5-24.

[Godefrey of St. Victor]. *Godefroy de Saint-Victor Microcosmus.* Edited by P. Delhaye. Mémoires et travaux publiés par les professeurs des Facultés Catholiques de Lille, LVI. Lille/Gembloux, 1951. Idem, *Le microcosmus de Godefroy de Saint-Victor. Etude théologique.* Ibid. LVII, 1951.

Grabmann, M. *Die Geschichte der scholastischen Methode. Nach den Gedruckten und Ungedruckten Quellen dargestellt.* 2 vols. Freiburg im Breisgau, 1909-11.

————. "Handschriftliche Forschungen und Mitteilungen zum Schrifttum des Wilhelm von Conches und zu Bearbeitungen seiner naturwissenschaftlichen Werke." *SB München, phil.-hist. Abt.*, 10 (1935).

Graf, A. *Miti, leggende e superstitioni del medio evo*. 2nd edn. Torino, 1925.

Gregory, T. "L'idea di natura nella filosofia medievale prima dell'ingresso della fisica di Aristotele il secolo XII." *La filosofia della natura nel medioevo. Atti del terzo congresso internazionale di filosofia mediovale, Passo della Mendola (Trento) 31 Agosto-5 Settembre 1964*, pp. 27-65. Milano, 1966.

————. *Platonismo medievale. Studi e ricerche*. Istituto Storico Italiano per il Medio Evo, studi storici, 26-27. Roma, 1958.

Handschin, J. "Ein mittelalterlicher Beitrag zur Lehre von der Sphärenharmonie." *Zeitschrift für Musikwissenschaft* 9 (1927), 193-208.

Haring, N. "Thierry of Chartres and Dominicus Gundissalinus." *MS* 26 (1964), 271-86.

Hauréau, B. *Histoire de la philosophie scholastique. Première partie (de Charlemagne à la fin du XIIe siècle)*. Paris, 1872.

[Hermann of Carinthia]. *Hermann de Carintia, De Essentiis*. Edited by P. Manuel Alonso. Miscelánea Comillas v, 7-107. Comillas, Santander, 1946.

Huygens, R.C.B. "Mittelalterliche Kommentare zum *O qui perpetua....*" *Sacris Erudiri* 6 (1954), 373-427.

Jeauneau, E. "Gloses de Guillaume de Conches sur Macrobe. Note sur les manuscrits." *AHDLMA* 27 (1961), 17-28.

————. *Jean Scot. Homélie sur le prologue de Jean*. Sources chrétiennes, 151. Paris, 1969.

————. "La lecture des auteurs classiques à l'école de Chartres durant la première moitié du XIIe siècle. Un témoin privilégié: les *Glosae super Macrobium* de Guillaume de Conches." In R. R. Bolgar, ed., *Classical Influences on European Culture A.D. 500-1500. Proceedings of an International Conference Held at King's College, Cambridge, April 1969*, pp. 95-102. Cambridge, 1971.

———. "Le *Prologus in Eptatheucon* de Thierry de Chartres." *MS* 16 (1954), 171-75.

———. "L'usage de la notion d'*integumentum* à travers les gloses de Guillaume de Conches." *AHDLMA* 24 (1958), 35-100.

———. " 'Nani gigantum humeris insidentes.' Essai d'interprétation de Bernard de Chartres." *Vivarium* 5 (1967), 79-99.

———. "Note sur l'Ecole de Chartres." *SMed*, 3rd ser., 5 (1964), 821-65.

———. "Simple notes sur la cosmogonie de Thiérry de Chartres." *Sophia* 23 (1955), 172-83.

———. "Un commentaire inédit sur le chant 'O qui perpetua' de Boèce." *Rivista critica della storia della filosofia* 14 (1959), 60-80.

[John Scottus Eriugena]. *Joannis Scoti Opera quae supersunt omnia ad fidem italicorum, germanicorum, belgicorum franco-gallicorum, brittanicorum codicum*. Edited by H. J. Floss. *PL* 122.

[John of Salisbury]. *Ioannis Saresberiensis episcopi carnotensis Metalogicon libri IIII*. Edited by C.C.J. Webb. Oxford, 1929.

Klibansky, R. "Standing on the Shoulders of the Giants." *Isis* 26 (1936), 147-49.

———. *The Continuity of the Platonic Tradition during the Middle Ages*. London, 1950.

———, E. Panofsky, and F. Saxl. *Saturn and Melancholy. Studies in the History of Natural Philosophy, Religion, and Art*. London, 1964.

Lacombe, G., *et al. Aristoteles Latinus*. Union Académique Internationale. Corpus Philosophorum Medii Aevi. Pars prior, Roma, 1939; pars posterior, Cambridge, 1954.

Ladner, G. B. *The Idea of Reform. Its Impact on Christian Thought and Action in the Age of the Fathers*. Cambridge, Mass., 1959.

Langlois, Ch.-V. "Maître Bernard." *Bibliothèque de l'Ecole des Chartes* 54 (1893), 225-50.

Lemay, R. *Abu Ma'shar and Latin Aristotelianism in the Twelfth Century. The Recovery of Aristotle's Natural Philosophy through Arabic Astronomy.* American University of Beirut, Publication of the Faculty of Arts and Sciences, Oriental Series, 38. Beirut, 1962.

Leonardi, C. *I codici de Marziano Capella.* Milano, 1959-60. (= *Aevum* 33 [1959], 443-89; 34 [1960], 1-99; 411-524.)

Lewis, C. S. *The Allegory of Love. A Study in Medieval Tradition.* Oxford, 1938.

Liebeschütz, H. *Das allegorische Weltbild der heiligen Hildegard von Bingen.* Studien der Bibliothek Warburg, XVI. Leipzig/Berlin, 1930.

———. "Kosmologische Motive in der Bildungswelt der Frühscholastik." *Vorträge der Bibliothek Warburg 1923-1924,* pp. 83-148. Leipzig/Berlin, 1926.

Lubac, H. de. *Exégèse médiévale. Les quatre sens de l'Ecriture.* Théologie . . . , vols. 41, 42, 59; 4 vols. Paris, 1959-64.

———. " 'Typologie' et 'allégorisme.' " *Recherches de science religieuse* 34 (1947), 180-226.

[Manilius]. *M. Manilii Astronomicon.* Edited by A. E. Housman. 4 vols. London, 1903-30.

Manitius, M., and P. Lehmann. *Geschichte der lateinischen Literatur des Mittelalters,* vol. 3. Handbuch der Altertumswissenschaft, 9.2.3. München, 1931.

Martianvs Capella. *[De Nuptiis Philologiae et Mercurii].* Edited by A. Dick and J. Préaux. Leipzig, 1969.

Massignon, L. "Inventaire de la littérature hermétique arabe." In A.-J. Festugière, *La révélation d'Hermès Trismégiste I, L'astrologie et les sciences occultes,* pp. 384-400. Etudes bibliques. Paris, 1944.

McCrimmon, M., "The Classical Philosophical Sources of the *De Mundi Universitate* of Bernard Silvestris." Dissertation, Yale University, 1952.

McKeon, R. "Poetry and Philosophy in the Twelfth Century: the Renaissance of Rhetoric." *Modern Philology* 43 (1945-46), 217-34.

Miller, K. *Mappaemundi, die ältesten Weltkarten.* 6 vols. Stuttgart, 1895-98.

Minio-Paluello, L. "Aristotele dal mundo arabo a quello latino." *L'occidente e l'Islam nell'alto medioevo.* Settimane di studi del centro italiano di studi sull'alto medioevo XII, 2-8 aprile 1964. Vol. 2, 603-37. Spoleto, 1965.

————. "Iacobus Veneticus Grecus, Canonist and Translator of Aristotle." *Traditio* 8 (1952), 265-304.

[Moses Maimonides]. *Rabi Mossei Aegyptii Dux seu Director dubitantium aut perplexorum, in treis Libros diuisus, & summa accuratione Reuerendi patris Augustini Iustiniani ordinis Praedicatorii Nebiensium Episcopi recognitus. Cuius index seu tabella ad calcem totius apponetur operis.* [Lipsiae, 1522].

Müller, M. "Die Stellung des Daniel von Morley in der Wissenschaft des Mittelalters." *Philosophisches Jahrbuch auf Veranlassung und mit Unterstützung der Görres-Gesellschaft* 41 (1928), 301-37.

Munari, F. "Mediaevalia I-II." *Philologus* 104 (1960), 279-92.

[Mythographus Vaticanus]. *Scriptores Rerum Mythicarum Latini Tres Romae Nuper Reperti.* Edited by G. H. Bode. 2 vols. Cellis, 1834.

Nardi, B. *Dante e la cultura medievale. Nuovi saggi di filosofia dantesca.* Bari, 1942.

Nau, F. "Une ancienne traduction latine du Bélinous arabe (Apollonius de Tyane) faite par Hugo Sanctelliensis et conservée dans un MS. du XIIe siècle." *Revue de l'orient chrétien,* 2nd ser., 12 (1907), 99-106.

Nuchelmans, G. "Philologia et son mariage avec Mercure jusqu'à la fin du XIIe siècle." *Latomus* 16 (1957), 84-107.

O'Donnell, J. R. "The Meaning of 'Silva' in the Commentary on the *Timaeus* of Plato by Chalcidius." *MS* 7 (1945), 1-20.

————. "The Sources and Meaning of Bernard Silvester's Commentary on the *Aeneid.*" *MS* 24 (1962), 233-49.

Padoan, G. "Tradizione e fortuna del commento all' "Eneide" di Bernardo Silvestre." *Italia medioevale e umanistica* 3 (1960), 227-40.

Parent, J. *La doctrine de la création dans l'école de Chartres. Etude et textes.* Publications de l'Institut d'Etudes Médiévales d'Ottawa, VIII. Paris/Ottawa, 1938.

[Paschalis Romanus]. "Le *Liber Thesauri occulti* de Paschalis Romanus." Edited by S. Collin-Roset. *AHDLMA* 30 (1964), 111-98.

Pellicer, A. *Natura. Etude sémantique et historique du mot latin.* Université de Montpellier, Faculté des Lettres, publication 27. Paris, 1966.

Pépin, J. *Mythe et allégorie. Les origines grecques et les contestations judéo-chrétiennes.* Paris, 1958.

Poole, R. L. "The Masters of the Schools of Paris and Chartres in John of Salisbury's Time." *English Historical Review* 35 (1920), 321-42.

Post, G. *Studies in Medieval Legal Thought, Public Law, and the State, 1100-1322.* Princeton, 1964.

[Ptolemy]. *Ptolemaeus. Opera astronomica minora.* Edited by J. L. Heiberg. Leipzig, 1907.

Raby, F.J.E. "*Nuda Natura* and Twelfth-Century Cosmology." *Speculum* 43 (1968), 72-77.

———. *A History of Secular Latin Poetry in the Middle Ages.* 2 vols. 2nd edn. Oxford, 1957.

[Radulfus de Diceto]. *Radulfi de Diceto Decani Lundoniensis Opera Historica.* 2 vols. Edited by W. Stubbs. Rerum Britannicarum Medii Aevi Scriptores. London, 1876.

Reinhardt, K. *Poseidonios.* München, 1921.

Rico, F. *El pequeño mundo del hombre. Varia fortuna de una idea en las letras españolas.* Madrid, 1970.

Robertson, D. W., Jr. *A Preface to Chaucer. Studies in Medieval Perspectives.* Princeton, 1963.

Rossi, P. *Francis Bacon, from Magic to Science.* London, 1968. (= *Francesco Bacone: dalla magia alla scienza.* Bari, 1957.)

Saecvli noni avctoris in Boetii Consolationem philosophiae Commentarius. Edited by E. T. Silk. Papers and Monographs of the American Academy in Rome, IX. Roma, 1935.

Sambursky, S. *Physics of the Stoics.* London, 1959.

Sandys, J. E. "Notes on Mediaeval Latin Authors." *Hermathena: A Series of Papers on Literature, Science, and Phi-*

losophy by Members of Trinity College, Dublin 12 (1903), 428-40.

Saxl, F. *Verzeichnis astrologischer und mythologischer illustrierten Handschriften des lateinischen Mittelalters II. Die Handschriften der National Bibliothek in Wien. SB Heidelberg, phil.-hist. Kl.,* 1925/1926 2. Abh. Heidelberg, 1927.

Schipperges, H. "Die frühen Übersetzer der arabischen Medizin in chronologischer Sicht." *Sudhoffs Archiv für Geschichte der Medizin* 39 (1955), 53-93.

————. "Einflüsse arabischer Medizin auf die Mikrokosmosliteratur des 12. Jahrhunderts." In P. Wilpert, ed., *Antike und Orient im Mittelalter. Miscellanea Medievalia I,* pp. 129-53. Berlin, 1962.

Schmid, T. "Ein Timaioskommentar in Sigtuna." *Classica et Mediaevalia* 10 (1949), 220-66.

Scott, W., and A. S. Ferguson. *Hermetica. The Ancient Greek and Latin Writings which Contain Religious or Philosophic Teachings Ascribed to Hermes Trismegistus.* 4 vols. Oxford, 1924-36.

Silk, E. T. "Pseudo-Johannes Scottus, Adalbold of Utrecht, and the Early Commentaries on Boethius." *Mediaeval and Renaissance Studies* 3 (1954), 1-40.

Silverstein, T. "Adelard, Aristotle and the *De natura deorum.*" *Classical Philology* 47-48 (1952-53), 82-85.

————. "Daniel of Morley, English Cosmogonist and Student of Arabic Science." *MS* 10 (1948), 179-96.

————. "*Elementatum*: Its Appearance Among the Twelfth-Century Cosmogonists." *MS* 16 (1954), 156-62.

————. "Liber Hermetis Mercurii Triplicis de VI rerum principiis." *AHDLMA* 22 (1956), 217-301.

————. "The Fabulous Cosmogony of Bernardus Silvestris." *Modern Philology* 46 (1948-49), 92-116.

Silvestre, H. "Le commentaire inédit de Jean Scot Erigène au mètre IX du livre III du 'De consolatione Philosophiae' de Boèce." *Revue d'histoire ecclésiastique* 47 (1952), 44-122.

Smalley, B. *The Study of the Bible in the Middle Ages.* 2nd edn. Oxford, 1952.

Souter, A. *A Glossary of Later Latin to 600 A.D.* Oxford, 1949.

Spicq, C., *Esquisse d'une histoire de l'exégèse latine au moyen âge.* Bibliothèque thomiste, XXVI. Paris, 1944.

Steinschneider, M. *Die Europäischen Übersetzungen aus dem Arabischen bis Mitte des 17. Jahrhunderts.* Reprint. Graz, 1956. (= *SB Wien, phil.-hist. Cl.*, 1904, 1905.)

Stock, B. "A Note on *Thebaid* Commentaries: Paris, B.N., lat. 3012." *Traditio* 27 (1971), 468-71.

———. "Cosmology and Rhetoric in *The Phoenix* of Lactantius." *Classica et Mediaevalia* 26 (1965), 246-57.

———. "Hugh of St. Victor, Bernard Silvester and MS Trinity College, Cambridge, O.7.7." *MS* 34 (1972), 152-73.

———. "Observations on the Use of Augustine by Johannes Scottus Eriugena." *Harvard Theological Review* 60 (1967), 213-20.

———. "The Philosophical Anthropology of Johannes Scottus Eriugena." *SMed*, 3rd ser., 8 (1967), 1-57.

Taylor, J. *The Didascalicon of Hugh of St. Victor. A Medieval Guide to the Arts.* Records of Civilization Sources and Studies, LXIV. New York/London, 1961.

[Thierry of Chartres]. "A Commentary on Boethius' *De Trinitate* by Thierry of Chartres (*Anonymus Berolinensis*)." Edited by N. Haring. *AHDLMA* 23 (1957), 257-325.

———. "The Creation and Creator of the World according to Thierry of Chartres and Clarenbaldus of Arras." Edited by N. Haring. *AHDLMA* 22 (1956), 137-216.

Thorndike, L. *A History of Magic and Experimental Science During the First Thirteen Centuries of Our Era*, vol. 2. New York, 1929.

———. and P. Kibre. *A Catalogue of Incipits of Mediaeval Scientific Writings in Latin.* Revised and augmented edition. The Mediaeval Academy of America, Publication No. 29. Cambridge, Mass., 1963.

Tierney, B. "Natura Id Est Deus: A Case of Juristic Pantheism?" *Journal of the History of Ideas* 24 (1963), 307-22.

Weisheipl, J. "Classification of the Sciences in Medieval Thought." *MS* 27 (1965), 54-90.

White, L., Jr. "Natural Science and Naturalistic Art in the Middle Ages." *The American Historical Review* 52 (1947), 421-35.

[William of Conches]. "Des commentaires inédits de Guillaume de Conches et de Nicolas Triveth sur la Consolation de la philosophie de Boèce." Edited by C. Jourdain. *Excursions historiques et philosophiques à travers le moyen âge.* Paris, 1888.

————. *Guillaume de Conches. Glosae super Platonem. Texte critique avec introduction, notes et tables.* Edited by E. Jeauneau. Textes philosophiques du moyen âge, XIII. Paris, 1965.

————. *De Philosophia Mundi libri quatuor, PL* 172, 39-102.

Wilmart, A. "Poèmes de Gautier de Châtillon dans un manuscrit de Charleville." *Revue bénédictine* 49 (1934), 121-69, 322-65.

Winden, J.C.M. van. *Calcidius on Matter, his Doctrine and Sources. A Chapter in the History of Platonism.* Leiden, 1959.

Wolfson, H. *Philosophy of the Church Fathers.* Vol. I. Cambridge, Mass., 1956.

Woolsey, R. B. "Bernard Silvester and the Hermetic *Asclepius.*" *Traditio* 6 (1948), 340-44.

Wright, J. K. *The Geographical Lore of the Time of the Crusades. A Study in the History of Medieval Science and Tradition in Western Europe.* American Geographical Society Research Series, No. 15. New York, 1925.

Wulf, M. de. *Histoire de la philosophie médiévale I, Des origines jusqu'à Thomas d'Aquin.* 5th edn. Louvain, 1924.

————. *Histoire de la philosophie médiévale I, Des origines jusqu'à la fin du XIIe siècle.* 6th edn. Louvain/Paris, 1934.

Vernet, A. "Un remaniement de la *Philosophia* de Guillaume de Conches." *Scriptorium* 1 (1947), 243-59.

Yates, F. *The Art of Memory.* London, 1966.

Index of Manuscripts

Index

301

eternity, 93, 137-50, 161,
246; and nature, 150, 152,
203, 224 (*see also* fate);
and number, 159; and
order, 131, 159 (*see also*
order)
Tiresias, 34, 57, 58n
topos, *see* complaint, dignity of
man, dialogue, *locus amoenus*,
secrets of nature
touch, sense of, 214
Tours, 13, 37, 60n, 135, 263
translation, *see* Arab science
travel, influence upon science
of, 24
trigonometry, Arabic, 25
trinity, as analogy between
world and man, 209-11;
Christian, 22, 178, 242n,
265; as four causes of
creation, 252; non-Christian,
176, 177&n, 178
trivium, 9, 31, 32, 49, 59,
229, 277
truth, moral, 23, 40, 42, 45,
58; natural-philosophical,
23, 40, 48, 58, 109
Tugaton, 16, 123n, 163, 172,
173, 174, 175, 182
tumultus, 69, 75n, 179, 203n
Tu quem psallentem . . .
(Mart. Cap. i.1), 33
turpitudo, 116. *See also* evil

ὕλη, 104n, 179. *See also hyle*
Ullman, B. L., 36n
ultramundanus, 132n, 177n.
*See also extramundanus,
superessentialis*
unitas, 113n, 147, 247n
unitas et diversum, 112, 213n.

See also one and many, unity
and diversity
unity, 113, 148, 154, 246,
247
unity and diversity, 112, 153,
186, 192, 245-47, 248.
See also one and many
universe, the, 16, 23, 26, 28,
40, 45, 63, 66, 67, 68, 75,
77, 83, 90, 99, 100, 114,
117, 119, 120, 127, 128,
132, 142
universitas, 125f, 137, 141;
mundi, 126n, 197; *rerum*,
98, 132, 143, 145. *See also*
universe
Urania, 16, 18, 22, 23, 35,
71, 163, 164-67, 172, 179,
187&n, 189, 192, 195f,
203&n, 204, 220, 223, 226,
228, 229, 236n
usia, 69, 89, 141, 143&n,
144, 149, 170, 192. *See
also* being, matter, *ousia, silva*
uterus, 89, 98, 99
utopia, 133, 189, 282. *See also*
paradise

van Winden, J., 109n, 111n,
114n
vates, 42n. *See also* poet
vegetatio, 145, 260n
velamentum, 51
Venus, 85, 168n, 179
verification, of myth, 82; of
propositions, 109
veritas, 43n, 45n. *See also* truth
Vernet, A., 7n, 12&n, 22n,
103n, 120, 132n, 134n,
172n, 196&n, 278n, 282n